29 95

Sitting in the
Hot Seat

Sitting in the Hot Seat

Leaders and Teams for Critical Incident Management

RHONA FLIN

The Robert Gordon University

JOHN WILEY & SONS

Chichester · New York · Brisbane · Toronto · Singapore

Other Wiley Editorial Offices

John Wiley & Sons, Inc., 605 Third Avenue,
New York, NY 10158-0012, USA

Jacaranda Wiley Ltd, 33 Park Road, Milton,
Queensland 4064, Australia

John Wiley & Sons (Canada) Ltd, 22 Worcester Road,
Rexdale, Ontario M9W 1L1, Canada

John Wiley & Sons (Asia) Pte Ltd, 2 Clementi Loop #02-01,
Jin Xing Distripark, Singapore 129809

Library of Congress Cataloging-in-Publication Data

Flin, Rhona H.
    Sitting in the hot seat : Leaders and Teams for Critical Incident Management /
Rhona Flin.
        p. cm.
    Includes bibliographical references and index.
    ISBN 0-471-95796-8 (cloth)
    1. Emergency management. 2. Leadership. I. Title.
HV551.2.F58   1996
658.4'77—dc20   96–12076
                                                      CIP

British Library Cataloguing in Publication Data

A catalogue record for this book is available from the British Library

ISBN 0-471-95796-8

Typeset in 10/12pt Palatino from the author's disks by Acorn Bookwork, Salisbury, Wiltshire
Printed and bound in Great Britain by Biddles Ltd, Guildford and King's Lynn
This book is printed on acid-free paper responsibly manufactured from sustainable
forestation, for which at least two trees are planted for each one used for paper production.

Contents

Preface

While human life has always encountered hazards from man-made and natural threats, the United Kingdom is fortunately remote from the risk of catastrophe caused by volcanoes, earthquakes, cyclones and hurricanes. Nevertheless, major peacetime tragedies have occurred throughout our history due to fire, landslide (e.g. Aberfan), crowds (e.g. Ibrox stadium), transportation (e.g. the *Titanic*, the Tay Bridge) or occupational hazards, especially in fishing, mining and chemicals (e.g. Flixborough). In the 1980s an unprecedented sequence of British disasters (e.g. Bradford, Hillsborough, Kings Cross, *Piper Alpha*, Clapham, Lockerbie, Kegworth, the *Marchioness*, the *Herald of Free Enterprise*), resulting in hundreds of fatalities, focused attention on the management of civil emergencies. This book examines the role of the individual who acts as incident or on-scene commander in an event with life threatening potential, such as a fire or an explosion, or in a major incident involving all of the emergency services.

My interest in this topic began when I approached the Department of Energy in 1990 with a request for research funding to study the job of the offshore installation manager (OIM) on the UK offshore oil and gas fields. I had spent time offshore, working on applied psychology research and consultancy projects for the oil industry, and was intrigued by this unusual offshore management position. The result was that my former colleague Georgina Slaven and I received funding from the newly created Offshore Safety Division of the Health and Safety Executive (HSE) to look at one unusual aspect of this manager's job – the ability to take command in the event of an offshore emergency (Flin and Slaven 1994). This particular focus was a result of the findings and recommendations of the public inquiry into the *Piper Alpha* disaster (Cullen 1990), which directed the oil companies to review their selection and training procedures for the offshore managers, who, as had been tragically demonstrated, have a critical role to play in an emergency.

The project scope required a survey not only of the oil industry's procedures for selection and training in crisis management but also of the methods used by a range of other agencies that employ on-scene comman-ders. This volume was developed from that investigation and from my initial disappointment that there was no standard reference I could consult on the subject of incident command. In an attempt to fill that gap I have gathered information on the techniques used to select, train and assess the competence of incident commanders, and highlighted common principles that are the foundations for successful incident management across a range of occupations and emergency scenarios. Several fundamental aspects of incident command, namely leadership, decision making, team working and stress management, are examined in greater detail from a psychological perspective. The book is not about emergency planning or large-scale disaster management (which have been comprehensively discussed elsewhere). I should also like to emphasize that this book has been written from the viewpoint of a detached observer rather than an expert. I have no personal experience of incident command and the knowledge I have of the subject has been gleaned entirely from watching or talking to commanders.

PREVIOUS RESEARCH ON INCIDENT COMMAND

The first stage of any research study is to conduct a literature review in order to identify material already published. A search for articles and books specifically dealing with incident commanders (i.e. their role, selection, training and assessment), carried out using international on-line reference databases as well as the emergency service college libraries, did not prove to be a fruitful exercise. While emergency response professionals – the ambulance service, the fire service, the police and the coastguard – have a long history of efficient operations, there are few standard texts on incident command, although any organization with emergency command responsibilities will have its own emergency procedures manual. There are also specialist journals (e.g. *Ambulance UK, Coastguard, Policing, Fire Professional, Emergency* (Institute of Civil Defence and Disaster Studies), *Civil Protection* (Home Office)), which do carry pertinent material, particu-larly case reports of relevant incidents, but surprisingly few articles or research reports examine critically the job of the on-scene commander.

When searching more generally for books or articles on emergency management, titles that appeared promising at an initial glance (e.g. "crisis management") generally turned out to be disappointing, as the topics were usually business or political crises. Admittedly, many libraries could be filled on the subject of military command (e.g. Montgomery 1958, 1961; Slim 1956; van Creveld 1985; Von Clausewitz 1968; Woodward 1992) but warfare command has different objectives and is generally beyond the scope of this book. There are innumerable volumes on emergency response (e.g. Lagadec 1991; Wallace, Rowles and Colton 1994), disaster management (e.g. Hodgkinson and Stewart 1991; Raphael 1986; Rosenthal, Charles and Hart 1989; Toft and Reynolds 1994), corporate crisis management (e.g. Cameron 1994; Darling 1994; Fink 1986; Regester 1987) and operational techniques, such as firefighting (e.g. Grimwood 1992; MoD 1994b), but they contain very little, if anything, on the practice of on-scene command and on the selection and training of individuals for this position. Another possible source of reference material was from a growing academic interest in risk management, emergency planning and disasters exemplified by a clutch of new journals (e.g. *Disaster Prevention and Management, Disasters, Emergency Management Today, Industrial and Environmental Crisis Quarterly, International Journal of Mass Emergencies and Disasters, Journal of Contingencies and Crisis Management*), but although these occasionally contained case studies of major incidents, the focus was rarely on the incident commander.

As a result of the dearth of published work on this topic, much of the material presented in this book has been gathered from interviews with incident commanders and visits to observe incident command selection, training or competence assessment procedures. This was not intended to be a fully comprehensive survey, and the selection of organizations has, to some extent, been based on their relevance to our ongoing research into emergency management on offshore oil installations (Flin, Slaven and Stewart, 1996). The types of situation that will involve an incident commander include non-routine events involving large crowds, bomb threats, fires, flooding, explosions, building collapse, industrial accidents, transport accidents (roads, aviation, railway, marine), public order problems, and terrorist or criminal incidents with firearms or hostage taking. The first three chapters describe the principles and practice of incident command from different organizations' perspectives. Chapters 4–6 examine the psychological research that has most relevance to incident command, namely naturalistic decision making, team working and stress management. The final chapter presents an overview and considers future developments.

Acknowledgements

I would like to thank all the incident commanders who provided with me with information for this book. Many OIMs, pilots and emergency services commanders discussed at length their experiences of incident management with me, especially DO Brian Murray (Warwickshire Fire and Rescue Service), Inspector Ewan Stewart (Grampian Police), Captain Glyn David (Bond Helicopters), ACO Brian Hesler (Fife Fire and Rescue Service), Bob Gleason (FBI Academy), and SDO John Bonney (London Fire Brigade). I am also grateful to those commanders, managers and psychologists who provided materials or feedback on early drafts of the manuscript, particularly: Dr Jonathan Crego (Metropolitan Police), DO Darran Gunter (Fire Service College), M Frank Albert (Cote San Luc Fire Department, Quebec), Commander Vincent Dunn (New York Fire Department), Superintendent Andy Tyrrell (Police Staff College, Bramshill), Mr Joe Paul (State Emergency Service, Tasmania), Sergeant Allan Schepers (Queensland Police), Professor Joe Scanlon (Carleton University, Ottawa), Professor David Gaba (Stanford University), ACC Tom Woods (Lothian and Borders Police), Professor David Alexander (University of Aberdeen), Colonel Christian Pourny (Ecole Nationale Superieure des Officiers Sapeurs-Pompiers, France), David Cook (Mobil North Sea), Mary Manolias (Home Office), and Professor Lars Weisaeth (University of Oslo). Three distinguished military commanders were interviewed – Lord George Mackie (RAF Bomber Command, WW2), the late Brigadier Alastair Pearson (Paratroop Regiment, WW2), and Admiral Sir John Woodward (RN, Falklands Battle Group Commander) – and I am most grateful for their cooperation and the insights they provided. Fellow psychologists across the Atlantic – especially Gary Klein, Judith Orasanu and Ed Salas – provided inspiration and a formidable stream of research papers. I am indebted to a number of organizations which permitted me to meet with commanders or to observe command training and these are listed in Appendix 1. In addition, I would like to acknowledge the help of Grampian Fire Brigade, Grampian Police, the Fire Service College,

Montrose Fire and Emergency Training Centre, Mobil North Sea, Scottish Police College, Shell Expro and the Offshore Safety Division HSE who have granted access or funding for our research endeavours. I would particularly like to acknowledge the support of my secretary, Evelyn McLennan; my colleagues on this project, Georgina Slaven, Keith Stewart, Jan Skriver and Lynne Martin; Ian Calder for graphics; Anne Nicol for retrieving endless obscure literature requests; and Aberdeen Business School's very own incident commander, David Sagar. Finally, the book would never have reached production without the encouragement and patience of Diane Taylor and Claire Plimmer at Wiley. Any errors or inaccuracies in the book are entirely of my own making and if readers could offer enlightenment, I would be extremely grateful.

1
The Role of the Incident Commander

"The failure of the OIMs [offshore installation managers] to cope with the problems they faced on the night of the disaster clearly demonstrates that conventional selection and training of OIMs is no guarantee of ability to cope if the man himself is not able in the end to take critical decisions and lead those under his command in a time of extreme stress."

(Cullen 1990, para 20.59)

INTRODUCTION

This book examines the role of the on-scene commander, who has the key role to play in the management of an emergency. Traditionally this has been regarded as the province of the emergency services, with associated expertise available in the armed services. Recent events have demonstrated that with the development of high hazard industries, mass transport systems and ever larger entertainment venues, an increasing number of site managers may also find themselves responsible for incident command, particularly in the opening stages of a crisis, which is usually the most critical phase. A surprising range of individuals may be required to act as the key decision maker in a crisis, most obviously officers from the police, fire, ambulance services and coastguards but also airline captains, merchant navy captains, Royal Navy damage control officers, casualty doctors, anaesthetists, prison officers, and managers of industrial plants, entertainment venues, football grounds, hotels, hospitals and other public buildings. As described in the Preface, there is a notable absence of written material on incident command. Drabek (1986), in an American study of human responses to disaster, commented that, "Curiously, both media and medical organizations have been studied much more since our

1975 inventory was completed, but police, fire, public works, military and other first-responder organizations have not been pursued much" (p. 157). This is endorsed in a more recent article by a divisional officer at the Fire Service College, who argued that "the senior fireground commander is a neglected species", and pointed out that there is little official guidance available for the fireground incident commander (Murray, 1994a, p. 22). This volume is based on a study of incident commanders from different professions. It reviews their selection and training, then discusses the relevant psychological research dealing with stress, decision making and teamwork.

Defining Emergencies, Major Incidents and Disasters

Throughout this book, the terms "emergency", "accident", "critical incident", "major incident" and "disaster" are used as they appear in the original source material. While there have been many attempts to provide distinctive definitions, there is no universally accepted classification or terminology. In the literature these terms are used interchangeably to describe equivalent events, although disasters and major incidents are generally regarded to be on a larger scale than incidents, emergencies or accidents (Parker and Handmer 1992). An emergency, according to the *Oxford English Dictionary*, is, "A juncture that arises or 'turns up'; esp. a state of things unexpectedly arising, and urgently demanding immediate action", whereas a disaster is defined as "Anything that befalls of ruinous or distressing nature; a sudden or great misfortune; a calamity". Keller (1990) defines a disaster as "when ten or more fatalities result from one event over a relatively short period of time" (p. 3). Not all researchers would agree with this fatality-count definition; some differentiate accidents, disasters and catastrophes in terms of their social impact. Disasters are widely regarded to be qualitatively as well as quantitatively different from other types of incident or emergency. Quarantelli (1988), Director of the University of Delaware Disaster Research Center, who has studied more than 500 disasters and mass emergencies over the past 30 years, has argued that there is an essential difference in kind and not just in degree. That is, accidents are not little disasters, nor are disasters big accidents. He believes that the characteristics of disasters or crises produce a different social order, and that they cannot be managed by the same organizational structures used to deal with what he calls "everyday emergencies" (Quarantelli 1995). Similar views have been expressed by other authors (Dynes 1994; Horlick-Jones 1994; Parker and Handmer 1992). Disaster researchers tend to examine prolonged, extensive natural catastrophes such as earthquakes, volcanic eruptions, tidal waves, flash floods and forest fires, which involve thousands of victims, a multinational emergency response and an aftermath lasting for several years (e.g. Horlick-Jones, Amendola and Casale 1995). These large-scale, long duration calamities are not discussed here, and my use of the term "disaster" equates to the use of the terms "disaster" and "major incident". According to publication *Dealing with Disaster*, the police and fire service definition of a "major incident" is as follows:

> "A major incident is any emergency that requires the implementation of special arrangements by one or more of the emergency services, the NHS or the local authority for:
> a. The initial treatment, rescue and transport of a large number of casualties;
> b. The involvement either directly or indirectly of large numbers of people;
> c. The handling of a large number of enquiries likely to be generated both from the public and the news media usually to the police;
> d. The need for the large scale combined resources of two or more of the emergency services;
> e. The mobilisation and organisation of the emergency services and supporting organisations, eg local authority, to cater for the threat of death, serious injury, or homelessness to a large number of people."
>
> (Home Office 1994, p. 38)

This definition will not strictly apply to all industrial, military, aviation or marine emergencies, and this volume will consider on-scene command at critical incidents, ranging from routine emergencies to major incidents. These events can be described in terms of their life cycle: Sarna (1984), a Californian police captain who trains British and American officers in critical incident management, uses the following three-stage model:

1. Response phase (threat evaluation and containment)
2. Resolution phase (contingency management)
3. Recovery phase (restoration of normality)

This pattern is common to a wide range of critical incidents. However, there are a number of differences between a routine emergency (for the emergency services) and a major incident, as shown in Table 1.1; the distinction is not just in terms of scale – the nature of the emergency response is changed, with additional demands placed on those tasked with command and control.

Many of the issues raised in Table 1.1 relate to the requirement for the three emergency services (and sometimes a host of other agencies) to work together at a major incident. For example, at the Kegworth plane crash in 1989, there were at least four fire services, four ambulance services, three police forces, as well as RAF helicopters, mountain and mining rescue teams, the army and the Salvation Army, plus the passing

Table 1.1 *Distinctions between a Routine Emergency and a Major Incident (based on Auf der Heide 1989, table 4.1; Lagadec 1990, p. 12; Sarna 1984, p. 5).*

Routine emergency	Major incident
Familiar event, standard procedures (SP)	Unusual event, SPs may be inadequate
Known faces, tasks, procedures	Unfamiliar "teams"; unknown elements
Coordination within own organization	Inter-organizational coordination
Adequate communications	Overload of telephones, radios and roads
Communicate in-house	Share with other agencies
Familiar terms/language	Different terminologies
Local press/media	National/international press
Adequate resources	Diverse resources required; resources may be inadequate or exceed managerial capacity
"Do it all"	Work with multiple agencies
Relatively contained, scale and duration are limited	Large-scale risks, high variability, longer time scale, wide area affected
Orderly procedures	Limited control
Limited number of parties involved	Hundreds of rescue personnel, media etc.
Little impact on local services	Major disruption of local infrastructure and services

motorists who began the rescue operation (AAIB 1990). Scanlon and Prawzick (1991) discuss this "convergence" or "mass assault" effect in a study of a massive fire at Nanticoke in Canada in 1990, where 14 million rubber tyres burned for 18 days. They found that 346 different organizations (e.g. government departments, emergency services, hospitals, self-help groups) were on the site of the disaster (at the scene, within the evacuation perimeter or crossing the police checkpoint). The complex coordination of such activities is discussed later, in the section entitled "Incident Command and Control Procedures".

Emergencies and major incidents vary on a number of key dimensions (not all of which distinguish routine and major events as in Table 1.1), which determine the difficulty of the command and control operation. These are listed in Table 1.2 which indicates that the problems facing an incident commander do not come in a standard size or shape and, almost by definition, they have unusual, unanticipated and unexpected elements. One further distinction is that the incident commander may be involved at different stages of an emergency.

Prior Warning

In some cases, the commander will have been alerted to a developing problem; for example, police and prison incidents can have intelligence

Table 1.2   *Event Characteristics that Influence the Difficulty of Incident Command.*

Event characteristic	Easiest to command	Worst to command
Speed of onset	Slow – days	Fast – minutes
Warning	Prior indications	None
Preparation time	Months – regular event	None
Hazard status	Low	High
Risk to responders	Low	High
Casualties	None	Hundreds
Access	Good	Remote/awkward
Number of responders	Few: 20–30	Hundreds
Stage	Initiating event completed	Events escalating
Major risks	Single	Multiple
Services involved	One	All
Incident commanders	One	Several
Decision demands	Routine, familiar	Complex, unfamiliar
Resources	Adequate	Insufficient
Knowledge of site	Very familiar	Unfamiliar
Time of onset	Day-time (light and more people on duty, although possibly more casualties)	Night-time (easier under some circumstances)
Location	Single site	Multiple sites/incidents, or moving (e.g. bus hijack)

indications (forewarning), e.g. prison riot, public order disturbance. For natural disasters, such as storms or flooding, there may be weather warnings, and in industry or on a flight deck, a developing emergency may be signalled by preliminary hazard alarms, allowing avoidance or controlling actions to be taken.

On-Site at the Time of the Initiating Event

Sometimes there is no prior notification. If there is an explosion on a ship, a plane or an offshore oil installation, the captain or offshore manager will already be on-site at the start of the event. This could also be the position for police football match commanders on duty with a large crowd. These individuals have to take immediate command of the situation while they are attempting to figure out the cause of the problem and to assess the extent of the damage and danger. Even if the cause has not been diagnosed, they should be able to implement standard emergency response procedures to deal with the event, minimize further damage and effect a rescue, if necessary. Incident commanders at the scene of the event may themselves be in danger or may place themselves at risk to rescue others. A more stressful circumstance applicable to industrial managers, transport captains and police commanders is when they are not only present when the emergency occurs but they are also alleged to have some responsibility for it. For a police commander (e.g. at a football match or a riot), or even a fireground commander, this could create additional risks of an escalating public order problem or overt attacks during a rescue operation. Concern about their own culpability in failing to prevent the unfolding emergency may increase the commander's anxiety (the question of stress for incident commanders is discussed in Chapter 4).

Called to the Scene

In many cases, particularly for the emergency services, the duty incident commanders are notified after the initiating event has begun and they travel to the incident scene. Consequently, they have the chance to prepare mentally *en route* to the incident, and to monitor situation reports by radio enabling them to formulate an initial assessment and prioritize reactions. Several commanders told me that this was a welcome opportunity to gather their thoughts and to brace themselves for the scene ahead. On arrival, they are typically briefed as to what has happened and what immediate actions have been taken by the first responders. In this case, an incoming commander may well be taking over from a more junior officer who has already implemented an action plan. Brunacini (1985), discussing fireground command, says, "You must be prepared to inherit ongoing scenarios. This means that you must be prepared to evaluate the initial commitments and actions of others and make the necessary changes to fit your fire plan. Learn to do so with both grace and confidence" (p. 8).

There are additional cross-cultural and logistical problems for commanders who have to travel abroad to become involved in a major incident involving British civilians (e.g. a transport accident or a hostage taking). The intricacies of international collaboration in incident management would by all accounts justify a volume on their own, and this is not discussed further.

In all of these situations, significant demands are placed on the incident commanders; the next section considers the organizational systems of command and control or emergency response that are designed to enable commanders to achieve a swift and effective response.

INCIDENT COMMAND AND CONTROL PROCEDURES

Most organizations with responsibility for the management of emergencies on a routine or contingency basis will have developed incident command

and control procedures. Where agencies have to work together at the same event, it is particularly important that they understand each other's command and control systems, and in recent years a number of more formal structures and standardized systems of incident command have been developed. The Home Secretary, Michael Howard, has emphasized the need for consistency in these command procedures:

> "Experience in the light of recent disasters has shown a need for a common approach to be adopted between the agencies involved in order to achieve an effective response. Crucial to this is a multi-agency approach to command and control."
>
> (quoted in *Civil Protection*, winter, 1995, p. 3)

The following subsection explains the command and control procedures employed by the emergency services for major incidents. This is followed by descriptions of emergency response procedures in hazardous industries, procedures for damage control in the Royal Navy, and the general use of standard operating procedures.

The Emergency Services

In the UK, major incidents are dealt with by the emergency services: there is no civil defence, national disaster force or military response, as there is in a number of other countries. Following the unprecedented spate of major emergencies in the 1980s (and the end of the Cold War, which reduced the threat of attack on the UK), a government review of arrangements for peacetime emergency planning was undertaken in 1988 (see Kornicki 1990; Parker and Handmer 1992). This concluded that there was no requirement for a national specialist disaster response force, and confirmed that emergency management should continue to be coordinated at a local level (a decision that has not met with universal approval; see Jackson 1994). The Civil Defence and Royal Observer Corps were disbanded and the funding reallocated to civil emergency planning, which is coordinated on a regional basis by emergency planning departments in local authorities, with an emphasis on an integrated emergency management approach between them and the emergency services (Home Office 1994).

> "The starting point must be the development of flexible management arrangements for handling a crisis, whatever its cause, identifying responsibilities and chains of command. It therefore follows that the crisis management arrangements must align with the normal management arrangements of the authority or organisation, not least because it will be faced with the task of trying to maintain normal services as well as handling the emergency."
>
> (Bawtree 1995a, p. 1)

What are the management (command and control) arrangements for handling an emergency or major incident? Each of the major emergency services has its own emergency operational procedures guide. For example, the Association of Chief Police Officers (ACPO) *Emergency Procedures Manual* (ACPO 1991) provides detailed guidance for police forces dealing with major incidents, covering casualty information management, dealing with the media, investigation, officers' welfare and liaison with other agencies. The fire service has a similar volume, prepared by the Chief and Assistant Fire Officers Association (CACFOA), the *Major Incident Procedures Manual* (CACFOA 1991), and the Scottish Ambulance Service has *Arrangements for Civil Emergencies* (Scottish Ambulance Service 1990). There are also locally devised police force, fire brigade and ambulance service operational manuals with contingency plans to cope with emergencies that are peculiar to the hazard profile of each region. These guidelines indicate the command structure that will be employed, standard response procedures and the roles of particular commanders and support personnel. See Figure 1.1, which shows the incident command structure of Grampian Fire Brigade.

The best (unrestricted) description of the emergency services' command structures and procedures for a major incident can be found in the Home Office (1994) publication *Dealing with Disaster*, first published in 1992 and now in a second edition with an accompanying video training package entitled *"Strategic" – Command and Control of a Major Incident*. The booklet gives general principles for the operational management of major incidents, and defines command as "the authority for an agency to direct the actions of its own resources (both personnel and equipment)". The term "control" is defined as "the authority to direct strategic and tactical operations in order to complete an assigned function and includes the ability to direct the activities of other agencies engaged in the completion of that function". The police typically have a coordinating role and responsibility for control of the disaster site, although control of specific functions, e.g. rescue or medical evacuation, may be assigned to one of the other emergency services. All agencies are deemed to be working with a set of common objectives, which include saving life, preventing escalation of the disaster, relieving suffering, safeguarding the environment and protecting property.

According to the guide the personnel and resources of each emergency service remain under the command of its senior officers, so that they can execute their primary duties. Apart from coordination and site control (e.g. cordons and traffic), the police have responsibility for dealing with casualty information, and protection of life and property. They also have to oversee any criminal investigation and assist in any formal accident investigation. The fire service is primarily concerned with rescuing people trapped by fire or wreckage and preventing further escalation of the incident by extinguishing fires, as well as dealing with chemicals and contamination. The

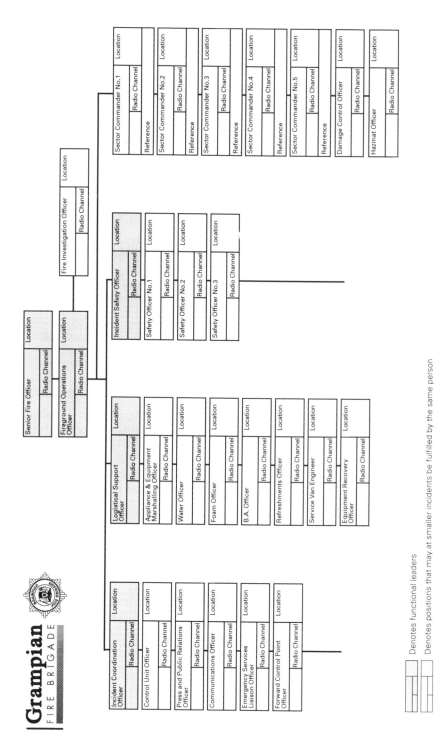

Figure 1.1 *Grampian Fire Brigade Incident Command Structure. Reprinted with permission of Grampian Fire Brigade.*

ambulance service, in conjunction with medical teams, provides the on-scene medical aid and transportation of the injured to hospital. Maritime search and rescue operations are the responsibility of the Coastguard Agency, which operates from six Maritime Rescue Coordination Centres around the British coast. The roles and functions of local authorities, volunteers, industrial and commercial organizations, military assistance and central government are also briefly outlined. Special advice is available for those managing large crowds at sporting or musical events.

In terms of response to a disaster at a single site, the following advice is given:

> "The scene immediately after disaster has struck is likely to be confused. To bring some order to this confusion it is important that the emergency services establish control over the immediate area and also build up arrangements for co-ordinating the contributions to the response. Experience has shown that an effective response depends on the timely receipt of accurate and complete information and on sound decisions being made and set in train at the onset.
>
> It is generally accepted that the first member of the emergency services at the scene should not immediately become involved with rescue but should make a rapid assessment of the disaster and report to that service's control. Such information as is immediately available should be provided about the nature of the disaster and its location; the number of dead, injured and uninjured; hazards actual and potential; access to the site and possible rendezvous points; and which emergency services are present or required. Additionally, each of the emergency services has its own requirements; for example, in the case of the fire service, the number of appliances and personnel to be needed."
>
> (Home Office 1994, p. 6, sections 2.9 and 2.10)

Arrangements have to be activated rapidly to establish inner and outer cordons, collection points for survivors and casualties, various rendezvous points, traffic routing, emergency flying restrictions, a temporary mortuary and a media liaison point. The overall command organization adopted by the emergency services at a major incident is shown diagrammatically in Figure 1.2, which illustrates that each emergency service will establish its own incident control posts and forward control posts (specially equipped vehicles are sometimes used as incident control centres) which are staffed by incident commanders. The three organizations should attempt to locate their incident control posts in close proximity, if possible, in order to facilitate liaison.

Command and Control Systems

There are many different command and control systems adopted by the emergency services, although they are all essentially designed for the

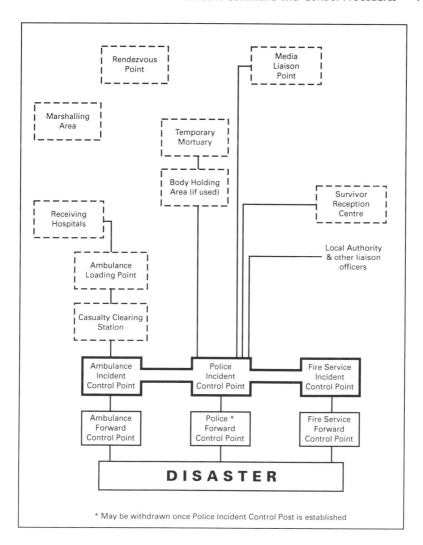

Figure 1.2 *Example of a Typical Organization for Dealing with Disaster. Home Office 1994 (figure 1). Reproduced by permission of the Home Office. Crown Copyright.*

same purpose, which is to deploy available resources to maximum effect to save lives and to bring an emergency under control. Frequently the differences are more apparent than real, with a variety of terminology employed to label the same roles and operations. Precisely to avoid the confusion that is inevitable when different forces, brigades and services, each with its own incident command systems and operational languages, have to work together at a major incident, the Home Office has now issued general guidelines on incident command based on a framework of command and control structures agreed nationally between the emergency services and local authorities. These are reprinted as an appendix in *Dealing with Disaster* (Home Office 1994). The guidelines constitute "a principles paper which: a) allows each agency to tailor its own response plans to interface with the plans of others; b) allows all parties involved to understand their role in the combined response; c) explains how the differing levels of management relate to each other; and d) retains flexibility of option to suit local circumstances" (Home Office 1994, p. 12).

The system that has been adopted was developed by the police following a series of inner city disturbances (riots) in England during the 1980s. It is a three-tiered command and control structure, which defines the strategic, tactical and operational management levels of incident command. These are known as Gold, Silver and Bronze, respectively (Table 1.3). Similar three-tier hierarchical command structures are now used by police forces in England and Wales, and in Scotland (although the Scots have not adopted the metallic labels).

The advantage of this nationally agreed system is that it provides a common framework and shared understanding of incident command. For the purpose of this book, the commanders of most interest are those at the Silver (tactical) and Bronze (operational) levels. The actual implementation

Table 1.3 *Incident Command and Control Structure (Home Office 1994).*

Command	Level	Management Function
Bronze	Operational	This corresponds to the normal operational response provided by the emergency services where the management is of routine tasks. The initial response to most incidents is at this level. In a major incident the Bronze Commanders are likely to be in charge of front line teams.
Silver	Tactical	Their command objective is to determine priority in allocating resources, to plan and coordinate actions. At a major incident the Silver Commander is likely to be the incident commander and located at the incident control post.
Gold	Strategic	Their purpose is to formulate the overall policy for the incident response, ensuring that priorities for demands from the tactical commanders are met. They are responsible for government and media liaison. The Gold Commanders are chief or senior officers, who are likely to be located at a headquarters incident room rather than at the scene. They do not take tactical decisions.

of the system in routine operations is not without its critics. Morrell (1994), a superintendent with Greater Manchester Police, argues that the Gold, Silver and Bronze system should reduce "the normal plethora of senior officers at public order events" but has failed to do so because "the introduction of sub bronzes and sub sub bronzes effectively undermined the concept at an early stage. The desire to employ a large number of senior officers to deal with public order seems to be based on a cultural insurance policy, rather than sound command philosophy" (p. 7). He proposes that optimum command ratios should be incorporated into the command structures for police support units employed in crowd supervision to improve communication and incident management.

A number of fire brigades have adopted the Gold, Silver and Bronze system, while others have retained the more traditional labels of Strategic, Tactical and Task levels of fireground command. The principles of operational command and control at fire incidents and the role of the incident commander (officer in charge) can be found in the *Manual of Firemanship* (Home Office 1981) and the Fire Service Circulars (e.g. Home Office 1978). These state that:

> "at the start of an incident the officer in charge of the first attendance, who is the senior member of the Brigade present, will remain in charge until such time as a more senior officer takes command. The officer in charge is responsible for the control of the incident and the action taken; he must therefore concern himself with an assessment of the situation, an assessment of how the incident might develop and the necessity or otherwise of calling for additional resources."
>
> (Home Office 1978, p. 1)

To exercise effective control, a series of basic steps are recommended: prepare, assess, plan, resources, implement, control and evaluate. The command structure should be designed for situation reports to flow upwards and orders to flow downwards:

> "From the outset of the incident the officer in charge should direct operations and relate brigade strategy and tactics to accepted pre-planning measures. Care must be taken to ensure central direction of the operational plan with a practical measure of control, whilst at the same time ensuring that appropriate initiative in the prescribed plan is not denied to subordinates."
>
> (Home Office 1978, p. 3)

Additional guidance is given relating to the establishment of control points, communications, safety and special duties. (The *Manual of Firemanship* is currently being updated).

Incident command systems are used worldwide, especially by police and fire departments. One example is the incident command system (ICS), which was developed following the FIRESCOPE project initiated after the California brush fires of 1970. According to Cardwell (1994), both fire agencies and law enforcement agencies have adopted this system, with significant benefits in communication and coordination of operations. See Irwin (1989) for further details, and Wenger, Quarantelli and Dynes (1990) for a very critical review of its limitations. In the United States, the National Fire Protection Association (NFPA) stated that "The consequences of operating without an effective incident management system have been documented in numerous deaths and injuries to firefighters" (NFPA 1990, p. 1). They consequently developed a standard Fire Department Incident Management System (NFPA 1990) to provide structure and coordination to the management of emergency incident operations, which is used in the USA and Canada. This defines key terms, such as incident commander, unified command and staging, and then goes on to outline system structure, system components, and roles and responsibilities. For example, the incident commander is responsible for overall coordination and direction of activities, establishing a command structure, assigning supervisory duties, delegating authority and for communicating the overall strategy and any subsequent changes to all supervisors. Many US fire departments have their own incident command systems, similar to the standard ICS. For example, in the New York Fire Department the command system is tailored to deal with specific problems, such as fires in high rise buildings (Dunn 1994).

Standard incident command systems do not meet with unanimous approval. Murphy (1993), a fire safety engineer in New York, complains that not all officers have fully accepted the incident command system:

> "It has been patronized by commanders who operate by the 'seat of their pants.' Their continual nontactical approach on the fireground causes misinterpretation, hostility, and disorder – which results in time lost, severe property damage, and injuries or deaths. Freelancing by companies on the fireground is a prime example of command breakdown. The most frightening aspect of patronizing ICS is that the commander is more vulnerable, as he is left to address complex fireground issues by himself."
>
> (p. 113)

Murphy advocates a STandard Incident Command Kit (STICK) method to assist in the mental process of establishing ICS protocol. This presents the core functions on laminated cards in a ring binder which can be used at the scene of the incident. (For further details of American fireground incident command procedures, see Brunacini 1985; NFPA 1990.) The French fire brigade uses a system called the Method of Tactical Reasoning (MTR) (Pandele 1994a, b), which specifies the command structure and detailed action planning. This prescriptive approach is described in Chapter 5.

Emergency Response Procedures in Hazardous Industries

The foregoing discussion was principally concerned with routine emergencies or major incidents dealt with by the emergency services, where the initiating event may be very sudden and unpredictable. In the case of industrial emergency planning (particularly for chemical or nuclear fixed location sites), the most probable types of incident, their consequences and the required emergency response procedures should already have been identified by hazard analysis and quantitative risk assessment. Such calculations and plans are required to be documented by the organizations concerned, as specified in the Control of Industrial Major Accident Hazards (CIMAH) regulations (HSE 1985b), the EC Directive on the Control of Major Accident Hazards (COMAH) (see De Cort 1994) and the Nuclear Installations Act (1965). For offshore oil and gas installations, similar requirements are stipulated in the Offshore Installations Safety Case regulations (HSE 1992). Individual companies have their own emergency response procedures manuals (see Dickson 1992) and disaster management plans (Lovas and Leitao 1991). The existence of such plans, according to the Home Office (1994) "reduces the likelihood of errors resulting from decisions taken under crisis conditions" (p. 2). In all cases the organization will need to have a proper command and control system in place to deal with any emergency, including a designated incident commander.

At hazardous sites, such as nuclear and chemical plants, these emergency response plans may be subject to independent scrutiny and their emergency exercises observed and assessed. A recent review by the HSE into the management of health and safety and standards of risk control at Atomic Weapons Establishments plc (main sites at Aldermaston, Burghfield, Cardiff and Foulness) provides a good example of this type of inspection. In this case, it resulted in a critical review that revealed a number of problems relating to the emergency response procedures (HSE 1994a). The company was criticized for not carrying out sufficient training or rehearsals of the emergency response plans, and the observed emergency exercise at Aldermaston showed that, while the site plan was put into action, one of the most important weaknesses was "poor command and control at the scene of the incident" (HSE 1994a, Vol. 2, p. 172):

> "It was clear that in an emergency the duty Nominated Senior Officer would take overall charge of events, but the command and control structure below that level was less well defined. At Aldermaston, for example, the

arrangements for command and control at the scene of an incident were not clear. Interviewees said that the separate location of a number of key command posts at that site hampered coherent command and control."

(p. 148)

The Aldermaston on-site emergency plan was judged to be:

"poorly structured, with no succinct top tier plan, little task oriented information, a plethora of annexes, an overly complex numbering system and limited cross-referencing.... There was only limited corporate guidance on important aspects of emergency preparedness such as the frequency and extent of training, the measuring of performance, and the reviewing and auditing of arrangements.... There were no structured corporate or local arrangements for the selection, training, and accreditation of a number of the people who had key roles in relation to site emergency preparedness, either in relation to planning or in relation to the response to an event."

(p. 151)

The preparation of the Nominated Senior Officers for their role as emergency commander was also criticized:

"As far as the review team could gather, their appointment was on the basis of rank, rather than any assessment of competence. They were given minimal training and there was no requirement that they should successfully take part in an emergency exercise before being appointed. These arrangements were inadequate and fell short of practice on licensed nuclear and other high hazard sites."

(p. 157)

This is an interesting deficiency, given the same concern regarding industrial managers having to function as emergency commanders on offshore oil platforms highlighted four years earlier in the Cullen report following the *Piper Alpha* disaster (described below). See also Dynes (1993), who criticizes the prescriptive and dysfunctional nature of the command and control models used for emergency plans at fixed site installations, arguing instead for a more flexible approach.

The Royal Navy

The Royal Navy has very well-developed organizational structures and procedures for dealing with damage control (peacetime emergencies or warfare damage) on their vessels. These are outlined in the *Ship NBCD [Nuclear, Biological, Chemical, Damage]) Manual* (MoD 1994a), which is akin to the emergency procedures manuals used by the police, fire and ambulance services. It covers not only the standard damage control organization, with control positions, communication and staff responsibilities, but also contains tactical and technical information on firefighting, leakstopping, ventilation, medical requirements and ship stability. Unlike an emergency service, whose sole focus will be to deal with the incident, or an industrial emergency response team, who can shut down their business operation (e.g. chemical processing) and concentrate on the incident, a warship crew may be engaged in a battle when the emergency occurs and they will have to continue to fight while the damage is being controlled. In this circumstance, the ship's captain does not take the role of incident commander, remaining instead in the operations room to manage the warfare command. Instead, the marine engineering officer (MEO) acts as the emergency commander (Action NBCD officer) in the ship's control centre. The first lieutenant (XO), second in command of the ship, acts as a roving support and will liaise between the MEO and the captain, as well as visit the scene of the damage and the forward control point. In each control station, specially trained incident board markers, wearing headsets, communicate with each other on an open communications net in order to provide an accurate information log on their status boards (see Atterbury 1992). The training of the NBCD officers is described in Chapter 3.

Standard Operating Procedures

In addition to strategy and planning documents for dealing with emergencies and major incidents, organizations usually have manuals of standard operating procedures (SOPs) to be adopted in response to a particular problem. These may form part of the general emergency procedures manual, or may be published as separate documents. As their name indicates, they are essentially at an operational level rather than tactical or strategic; they define the appropriate set and sequence of actions to be taken in a given situation, and are commonly used with complex technical systems such as production control rooms and flight decks. In some domains, the SOPs will be well known and can be recalled easily from memory; in other cases, officers or managers will rely on prompt cards (*aides-mémoire*, idiot's guides, cue cards) to remind them of the standard procedure. Such cards or check sheets are very widely employed, and their use is encouraged in training, where instructors emphasize that the effect of one's memory going blank under stress is a normal, and not an uncommon, reaction (see Chapter 4). SOPs are also used by the emergency services, but having a procedure in place does not necessarily guarantee compliance, as Dobson (1995) has recently demonstrated for the fire service. Moreover, it has been argued that in non-routine events they can stifle necessary creative thinking. Dror (1988), discussing decision making in disasters, makes the point that "The standard operating procedures accordingly should recognise the crucial importance of improvisation and provide suitable frameworks for it, rather than repressing it" (p. 269).

WHO IS THE INCIDENT COMMANDER?

Throughout this book, the terms "incident commander" and "on-scene commander" will be used interchangeably rather than "operational commander", which has a more ambiguous definition. The individuals who are the focus of discussion are those who hold a command role at the scene of an emergency or major incident. With regard to the emergency services at a joint operation, this will include the overall incident commander (who is usually a police officer), as well as the fire service and ambulance service incident commanders, who will have established their own command posts. These commanders have tactical responsibilities. In a typical incident command structure (discussed above), these people would be the Silver Commanders (the more senior Gold Commander would have strategic responsibilities and is likely to be located in an off-site command centre, such as headquarters). The more junior sector commanders, functioning as incident commanders for their own areas, have operational responsibilities and may be known as Bronze Commanders. They are more likely to be able to view the scene directly and will report their observations and judgements to the Silver Commander. This book is primarily concerned with the Silver and Bronze Commanders (tactical and operational commanders) who have management responsibilities at the scene of the event. It is acknowledged that there are occasions when a very junior officer can be the incident commander. Police constables or ambulance personnel will often be the first officers on the scene of what transpires to be a major incident; in these circumstances, their primary duty is to assess the situation and act as the communication link until more senior officers arrive. For smaller scale or routine incidents, they will be expected to take charge of the situation and thus begin to gain incident management experience early in their careers. Similarly, in the fire service, the first response to an emergency call may be one fire appliance and, in the event of a major fire, this crew commander will be the fireground commander until more senior officers arrive.

If an incident escalates, the on-scene commander from the initial emergency services response will typically transfer command to an officer of a more senior rank. At a major incident this can involve a rapid series of handovers. For example, at the King's Cross fire, a fire service divisional officer took command for three minutes before he had to hand over command to a more senior officer. The public inquiry directed

London Fire Brigade to review its procedures for handing over command at major incidents (Fennell 1988). This is an interesting facet of incident command procedures, particularly if a senior officer with little recent incident command experience takes over from an officer with considerable expertise who is handling the situation effectively. Wenger, Quarantelli and Dynes (1990), commenting on the American Incident Command System (ICS), say:

> "the one component of the system that is often selectively adopted and implemented in actual response situations is the weakest element in the model, i.e. the bumping of 'command' from initially-responding officers of lower rank to those of higher rank and the subsequent reversal of this pattern. ... In several of our studies, the position of incident commander changed a number of times and such action resulted in a loss of information about the earlier situation. This resulted not from incompetence of the officials involved, but from a structural flaw of the model."
>
> (p. 9)

For incident commanders who are not from the emergency services, the situation is rather different. An airline pilot, ship's captain or an industrial manager on a remote site, such as an offshore oil platform, will have to function as incident commander for the main duration of the incident without outside assistance (except by telecommunications links). The onshore hazardous plant manager (e.g. nuclear or chemical) will have the rapid assistance of professional incident commanders from the police, fire service and ambulance within minutes of notification. This still means that the early and often most critical phase of the emergency will have to be managed by the site emergency response teams from the on-duty shift, with a manager acting as incident commander. The issue of whether the plant manager should take the role of incident commander or whether another member of staff (e.g. the safety manager) should be specially trained to do so is frequently debated. Donovan (1992), discussing emergencies in chemical plants, says:

> "Plant managers are not always the most appropriate incident commanders. During an emergency they should retain their overall management positions but the actual emergency response is more effectively directed by an incident commander and an alternate who train regularly with the emergency response team."
>
> (p. 36)

Irrespective of which manager takes the role of commander at the start of the incident, the very welcome arrival of the professional emergency services can bring new problems in the form of maintaining communication and coordination with these agencies, who are likely to take over responsibility for incident management on a hazardous industrial site with which they are relatively unfamiliar.

What Is Command?

The focus of this book is incident command, but what exactly is command? Is it different from management, from leadership? The word command comes from the Latin *mandare*, meaning to entrust, and the Oxford dictionary definition is "to order, to exercise supreme authority over". The operation of command is the foundation of all warfare operations and is a prime topic of military writing (e.g. Keegan 1987; Montgomery 1958). Montgomery's doctrine of command is still taught to British armed forces' commanding officers. He equated command with leadership, which he defined as, "The capacity and the will to rally men and women to a common purpose, and the character which inspires confidence" (p. 80). The emergency services are organized on a militaristic model; they call their senior officers "commanders", and their literature also examines the nature and practice of command (e.g. Brunacini 1985). Murray (1994b), a fire service Divisional Commander, says "Operational Command separates the fire service from other organisations. The ability of the fire service officer to quickly make sense of the confused and dynamic picture presented at every incident, separates fire service management from other forms of management. Commanding critical resources when life, property and the environment are at risk is a very unique and demanding situation. The exercise of command at an operational incident is complex. Incident commanders must realise the responsibilities faced, recognise authority possessed, assess the situation, make decisions and take action which meets the expectations of all those they serve" (p. 67).

For the manager who is required to take the position of incident commander in an emergency, the concept of command may be rather less familiar; some of the oil companies have used ex-military commanders to train their offshore mangers in emergency command. One such company is the Offshore Command Training Organisation, established by ex-Falklands naval officers Admiral Sir John Woodward and Rear-Admiral Jeremy Larken. They emphasize that command in an emergency is different from routine management:

"But when time is at a premium and when danger immediately threatens, command has to encompass a whole range of extra skills, mostly concerned with the rapid assessment of people who have changed under pressure and of things which have failed to operate or activate as might have been expected. Command is predominately subjective and directive. Management is predominately objective and consultative.... An important subsidiary conclusion is that the application of conventional management techniques can ironically be quite dangerous in an emergency."

(Larken 1992, p. 31)

The available literature on emergency management appears to agree on the role and function of the incident commander. For the purposes of major incident management, the Home Office (1992) provides this definition: "Command means the authority for an agency to direct the actions of its own resources (both personnel and equipment)" (p. 52). As mentioned above, incident commanders are ranked in relation to their operational, tactical and strategic responsibilities. Brunacini (1985), examining the role of the American fireground commander who has overall responsibility for incident command, says, "As a Commander, he is expected to choose command over action, working from strategic levels rather than the task level" (p. 4), and he goes on to define the fireground command functions as follows (p. 11):

"1. Assumption, confirmation and positioning of command.
2. Situation evaluation.
3. Initiation, maintenance, and control of the communications process.
4. Identification of the overall strategy, development of an attack plan, and the assignment of units.
5. Development of an effective fireground organization.
6. Reviewing, evaluating, and revising the attack plan.
7. Providing continuation command, transferring command (as required), and termination command."

Having established some general agreement as to the role of the on-scene commander, the following section examines incident command in action.

COMMAND AND CONTROL AT MAJOR INCIDENTS

The following review of demonstrated strengths and weaknesses in on-scene command is based on public investigations of European accidents that occurred in the late 1980s and early 1990s, in each case resulting in multiple fatalities. In each case, command problems have been identified; of particular interest are those that reappear in different environments and with different agencies involved. The themes relate to poor decision making, lack of training, disorganized teamwork, inadequate incident command preparation, plans or procedures, and coordination and communication problems. It should be acknowledged that in the vast majority of cases, the successful incident commanders rarely see their skills and effort lauded, because the incident has been so well managed that it does not escalate, and hence does not reach the pages of the press. The media are much more interested in mismanaged calamity than in a smooth running and controlled operation. It is surprisingly difficult to find good documentation of successful incident command because it is typically the failures that are scrutinized minutely when a formal investigation is commissioned. We usually have more to learn from our errors than from our triumphs, but sometimes, particularly when detailed evidence is available such as voice recordings, a difficult but well-managed incident will also provide valuable indicators of effective incident command. The final accident discussed is of this genre. The other incidents chosen for inclusion were either of such magnitude that command resources were tested to an extreme or were found to have been incompetently managed.

The material presented in the examples to follow is based not on personal interviews with the responsible commanders but on the reports of public inquiries. The subsection is therefore prefaced by the caution that the power of hindsight granted to those tasked with reviewing the incident was not available to the on-scene commanders at the time of these exceptionally difficult incidents. The potential limitations of such post-event reviews were acknowledged by Anthony Hidden, who chaired the public inquiry into the Clapham rail crash:

> "In my review I have attempted at all times to remind myself of the dangers of using the powerful beam of hindsight to illuminate the situations revealed in the evidence. The power of that beam has its disadvantages. Hindsight also possesses a lens which can distort and can therefore present a misleading picture: it has to be avoided if fairness and accuracy of judgement are to be sought."
>
> (Hidden 1989, p. 3)

In the same vein, Brunacini (1985) says, "Considering what was going on at the time a decision was made will many times effectively refocus 20–20 hindsight", and "The number of faults in a fire operation is in direct proportion to the number of viewers; the intelligence of the viewers is in direct proportion to how late they arrive" (p. 245).

It is accepted that the following extracts are to some extent presented out of context, but they have been selected to illustrate the particular problems facing the incident commander, especially at a major incident. For a more complete picture, the original inquiry reports, which often contain a chapter on the emergency response, should be consulted. It should also be noted that many lessons have been learnt from these disasters, and that the organizations in question have taken significant steps to address problems in operating procedures or incident command training. These developments are outlined in subsequent chapters.

The *Piper Alpha* Platform

Not all incident commanders are from military or emergency service occupations. Managers, particularly those who work in remote locations such as mines or construction sites, may have several hundred staff under their charge and will be required to act as the on-scene commander should an emergency arise. Oil industry maritime disasters such as the loss of the *Alexander Keilland* flotel rig in 1980 with 123 lives (Norwegian Public Reports 1981) and the sinking of the drilling rig *Ocean Ranger* off Newfoundland in 1982 with her entire crew of 84 men (Canadian Royal Commission 1984) had demonstrated the potential dangers and the need for emergency training of key personnel. But one of the worst accidents experienced by the offshore oil industry highlighted the critical role of the on-scene commander.

The *Piper Alpha* oil and gas production platform, operated by Occidental Petroleum (Caledonia) Ltd, was located 110 miles north-east of Aberdeen, in the British sector of the North Sea. At around 22.00 hours on 6th July 1988 there was an explosion on the production deck of the platform, which, evidence presented at the public inquiry suggests, was caused by the ignition of a cloud of gas condensate leaking from a temporary flange. The resulting fire spread rapidly and was followed by a number of smaller explosions. At around 22.20, there was a major explosion caused by the rupturing of a pipeline carrying gas to the *Piper Alpha* from the nearby Texaco *Tartan* platform. Over the course of the next few hours an intense high pressure gas fire raged, punctuated by a series of major explosions that served to hasten the structural collapse of the platform. Of the 226 persons who were on board the installation, only 61 survived. The great majority of the survivors escaped by jumping into the sea, some from as high as 175 feet.

It appears that the crisis on board the *Piper Alpha* could have been managed more effectively. Dr Allan Sefton, operations director of the Offshore Safety Division of the HSE, made the following observation:

> "The explosion on *Piper Alpha* that led to the disaster was not devastating. We shall never know, but it probably killed only a small number of men. As the resulting fire spread, most of the *Piper Alpha* workforce made their way to the accommodation where they expected someone would be in charge and would lead them to safety. Apparently, they were disappointed. It seems the whole system of command had broken down."
>
> (Sefton 1992, p. 6)

The report of the ensuing public inquiry, chaired by Lord Cullen (1990), contained a number of criticisms relating to the performance of *Piper Alpha's* OIM on the night of the disaster, as well as the OIMs on duty on the adjacent *Claymore* and *Tartan* platforms. These installations were linked to the *Piper Alpha* by hydrocarbon pipelines, the rupturing of which caused massive explosions and the rapid spread of the fire on the *Piper Alpha*. It was suggested that, had the production of hydrocarbons by these platforms been stopped sooner, the situation on the *Piper Alpha* might have deteriorated less rapidly. The report pools the evidence of survivors from the disaster and describes in as much detail as is possible the actions of the *Piper Alpha* OIM during the early stages of the crisis. Evidence is also presented regarding the actions of the *Claymore* and *Tartan* OIMs during the same period:

> "The OIM had been gone 'a matter of seconds when he came running back' in what appeared ... to be a state of panic ... The OIM made no specific attempt to call in helicopters from the *Tharos* or elsewhere; or to communicate with vessels around the installation; or with the shore or other installations; or with personnel on *Piper*."
>
> (para. 8.9)

> "The OIM did not give any other instruction or guidance. One survivor said that at one stage people were shouting at the OIM and asking what was going on and what procedure to follow. He did not know whether the OIM was in shock or not but he did not seem able to come up with any answer."
>
> (para. 8.18)

> "it is unfortunately clear that the OIM took no initiative in an attempt to save life ... in my view the death toll of those who died in the accommodation was substantially greater than it would have been if such an initiative had been taken."
>
> (para. 8.35)

> "The OIM on *Claymore* had full authority to shut down oil production and was under no constraint from management in this respect. ... I consider that he should have shut down earlier than he did ... From the evidence I conclude he was reluctant to take responsibility for shutting down oil production."
>
> (para. 7.49)

> "The strong impression with which I was left after hearing the evidence as to the response of *Tartan* and *Claymore* was that the type of emergency with which the senior personnel of each platform was confronted was something for which they had not been prepared."
>
> (para. 7.52)

Two months after the *Piper Alpha* disaster, on 22nd September 1988, there was a blowout and an evacuation of the Odeco rig *Ocean Odyssey*, which was drilling in the North Sea 150 miles east of Aberdeen. Her radio operator did not escape from the installation and was killed in the fire. The report from the resulting fatal accident inquiry (Ireland 1991) again highlighted the important decision making role of the OIM during an offshore emergency:

> "The death of Timothy Williams might reasonably have been prevented (i) if the Offshore Installation Manager (OIM) had not ordered him from the lifeboat to the radio room; (ii) if the OIM, having ordered Timothy Williams back to the radio room, had countermanded that order when the rig was evacuated, and taken steps to see that the countermanding order was communicated to him."
>
> (12.5)

In the *Piper Alpha* public inquiry report, Lord Cullen (1990) made over 100 recommendations regarding the safe management of offshore installations, two of which related specifically to OIMs:

> "The operator's criteria for the selection of OIMs, and in particular their command ability, should form part of its SMS [Safety Management System]. There should be a system of emergency exercises which provides OIMs with practice in decision-making in emergency situations, including decisions on evacuation. All OIMs and their deputies should participate regularly in such exercises."
>
> (98.99)

The offshore oil manager is not the only professional in a remote workplace who may find it necessary to switch from routine technical or managerial activities into the role of on-scene commander. A series of transport accidents since the mid-1980s, in rail crashes, plane crashes and ship collisions or sinkings, has emphasized dramatically that aircraft captains and ships' captains are also incident commanders in the event of an emergency. Major passenger shipping accidents in recent years have included the collision on the River Thames between the passenger launch *Marchioness* and the dredger *Bowbelle*, resulting in 51 fatalities (MAIB 1991), the sinking of the P&O ferry *Herald of Free Enterprise* when she sailed from Zeebrugge in Belgium with her bow doors open and capsized, killing 188 (Crainer 1993), and the sinking of the passenger ferry *Estonia* in a storm off Finland in September 1994, with 780 fatalities (Bawtree 1995b). Such tragedies have raised issues relating to emergency training of non-marine crew (*Marchioness* collision), international coordination and communication (*Estonia* rescue) and operational command (the sinking of the fishing boat *Antares* by the nuclear submarine HMS *Trenchant*, with a student commander on duty; MAIB 1992). The most salient illustration of a captain and his crew who probably could have mitigated the scale of a marine emergency comes from a fire on a Norwegian passenger ferry.

The *Scandinavian Star*

On Friday 6th April 1990, the *Scandinavian Star* left Oslo bound for Fredrikshavn at 21.45. She was carrying a crew of 99 and had 383 passengers on board. Between 01.45 and 02.00 on 7th April, a fire started in a pile of bedclothes outside a cabin on deck 4. This fire was put out. A little after 02.00, a new fire started, aft in the starboard corridor of deck 3 (which was almost certainly started by a naked flame). Within a few minutes of ignition, flames and toxic smoke spread rapidly through the cabin sections and further into the ship. As a result, 158 people died in the fire, probably by 02.45. At 03.20 the crew abandoned the ship. The Committee of Inquiry's report (Norwegian Public Reports 1991) concluded that the ship's command had failed on several points during the disaster, namely (i) their inability to maintain an overview of the situation, (ii) failures to direct and command the crew – "many of the senior group leaders had no idea which emergency plan group they belonged to or what functions they were supposed to carry out" (p. 131), (iii) lack of information given to the crew and the passengers and (iv) insufficient information provided to the outside world (e.g. to adjacent vessels). Their emergency command procedures were severely criticized and deemed to be a contributing factor to the scale of the tragedy:

> "None of the key officers attempted at any time to actively acquire a systematic picture of the situation. No coordinated channels of information were set up, no arrangements were made for effective communication (e.g. by walkie-talkie), and no attempts were made to obtain status reports from various parts of the ship. Since no operational groups were established either, as presupposed by the emergency plan, no organized reports were made of what was being done. Even under the difficult conditions prevailing, the information possessed by senior officers was at all stages more haphazard than it need have been."
>
> (Norwegian Public Reports 1991, p. 132)

The above examples are situations where the on-scene command responsibility is a feature of a site manager's or transport captain's job, where he or she requires these skills but is not going to be asked to demonstrate them too often, if at all. But other disaster inquiries have also questioned the ability of incident commanders employed by agencies for whom crisis management is a central part of their job, if not their *raison d'être*. The following accounts demonstrate the significant demands that may be placed on the incident commander by the police and fire service, and the consequences of inadequate command decision making or delayed action in implementing command and control once an incident begins to unfold. In some instances, the efficiency of incident command by a particular individual or organization is commended.

The Bradford Fire

At about 15.40 on Saturday 11th May 1985, a fire started (probably by a dropped match) in block G of the main stand of Bradford City football ground. In approximately five minutes the whole stand, holding just over 2000 people, was in flames. The fire developed with a speed and intensity that no one had thought possible. A total of 56 supporters died and many others were seriously injured. Mr Justice Popplewell's Committee of Inquiry Interim Report (Popplewell 1985) revealed a number of the difficulties for the incident commander and his team in this situation:

> "Considerable controversy emerged during the course of the public inquiry about the responsibility of the club *vis-à-vis* the police and vice versa. ... the police have to take the *de facto* responsibility of organising the crowd, with all that entails, during the game. The significance of this aspect was highlighted by a number of questions raised about the responsibility for evacuation. It is clear that neither this police force, nor many other police forces, as far as we can ascertain have received any training or briefing in the question of evacuation.
>
> In the situation which obtained at Bradford they behaved with commendable efficiency, even without formal training. They also behaved with enormous bravery. I recommend therefore that evacuation procedure should be a matter for police training and form part of the briefing by police officers before a football match.
>
> The difficulties of communicating in an emergency of this sort are illustrated by the fact that when a police officer asked for a fire extinguisher another officer thought he wanted the fire brigade. Although the communication difficulties played no part in this disaster, there is undoubtedly a greater sense of urgency if instructions are given by a loud-hailer.
>
> Because of the enormous noise at any football ground, particularly during an emergency, it is very difficult for the reporting officer to make himself understood by control. There was a considerable body of evidence of officers having relayed messages to control which were not received, and of messages which were received but not in full.
>
> Finally, I would like to commend the fire services for the efficient and expeditious way in which they dealt with this fire."
>
> (Popplewell 1985, extracts from 3.16–3.9)

A number of psychologists were involved in the aftermath (see, for example, Duckworth (1986), who worked with police officers suffering from post-traumatic stress). Canter, Comber and Uzzell (1989) examined the accident in relation to crowd behaviour and control at football matches. They highlighted a particular feature of emergencies, which can also be seen in hindsight for the management of other major incidents:

> "The first thing to happen is that there are some ambiguous cues that something – possibly life threatening – may be going on. This is an aspect of emergency events such as fires that is frequently misunderstood. In the early stages it is not clear what the nature of the problem may be. All that people know is that there is some possible danger or perhaps only that something unusual is happening.... In the early stages of the Bradford fire it was clear that people did not take the event very seriously. Spectators close to the fire moved away but then stood and turned to watch it.... In the initial stages people in authority may be equally unlikely to treat an incident as serious and so delay taking appropriate action. The police in particular may need time to assess what is going on. In the Bradford fire a senior police officer walked the length of the football pitch in order to examine the fire before he started giving orders for people to leave over the front of the stands on to the football pitch. In Brussels [see below] it would appear that the police never got properly organised to deal with the rushing rowdy young men who were chasing around. They appeared to have no clear way of recognising the likely consequences of the actions."
>
> (Canter, Comber and Uzzell 1989, pp. 98–100)

The Heysel Stadium (Brussels)

On the 29th May 1985 the European Cup Final was due to take place between the English football club, Liverpool and the Italian club, Juventus, at the Heysel stadium in Brussels. At about 19.30, English fans charged into block Z of the terracing. In the resulting panic among the spectators, 38 people died and 400 were injured. The Final Report of Inquiry into Crowd Safety and Control at Sports Grounds (Popplewell 1986) contains extracts of the translated Report of the Belgian Inquiry. While there is little doubt that the main cause of the disaster was the hooligan behaviour of the English football fans, the issue of incident command, by the Belgian gendarmerie, is raised and the problems of coordination between them and the local police force is discussed:

> "The provisions made were based on information which proved to be inaccurate. The error lay in the fact that the arrangements were not adapted quickly enough when they needed to be, and this is attributable to four factors: the command structure of the gendarmerie; lack of precision in the orders given; lack of messengers for the dissemination of information within the stadium and the element of 'unpredictability'."
>
> (p. 74)

Jacobs and t'Hart (1992), who studied this accident, highlighted several command problems:

> "At this critical juncture, a gap in the operational command structure occurred: the Alpha squadron's commander and his deputy had both left the stadium responding independently to a call about a robbery outside the arena. Gendarmerie's written and unwritten rules strongly forbade lower level personnel to surpass their direct commanders in calling for assistance. As a consequence, the platoon commander at the Z section spent some agonizing minutes deliberating whether or not to take such an initiative. When he finally acted, his call for reinforcements could hardly get through because of faulty equipment (worn-out batteries).... the Gendarmerie's supreme commander who was visiting the match as a guest, had the greatest difficulty in reaching the general commander who had decided to conduct the operation from Brussels headquarters."
>
> (p. 146)

Unfortunately, some of the command problems identified reappeared (in a different guise) at another major football incident in England four years later.

The Hillsborough Stadium Disaster

On 15th April 1989 a football match to decide a major cup semi-final competition was to be played between the Liverpool and Nottingham Forest clubs. The match had been a sell-out and 54000 fans were expected. The neutral venue chosen was Hillsborough football stadium in Sheffield. A serious crowd control problem before the kick-off, in the turnstile area, resulted in a police decision to open gates into the ground, causing disastrous overcrowding and crushing in one part of the terracing. Only six minutes into the game, play was stopped when it was realized that spectators on the terraces behind the Liverpool goal had been severely crushed. As a result 95 people died and 400 received hospital treatment (see Jacobs and t'Hart (1992) for one of a number of analyses of the disaster). The senior police officer responsible was a chief superintendent; under him were sector commanders (superintendents), who had a total of 801 officers on duty at the ground. The club had a control room which could communicate by VHF radio with its 376 stewards and the turnstiles were filmed by CCTV. In addition, the police had a small control room with a good view of the pitch and five screens displaying images from roving cameras, which was manned by a superintendent, a sergeant and two constables. The Rt Hon. Lord Justice Taylor was appointed to carry out an inquiry (Taylor 1989, 1990) into the disaster. While the bulk of the recommendations dealt with the design and management of football grounds, a number of issues relating to command and control were raised:

"... although there were other causes, the main reason for the disaster was failure of police control."

(Taylor 1989, 278, p. 49)

"with some notable exceptions, the senior officers in command were defensive and evasive witnesses. Their feelings of grief and sorrow were obvious and genuine. No doubt these feelings were intensified by the knowledge that such a disaster had occurred under their management. But, neither their handling of problems on the day nor their account of it in evidence showed the qualities of leadership to be expected of their rank."

(Taylor 1989, 280, p. 49)

The chief superintendent who was in overall command was criticized for "his aversion to addressing the crowd and his failure to take effective control of the disaster situation. He froze." (Taylor 1989, 284, p. 50).

In his final report, Lord Justice Taylor states:

"The ultimate control at any match must be that of the Police Commander. He has authority to decide how many officers he needs and to deploy them inside and outside the ground. He has if necessary to take such decisions as to delay kick off, to stop the match, to evacuate the ground or any area of it."

(Taylor 1990, 215, p. 38)

He recommended that:

"Consideration should be given to the provision of a specific training course for senior officers presently acting as Police Commanders and those in line to do so. Such a course should include training in the basic strategy of policing football matches."

(Taylor 1990, 52, p. 80)

The training courses used by the police to teach command and control for football crowds, public order and other situations are discussed in Chapter 3. However, it is not only oil managers and police officers who have received criticism in recent years for their emergency command performance; the fire service too has come under public scrutiny.

Fires at Brightside Lane, Gillender Street, Sun Valley and Villiers Road

Problems relating to incident command at fires have been identified in a number of fire incidents, two of which resulted in the deaths of firefighters. In Brightside Lane, Sheffield, in December 1984, a fire broke out in a furniture repository which was part of a massive warehouse complex. In two days the fire destroyed almost the entire warehouse (with an estimated £20 million damage), but there were no fatalities. The entire operation involved 300 firemen and 150 police officers over a period of six days. The following month, the Fire Brigade Union complained to the HSE of inadequacies during the fire fighting operation, particularly relating to the provision of breathing apparatus, which they alleged had resulted in some firemen being unnecessarily exposed to smoke and fumes. The subsequent investigation (HSE 1985a) confirmed that "there was a lack of control and communication at critical points, affecting compliance with the procedures for using breathing apparatus, and some failure also to react with due care for safety during firefighting" (HSE 1985a, p. 1). It also noted that:

> "The fire was unique in the experience of most firefighters entering the fireground: the number of appliances, the scale and duration of the operation were greatly in excess of anything tackled previously, although it is by no means rare for a fire of such magnitude to occur nationally. Lack of experience of such a fire might have contributed to the identified failures to carry out designated fireground tasks in accordance with set procedure although training and practice should have avoided such failures."
>
> (HSE 1985a, p. 34)

When two firefighters died after becoming lost and running out of air during firefighting operations at Hays Business Services, a large document depository in Gillender Street, London, in August 1991, the Coroner's Inquest returned a verdict of unlawful killing and highlighted major failings in command and control. The HSE imposed two improvement notices on the brigade in relation to assessment and training for command and operational competencies. As a result of these notices, one of the initiatives taken by London Fire Brigade was to commission a project into competence based training (see Chapter 2). They also introduced a new incident debrief procedure, in which the incident commander and the team discuss each operation after the event to uncover any particular operational, technical or command problems, which are admitted and discussed in a no-blame setting.

In September 1993, two firefighters died when the roof collapsed at the Sun Valley poultry factory in Hereford. Consequently, the HSE issued two improvement notices to Hereford and Worcester Fire Brigade, which also raised issues relating to risk assessment and command and control. In response, the brigade have developed new risk assessment and team work training procedures. A third improvement notice was issued to London Fire Brigade in February 1994, following a firefighter's death at Villiers

Road, which focused on the need for risk assessment in relation to the systems of command and tactical firefighting.

In major incidents, the emergency services do not work alone; they have to operate in conjunction with local authority personnel and many other agencies, to say nothing of spectators, the media and visiting dignitaries. Three incidents serve to illustrate the dimensions of the command and control problem facing not only the fire and ambulance services, but particularly the police, who are responsible for overall coordination.

The King's Cross Underground Fire

On the evening of 18th November 1987 at 19.30, a passenger reported a small fire on an escalator in London's King's Cross underground station. One of the staff on duty (not normally based at this station) went to inspect but informed neither the station manager nor the line controller. By chance, there were two police officers in the station, one of whom called the London Fire Brigade, and passenger evacuation began. However, the fire escalated, resulting in a flashover which engulfed the ticket hall while passengers were still trying to escape. According to the Investigation Report:

> "The first London Fire Brigade personnel reached the tube line's ticket hall about 19:43 only two minutes before the flashover. It was too late for them to do anything. Between 19:30 and 19:45 not one single drop of water had been applied to the fire which erupted into the tube line's ticket hall causing horrendous injuries and killing 31 people [including a London Fire Brigade Station Officer]."
>
> (Fennell 1988, p. 17)

The report identified a number of problems relating to command and control, as well as to liaison between the emergency services, and concluded with 157 recommendations relating to London Underground, London Fire Brigade, Metropolitan Police, Ambulance Service and coordination between the services. Some of these are listed below.

London Underground:

> "While the actions of individuals at the time were understandable, and in several cases involved presence of mind and courage, their overall response may be characterised as uncoordinated, haphazard and untrained.... More importantly, the training and instruction the supervisory staff had received was wholly inadequate for them to deal with passengers, staff and occupants in an emergency."
>
> (Fennell 1988, 15.4, p. 125)

"There seems to have been a lack of perception that fire demands a very rapid reaction if it is to be contained. He considered that the limited knowledge, confusion and lack of leadership placed all staff on the night in a very difficult position."

(Fennell 1988, 15.30, p. 131)

"Every two years all management and supervisory staff shall receive refresher training in controlling station emergencies, and the use of fire and communications equipment."

(Fennell 1988, recommendation 82, p. 171)

"Potential London Underground incident officers must be trained and practised in their duties."

(Fennell 1988, recommendation 90, p. 171)

London Fire Brigade:

"It is clear that a large number of members of London Fire Brigade behaved with conspicuous courage and devotion to duty during the disaster in which they lost a brave officer, Station Officer Townsley."

(Fennell 1988, 11.34, p. 83)

"The London Fire Brigade shall review its procedures and criteria for handing over and assuming command during major incidents."

(Fennell 1988, recommendation 26, p. 166)

"The London Fire Brigade shall review its instructions and training arrangements for command and control."

(Fennell 1988, recommendation 30, p. 166)

Metropolitan Police:

"It is apparent that the Metropolitan Police had a properly planned and coordinated emergency response procedure which Inspector Coleman was able to initiate with speed after a prompt reconnaissance. In the result an efficient and effective back-up was available to deal with the results of the disaster."

(Fennell 1988, 11.66, p. 90)

London Ambulance Service:

"The London Ambulance Service shall improve its arrangements for the attendance of a senior officer when a major incident may develop and shall review the procedure for the attendance of its command and control vehicle at major accidents."

(Fennell 1988, recommendation 34, p. 166)

Coordination between the services:

> "The court was left with the impression that there had been a breakdown of communication at command level between the emergency services. Each diligently pursued its own duty but there was a lack of liaison between them."
>
> (Fennell 1988, 31, p. 83)

> "A review shall be undertaken of Section 30 of the Fire Services Act 1947 to clarify the responsibilities of the police and the fire brigade."
>
> (Fennell 1988, 155, p. 177)

The particular demands of multiple agency operations are well recognized (Home Office 1994) and are considered below in two transport accidents. The Clapham Junction rail crash and the Kegworth air crash demonstrated not only the coordination required at a major incident, but also the role played in disasters by many other agencies and members of the public who willingly provide rescue and support services.

The Clapham Junction Rail Crash

At 08.10 on Monday 12th December 1988, a crowded commuter train ran head-on into the rear of a second train, which was stationary in a cutting just south of Clapham Junction, London. After the impact, the first train veered to the right and struck a third train coming down the other line. A fourth train managed to stop in time, coming to a standstill 20 yards from the rear of the first train. As a result of the accident, 35 people who were travelling in the first two coaches of the first train died and nearly 500 were injured, 69 of them seriously. The London Fire Brigade assumed overall command of the incident at the trackside (normally the police role), coordinating the efforts of several hundred fire officers, police officers, British Transport Police officers, and local authority staff, along with ambulance service personnel and doctors. A total of 67 ambulances and a police helicopter were involved in ferrying the casualties to hospitals. The Public Inquiry report (Hidden 1989) devoted a chapter to the response of the emergency services. In terms of command and control, it commented on communication delays and possible confusion from various coloured tabards worn at the incident. Overall, it concluded that the coordination of the rescue had proceeded very smoothly:

> "all the evidence ... indicated that the rescue operation carried out by the emergency services was done in an exemplary manner. It was effected with total cooperation between those services."
>
> (Hidden 1989, 5.13)

> "The Investigation heard of the regular exercises that take place involving all the emergency services and the use of table-top exercises as an addition.

These obviously have an important role in emergency planning. In view of the comments I have already, future exercises should specifically test communications and in particular the call-out procedures between the services."

(Hidden 1989, 5.93)

"The LFCDA [London Fire and Civil Defence Authority] made representations to the effect that consideration should be given to amending the Fire Services Act 1947 so as to recognise command and control duties and responsibilities of the Senior Fire Officer at any incident to which the fire brigade dedicates equipment and personnel. The overall command of the Clapham Junction incident at trackside was not disputed by the other services. However, the general principle of a statutory command and control role for a fire brigade at any incident where it commits personnel and equipment is not agreed by the other services. Discussion would need to continue at national level to ensure that all relevant types of incident are considered. Looking at the Clapham Junction incident alone, I cannot make a recommendation to create an extended statutory role for the fire brigades throughout the country on the basis of that rescue operation."

(Hidden 1989, 5.94–5.96)

"The emergency services shall recognise the primacy of the civil Police authority in accidents of this kind where there is no fire. This recognition does not preclude delegation to the LFB of control at trackside."

(Hidden 1989, recommendation 74)

The Kegworth Air Crash

On the evening of Sunday 8th January 1989, a British Midlands 737-400 aircraft *en route* from Heathrow to Belfast developed an engine fire, and, in a tragic sequence of errors, the pilots shut down the wrong engine, which resulted in the plane crashing on the M1 motorway near Kegworth, just short of East Midlands airport runway (AAIB 1990). From the crew of 8 and 118 passengers, including an infant, there were 47 fatalities and 79 injured; in addition, 5 firefighters were injured during the rescue operation. News film of the incident site clearly shows the scale of the emergency response, which was coordinated by the Leicestershire Constabulary. They estimated that there were 59 police vehicles and 301 police officers attending, 73 ambulances with 140 personnel, as well as 37 fire appliances with 247 firefighters and officers. These figures need to be supplemented by airport emergency response teams, the large numbers of civilians acting as rescuers, who were on the motorway when the accident happened, plus many other voluntary agencies and rescue teams who turned up to help, passengers' relatives and news reporters, who began to arrive within an hour of the accident. The AAIB accident report only provides brief details of the rescue operations (section 1.15.2) but it does note that it took eight hours to evacuate all of the passengers.

It should be acknowledged in this opening chapter that across professions, incident commanders typically perform to a high standard, thus preventing minor emergencies from developing into major disasters. However, as anyone in this role will be aware, it is only the major catastrophes which challenge command systems that receive intense public and media scrutiny followed by the minute analysis of a formal inquiry. For this reason, commanders, officers, managers and pilots who perform competently rarely receive the public recognition or accolades that they deserve for a job well done. Occasionally there are exceptions to this rule, and in an attempt to provide a degree of balance, the final case study demonstrates incident command and teamwork of the highest calibre during a very serious emergency.

United Airlines Flight 232

During United Airlines flight 232 from Denver to Chicago on 19th July 1989, there was a catastrophic failure of the DC10's centre engine, which resulted in the loss of all hydraulic systems and flight controls. Captain Haynes (1992) enlisted the help of a training pilot who happened to be travelling as a passenger, and together the flight deck crew developed their own emergency procedure based on asymmetrical engine thrust and managed to get the crippled airliner within a few feet of Sioux City airport before impact. The crash landing and resulting fire caused 112 fatalities (from 296 aboard), in a situation that would have been expected to have resulted in total loss of life. The accident report commended the flight crew and stated that their teamwork was "indicative of the value of cockpit resource management training which has been in existence in UAL [United Airlines] for over a decade" (NTSB 1990, p. 76). (Cockpit resource management training, now called crew resource management, is discussed in Chapter 6.) The level of command and crew performance demonstrated in this incident is frequently cited as a gold standard for team working. This was no ordinary feat, as Ginnet (1993) has pointed out: "Remarkably this crew performed even better than subsequent crews in simulator re-enactments" (p. 84). Cockpit voice recordings of this incident reveal a very composed captain performing at the highest level with the assistance of his flight crew, and a very calm and proficient air traffic controller. (See also Emery and Grimsted (1994) for a personal account of pilots dealing with an in-flight emergency on a cargo plane.)

CONCLUSION

The disasters described in this chapter were all situations in which the incident commanders were faced with extremely difficult decisions, characterized by ambiguous and conflicting information, shifting goals, time pressure, dynamic conditions, complex operational team structures, and poor communication and circumstances where every available course of action carried significant risk. These event features are now regarded as typical of situations requiring naturalistic decision making (Zsambok and Klein, in press). Despite the broad spectrum of incident types and conditions, the on-scene commander has to take charge of the site, assess the situation and implement a plan of action to bring events under control. The thesis of this book is that there is sufficient commonality in the roles of various incident commanders to merit an integrated examination of their selection (Chapter 2) and training (Chapter 3). Certainly from a psychological perspective, there is a fundamental consistency across professions in the three basic skills of incident command, namely coping with stress (Chapter 4), decision making (Chapter 5) and team management (Chapter 6). The final chapter presents general conclusions and recommendations for future research.

2
Selecting the Right Stuff

"At every level in one's progress up that staggeringly high pyramid, the world was once more divided into those men who had the right stuff to continue the climb and those who had to be left behind in the most obvious way."

(Wolfe 1991, p. 30)

Thus Tom Wolfe describes the selection process in the 1950s for the American jet fighter pilots, some of whom graduated as the first astronauts on the Mercury project. Psychologists subsequently discovered that the "right stuff" for a single-pilot fighter plane was precisely the "wrong stuff" when he became the captain of a three-man crew on the flight deck of a commercial aircraft (Helmreich 1987).

INTRODUCTION

This chapter examines the selection and competence assessment of incident commanders who have responsibility for managing an emergency at the scene of the event, be it a fire, a riot, battle damage or an aircraft with a technical problem in flight. Is it possible to define the "right stuff" – a set of generic characteristics and competencies for on-scene commanders? How are the desired attributes and skills identified during the selection process to "select in" candidates? What are the performance criteria for incident command? Such questions have increasing relevance, not only for the emergency services but also in an industrial context for site managers, particularly in chemical, petroleum and nuclear plants and in large entertainment venues.

Some of the material in this chapter is derived from a survey commissioned by the HSE Offshore Safety Division following the public inquiry report (Cullen 1990) into the *Piper Alpha* disaster, which raised concerns regarding the emergency command competence of offshore managers. The background to this project was described in the Preface, and full details of the survey can be found in Flin and Slaven (1994). Following a literature search for details of selection procedures for incident commanders, a number of organizations were contacted for information and in some cases visited (see Appendix 1). The objective was to discover the selection methods, training and assessment procedures used to appoint staff to incident command positions. The training of the "chosen ones" for emergency command is discussed in the next chapter, and team training (in the form of Crew Resource Management) is described in Chapter 6.

The emergency services have long established criteria for initial selection and promotion to more senior command positions. The Home Office provides a specialist Assessment Consultancy Unit, which not only designs and manages selection procedures for more senior candidates but also conducts personnel research and advises on selection criteria for the police, the fire service and the prison service (Murray and Harrison 1994). The armed forces place great emphasis on their standardized procedures for initial selection and they have employed psychologists to advise on assessment methods for the past 50 years (Hardinge 1989). The merchant navy has a well-developed system of training and qualification for navigation officers, linked to a structured progression from cadet deck officer to master. Its selection criteria for an appointment as a ship's captain are based on certificates of competence, as well as on relevant seagoing experience (Department of Transport 1988). Individual shipping lines have their own specifications for officer cadets or qualified officers; for example, in some companies, officers now need to have the ability to manage a multinational crew, or to work on a single-officer bridge. The selection of aircraft pilots continues to be one of the most rigorously researched topics, both from a civilian and a military perspective (Hunter and Burke, 1995). In the commercial world, industrial managers and hospitality venue managers may find themselves in the role of on-scene commander if an emergency arises. However, in the majority of organizations, their selection is based more on their technical, business and managerial skills than on command ability. Their command skills are rarely put to the test, but, as the *Piper Alpha* incident demonstrated, these can be a critical element of their job. In the offshore oil industry, these skills are now examined in new simulator-based assessment procedures (Flin and Slaven 1994).

SELECTION CRITERIA

The formal selection criteria used to appoint individuals to senior positions with incident command responsibilities are similar across organizations. In general terms, these are based on technical/professional qualifications, managerial or leadership experience and demonstrated ability to command and control emergencies (real or simulated). It is difficult to produce a generic set of qualifications or to stipulate the training and type of experience required by incident commanders, as these vary depending on the organization and the command position in question. In many cases, the selectors will be looking beyond qualifications, training and experience to find a particular type of individual or a certain leadership style. These informal criteria tend to be less well defined, and this section examines the personality characteristics and managerial skills that are deemed to be the basis of the "right stuff".

Command Personality

When psychologists talk of personality they are referring to a relatively stable set of characteristics (relating to behaviour, thoughts and feelings), which distinguish individuals and account for consistent patterns of responses to everyday situations. There has been a perennial, if not entirely conclusive, quest to discover the personality characteristics of the effective worker and manager across a range of occupations, and umpteen articles have been written on the subject (see Furnham 1992 for a good review). However, if one turns to the available literature on the personality of the effective commander, there are many anecdotal accounts but few empirical studies, especially in relation to incident command.

The armed forces (as well as the police and the fire service) look for evidence of leadership potential in their initial officer selection (Dobson and Williams 1989), and, according to Sale (1992, p. 26), Field Marshall Montgomery's dictum on leadership is still stressed today at the Army Regular Commissions Board:

> "The two vital attributes of a leader are: a) Decision in action; b) Calmness in crisis. Given these two attributes he will succeed; without them he will fail. Our great problem in peace is to select as leaders men whose brains will remain clear when intensely frightened; the yardstick of 'fear' is absent."
>
> (Montgomery 1958)

Field Marshall Slim, Commander of the 14th Army in Burma in the Second World War, believed that a leader should have the attributes of courage, will-power, initiative, knowledge and integrity (Slim 1956). Downes (1991, p. 145) lists the personal qualities believed to characterize a leader as follows:

"In its incorporation into naval leadership training, the functions approach has been married to the more traditional qualities approach to leadership, which proposes that leaders have certain inherent qualities which qualify them to lead. In the naval leadership training package, these are identified as: intelligence, common sense, integrity, judgement, initiative, tenacity, determination, enthusiasm, loyalty, cheerfulness, sense of humour, energy, fortitude, moral courage, physical courage, the will to dominate and decisiveness. Accepting that natural and inspirational leaders are rare, the view is that the Admiralty Interview Board seeks to select those candidates who possess qualities in sufficient measure to allow them to develop into effective leaders."

This comprehensive list of personality characteristics also encompasses the traits mentioned by the emergency services. For example, Brunacini (1985) says:

"The Fireground Commander's personality is a big factor in the command system. The desirable traits for a FGC include the required knowledge of command and the inclination to command, control of temper, the ability to provide a positive example, psychological stability, physical fitness, fairness, being straightforward when communicating, a willingness to take reasonable risks without compromising safety, concern for all personnel, knowledge of limitations (self, personnel, apparatus, the plan), respect for command, being an organization person, and being disciplined and consistent."

(p. 13)

Police officers whom I have interviewed mention the abilities to stay calm, to listen to others and to be adaptable as key characteristics of effective incident commanders. The national air forces and international commercial airlines have expended significant research effort into identifying the personal qualities desired on the flight deck (Hilton and Dolgin 1991; Hunter and Burke, 1995), and those selecting pilots appear to look for a fairly consistent set of characteristics. For instance, Stead (1995), who has carried out research for the airline Qantas, suggests the following personal qualities for pilots: "Influence/Leadership; Communication Skills; Organising/Planning; Motivation/Energy; Analytical; Empathy; Emotional Maturity; Decision Making" (p. 310). On a visit to British Airways, I was told that the following characteristics would be desirable in a pilot: competent, relaxed but alert, involves and listens to crew, influences behaviour before using authority, patient, sociable, prepared to help (Flin and Slaven 1994).

If the attributes of a successful incident commander are expressed in terms of personality characteristics (as opposed to skills), then there appear to be certain features of personality that are considered to be related to emergency command ability. These typically include the characteristics shown in Table 2.1.

Table 2.1 *Personality Characteristics of the Incident Commander.*

Willingness to take a leadership role
Emotional stability
Stress resistance
Decisiveness
Controlled risk taking
Self-confidence
Self-awareness

The key personality characteristics appear to be leadership (discussed further in Chapter 7), stable personality and decisiveness, and a more detailed definition of each as used in the context of incident command is given below. The meanings attached to each term are derived from discussions with those selecting incident commanders.

- Leadership ability: inspires trust, commands respect, acts with authority and impartiality, is diplomatic, minimizes potential conflict across a multidisciplinary team, is a good communicator, listens to others, shows integrity, directs and controls the efforts of others, takes charge confidently and competently even when under pressure.
- Stable personality: demonstrates emotional stability, maturity, steadiness, reliability, balanced attitudes, is well adjusted, level-headed, remains calm when under pressure.
- Decisive: prepared to formulate and implement decisions when under pressure, balanced, analytical and sound judgement, logical reasoning ability, can recognize and solve problems, knows when to use an authoritative or a consultative decision making style.

In the USA, NASA has funded extensive programmes of psychological research to define personality characteristics to "select in" astronauts and commanders for space missions (Helmreich et al. 1990; Santy 1994). These commanders will have to be able to deal with emergencies in very remote environments in order to ensure the survival of their crew and space station. There have been studies of optimum leadership characteristics for commanders using analogue space environments (e.g. remote Antarctic bases, underwater simulations), which suggest that there may be certain behavioural attributes that characterize the leaders of effective and high performing groups in confined, isolated environments (Penwell 1990). These leaders tend to be task and achievement orientated, have a flexible, though primarily democratic, leadership style, work to maintain group harmony and can tolerate intimacy and status levelling without losing authority or the respect of the group. Effective leaders are described as having self-confidence, emotional control, self-reliance and the strength of personality to maintain their authority during both sustained intimacy and moments of crisis.

This research into astronauts' leadership and command ability has produced some interesting results, although it too has apparently not generated a definitive set of personality characteristics for the ideal space commander (Penwell 1990, p. 2):

> "While Kubis describes the effective space crew commander as technically competent, goal oriented and interpersonally sensitive, we have no direct data about the effectiveness of leadership styles in space environments. The Space Station Operations Task Force has recommended that only NASA career astronauts be eligible for the position of space station commander. While the selection criteria for the pool include physiological and psychological screenings to 'select out' pathology, the selection criteria do not intentionally 'select in' leaders.... [E]xcept for the criterion of previous experience in space and the probable experience as a pilot of a previous shuttle mission, it is unclear, even to the astronauts, what methods are used to select mission commanders."

As Penwell points out, it may be more important to "select out" undesirable personality characteristics that make individuals unsuited to command positions. At NASA psychiatrists tend to be tasked with determining and identifying the "select out" characteristics, which include anxiety, depression and psychotic disorders, and use semi-structured clinical interviews for this purpose (Santy 1994). Pearson (1995, p. 140) discusses the Joint Aviation Authorities' regulations on psychological fitness for pilots, which state that an applicant shall have "no established psychological deficiencies, particularly in operational aptitudes or any relevant personality factor, which is likely to interfere with the safe exercise of the privileges of the applicable licence". Some countries routinely use psychological testing as part of their licensing process for commercial pilots but at present this is non-mandatory.

While selectors appear to be in reasonable agreement as to the "right stuff" and the "wrong stuff" in terms of personality characteristics, the relationship of these traits to incident command ability has rarely been tested. However, personality questionnaires are used for selecting personnel whose job may involve incident command (e.g. prison officers, naval captains, pilots), and they are administered to senior officers from the emergency services for enhancing self-awareness as part of a management development programme. (The use of psychometric tests in selection is discussed below.) Personality is essentially only one factor in the incident command equation, and specific leadership styles and command techniques also need to be taken into account.

Command Skills

In interviews (Flin and Slaven 1994), selectors tended to specify the competencies or skills that they would look for in an incident commander rather than a prescribed set of personality characteristics. A typical set of competencies required in an incident commander, compiled from our study and subsequent interviews, is shown in Table 2.2.

While there appeared to be general agreement as to the command skills required, the terms given are general labels and do not indicate a precise set of behaviours or attributes. The same terms may not mean the same thing in different organizations, or even to different respondents within the same organization. The parallel problem of defining managerial competencies is well documented (Dale and Iles 1992; Greatrex and Phillips 1989; Silver 1991). For instance, a study of managerial skills in British companies shows the problem of capturing the essence of a key attribute of emergency command, namely leadership:

> "The commonest single expressions were communication, leadership, judgement, initiative, organising and motivation.... By far the highest level of confusion surrounds the expression 'leadership', which is unfortunate as it was the second commonest term of all, found in over half the documents analysed. Some view it as synonymous with a whole set of behaviours needed in managing people, and therefore view it as a competence. Some see it as a skill with the implication that leaders are not born but can be taught. Many see it as more of a personality attribute but this may be in terms of personality type, intellectual approach to dealing with problems and situations, or even as a motivational or attitudinal attribute.... Assessment and training require a more precise skill language which describes how a good manager needs to perform in a specific role and environment."
> (Hirsh and Bevan 1991, p. 91)

Clearly, as Hirsh and Bevan argue, these generic terms require to be broken down into their component skills, knowledge and behaviours in

Table 2.2   *Skills Profile of the Incident Commander.*

Leadership ability
Communication skills, especially briefing and listening
Delegating
Team management
Decision making, under time pressure, and especially under stress
Evaluating the situation (situation awareness)
Planning and implementing a course of action
Remaining calm and managing stress in self and others
Preplanning to prepare for possible emergencies

order that they can be used to form the basis of a person specification and a standard of competence for a particular position. In the armed forces, this is done for initial officer selection where, for example, detailed checklists of behaviours are used to record observations during assessment centre exercises. However, for more senior command appointments, such as nuclear submarine command in the Royal Navy, the selection criteria are not tightly specified in a formal manner; rather, they are determined by senior officers making the selection decision:

> "The fundamental problem [in assessing suitability for command] is that it is not possible to have an absolute, objective marking system to cover something as wide ranging and as fluid as submarine command. One of the major advantages possessed by a Royal Naval submarine captain in comparison with others is his application of individual skill and flair, rather than strict adherence to doctrine or standard operating procedures."
>
> (Charlton 1992, p. 58)

Common to all lists of selection criteria is the requirement that the emergency commander should be able to function well as a decision maker and leader when under stress. Is it possible to identify individuals who are more likely to be stress resistant? To some extent, this is probably partly achieved by self-selection. Persons of a nervous disposition are hardly likely to seek employment as firefighters, police officers or space station commanders. But this may not be an adequate screening process, and an Association of Chief Police Officers' working party on stress in 1987 recommended that, "one element of the selection procedure for new recruits, and for specialist positions, should concern the identification of applicants obviously unsuited to dealing with stressful situations" (quoted in Elliott and Smith 1993). Elliott and Smith (1993) have argued that identification of stress resistance is an important element of selection in a number of occupations, but add, "For the emergency services, however it may be more critical, given the importance of teamwork in their operations and the fact that the lives of colleagues and the public may rest in the hands of one individual who is in charge of the event" (p. 36). They suggest that, in practice, only limited screening for stress resistance is undertaken, and they argue that certain aspects of personality (such as hardiness; Kobasa 1982) may be a useful predictor. They also emphasize that employing hardier individuals is only part of an effective stress management strategy for high stress occupations, and advocate that stress exposure training and post-incident counselling should also be provided by the emergency services (these are discussed further in Chapter 4).

In summary, the personality characteristics that are regarded as essential in an incident commander are not dissimilar across occupations, and these include self-confidence, decisiveness, independence, intelligence and emotional stability. The command skills that are required relate to leadership, communication, flexibility, team working, high-level decision making under pressure, and stress management.

SELECTION PROCEDURES

Given general agreement as to the "right stuff" for an on-scene commander, how are these characteristics identified in the available candidates? In the majority of the organizations contacted, the emphasis is on selection from external candidates for entry level, junior positions, whereas senior command appointments are typically chosen from existing staff. Leadership potential will already have been one of the criteria used as the basis for selection at initial recruitment to the organization; future commanders are often identified early in their career and then exposed to a carefully structured training and career plan to test their suitability for a senior command position. In the military, the large number of candidates and good personnel records have enabled these organizations to validate their initial selection criteria and assessment methods against subsequent performance in training. (See Hardinge 1989; Jones 1991; Sale 1992 for a review of military selection procedures.) For officer selection in the police, fire and prison services, occupational psychologists at the Home Office Assessment Consultancy Unit also carry out this type of research (Murray and Harrison 1994). In our survey of organizations (Flin and Slaven 1994), a range of selection methods was found, as listed in Table 2.3. These are

Table 2.3   *Methods of Selecting Incident Commanders.*

Selection method	Comments
Appraisals/ performance reports	As most incident commanders are selected from internal candidates, this is one of the most common methods
Interviews	Often used, with critical incident questions to assess command experience ability
References	Mainly for external candidates
Biodata	Used in some military selection; special application forms seek biographical data shown to function as predictors of job performance
Psychometric testing	Tends to be used for self-awareness rather than screening or selection; usually personality questionnaires
Assessment centres	Widely used by the military and the Home Office Assessment Centre for police and fire service appointments
Simulator exercises	Traditionally used by airlines and military but more for training purposes beyond *ab initio* selection; increasingly finding favour in the merchant navy and industry

discussed in more detail below in relation to incident commanders, but for a general description of these methods, see Cook (1993), Anderson and Herriot (1989) and Smith and Sutherland (1996).

In general, selection decisions for positions that include incident command responsibilities are typically reached on the basis of interviews, performance records and regular career appraisals, as well as personal recommendations from superiors. Assessment centres (see below) may be used for mid-career appointments to senior command positions, as is the case in the police force for entry to their Strategic Command Course and in the fire service for entry to their Brigade Command Course. Across organizations, the selection panels include senior officers with relevant command experience. Typically, the ability to take command in an emergency is judged by reports of performance in real incidents and/or observations of performance during training or formal competence assessment. In some cases, the selection procedure is extremely rigorous, involving not only staff reports but also observations of behaviour in high fidelity simulators as part of specially designed training and assessment courses. For example, the Royal Navy submarine command ("Perishers") course is of 21 weeks duration in onshore simulators and on exercise at sea. The failure rate for these mid-career officers is of the order of 20–25% of candidates (see Case Study 2.1; see also Charlton 1992; Lang 1986).

Extensive use is made of assessed performance in high-fidelity simulators for final selection and continuing qualification of airline pilots and merchant navy officers, and the larger oil companies, such as Shell, BP, Mobil and Conoco, now include formal competence assessment of emergency command ability in a simulator as part of their selection procedure for the position of offshore manager (see Case Study 2.2).

Assessment Centres

In recent years there has been a steady increase by British organizations in the use of the assessment centre approach (Boyle, Fullerton and Yapp 1993), which has been developed for the selection of military officers since the Second World War (Jones et al. 1991). At an assessment centre, a carefully chosen sequence of selection techniques is used, including psychometric tests, interviews and problem solving exercises, as well as practical exercises, group discussions and presentations, which are observed by the assessors and judged on the basis of predetermined checklists or score sheets. (See Feltham 1989; Woodruffe 1990, for a more detailed explanation of this method.) For example, at the assessment centre for British Airways pilot training, candidates are given aptitude tests, general IQ tests, a personality questionnaire, teamwork tests and interviews. (For qualified pilots this will include tests of flying on a cockpit simulator.) This assessment centre procedure has a very high validity and less than 5% of cadets will fail to qualify after training.

The Home Office Assessment Consultancy Unit is responsible for designing and running the assessment centre process known as the Extended Interview, which is used to identify candidates for accelerated promotion in the police and prison service and to select officers for senior management training in the police and the fire service. London Fire Brigade has recently overhauled its selection, training and promotion procedures, with particular emphasis on incident command. This was partly the result of having been served with HSE improvement notices, as discussed in Chapter 1. London has the largest fire brigade in the UK, with 6200 operational firefighters and officers, who have to deal with a high incident rate, often in difficult conditions, due to their metropolitan environment. London Fire Brigade not only developed its own competence standards framework (see below), but also recruited an occupational psychologist and revised the selection procedures for crew command, watch command and junior officers' training programmes, with selection criteria mapped from the standards. The London Fire Brigade selects candidates for the Fire Service College junior officers' course following an assessment centre that includes a personality questionnaire, aptitude tests, a role play session and two group exercises. The focus is on the candidate's ability to deal with situations, to deal with information and to deal with people.

Psychometric Tests

A psychometric (or psychological) test:

> "refers to a procedure for the evaluation of psychological functions. Psychological tests involve those being tested solving problems, performing skilled tasks or making judgements. Psychological test procedures are characterised by standard methods of administration and scoring. The results of psychological tests are usually quantified by means of normative or other scaling procedures but they may also be interpreted qualitatively by reference to psychological theory. Included in the term psychological test are tests of varieties of: intelligence; ability; aptitude; language development and function; personality, temperament and disposition; interests, habits, values and preferences."
>
> (*British Psychological Society Bulletin*, **36**, May 1983, p. 192)

For the purposes of managerial and officer selection, psychometric tests can broadly be divided into two types: personality questionnaires, which typically ask between 100 and 200 questions about how individuals see themselves, and tests of intellectual ability or aptitude, where candidates have to solve a number of problems in a limited time period. (See Kline 1993; Toplis, Dulewicz and Fletcher 1991, for readable introductions to the subject of psychological tests; see Bartram 1995 for full details of all the different personality questionnaires mentioned below.) The UK armed forces use psychometric tests of intelligence at initial selection and alloca- tion, which are designed to measure aptitude rather than achievement. These are in the form of general test batteries. For officers, the tests are typically: non-verbal/spatial reasoning, mathematics, verbal reasoning, speed and accuracy, and general and/or service knowledge.

The British armed services do not use personality questionnaires to select or assess personnel. A psychologist from the RAF summarizes the military position on the use of personality tests as follows:

> "Most personality tests were produced for clinical use or as research tools rather than as purpose built tools for military selection. They present problems of faking and of adverse candidate reactions but foreign experience suggests that these are not insurmountable. Other nations use personality tests, often in place of group exercises. The Dutch Army for instance, replaced group exercises in 1961 with measures of personality derived from personality tests, biodata and interviews. The UK services do not use person- ality tests but rely on interview assessments, references, weighted application blanks, and, in the case of officer selection, group exercises. From time to time the Services try out new tests but so far personality tests have not been able to add anything useful to the predictive power of the selection process."
>
> (Hardinge 1989, p. 18)

A Royal Navy psychologist supports this position:

> "The impact of leadership research has been perhaps to move psychologists away from attempting to assess personality traits as an indication of officer potential. One response has been to put more emphasis on assessing intellect, partly on the basis that the intelligent person can learn to be a leader."
>
> (Jones 1991, p. 64)

During the course of the research for this book, several senior naval officers expressed an interest in the use of personality measures for the selection and development of commanding officers, one of whom had already carried out a research study of personality involving senior commanders and pilots from the Falklands campaign (Jolly 1982). It appears that personality questionnaires are occasionally used in the military for research purposes – Bartram and Dale (1982) assessed over 600 Army Air Corps and RAF pilots with the Eysenck Personality Inventory (EPI) and found that those who were successful in training were more likely to be stable and extroverted than those who failed.

Cooper (1982) used the 16PF (16 Personality Factors) to study the personality characteristics of British Army bomb disposal experts, but this measure did not discriminate between successful operators and a control group who were not so highly rated. According to Hardinge (1989), personality assessments are used for officer selection by Australia, Belgium, France, Holland, India, Israel and New Zealand, and the US Army apparently uses the Myers Briggs Type Indicator (MBTI) up to very senior ranks. Sale (1992) has criticized the absence of objective personality measures in the selection of senior British army officers, and he carried out a small study of 49 commanders (at brigade level) using a computerized battery of personality questionnaires (MANSPEC), which did not produce particularly conclusive results. However, this was hardly surprising given his sample size. For a more detailed account of personality factors in military selection, see Milgram (1991).

Non-military organizations use personality assessments for selecting officers who may take senior command positions. For example, Maersk Shipping uses a personality questionnaire when selecting managers, including ship's officers. All of the major airlines use personality questionnaires as part of a battery of tests and procedures in pilot selection: British Airways uses the Jackson Personality Research Form (PRF). This is an American test which assesses 15 dimensions of personality, including anxiety, responsibility, risk taking, social participation and interpersonal affect. This test was chosen on the basis of job analysis and critical incident analysis to identify defined job requirements. Cathay Pacific uses the 16PF (Bartram and Baxter 1995), while Qantas uses the Occupational Personality Questionnaire (OPQ). Stokes and Kite (1994) describe a range of personality measures that have been used in research with pilots, including behavioural tests such as the Defence Mechanism test (Vaernes 1982), used by the Swedish and Danish air forces. The Fire Service College uses the MBTI in the development of self-awareness in senior officers, and police forces have used 16PF, OPQ and the California Personality Questionnaire (CPI) for selection and development purposes. The police staff college at Bramshill has administered the MBTI and the FIRO-B team roles questionnaire for self-development purposes. Personality questionnaires are now very widely used by the larger British companies for managerial selection and development (Shackleton and Newell 1991; Williams 1994), and several of the oil companies have used the 16PF or the OPQ for the selection and/or development of offshore managers. For Fire Service recruits, Elliott (1991) found a strong correlation between an anxious personality and a subsequent experience of stress during the basic training programme." (p. 36). Elliott and Smith (1993), discussing the selection of stress resistant individuals for firefighting and other emergency services, suggest that "A hardy personality, as measured by the Hardiness scale appears to be more resilient to the effects of stressful life events. The hardiness scale (Kobasa 1982) is a self-completion personality questionnaire, which focuses on commitment, control and challenge in an individual's interpretation of stressful events. Although it has been used in research with police officers to study occupational stress (Tang and Hammontree 1992), it does not appear to have been used in the selection of incident commanders, and validation data would be required to evaluate its application.

In summary, psychological tests are only used by the UK armed forces for intelligence testing at initial officer selection. The armed forces do not use personality questionnaires, notwithstanding the increasing use of these by other agencies. Many organizations use personality instruments to develop self-awareness in senior officers with a view to improving their performance as commanders, but without precisely defining a single leadership style. There does not appear to be any one definitive test of command ability or crisis management skill, and there appear to have been few published research studies using standard personality questionnaires to predict emergency command performance. One such study is summarized below, to illustrate how the relationship between a psychometric instrument and incident command performance can be assessed.

Testing for Command Ability: Ongoing Research

Lord Cullen (1990) suggested in the *Piper Alpha* report that, "While psychological tests may not appeal to some companies, the processes used and proven successful by the armed forces or the merchant navy, who have to rely on their officers to lead under stress, should be seriously considered by the operating companies" (20.59). As part of our study into crisis management, we carried out a validation exercise to assess whether a psychometric test could predict a manager's incident command performance in a simulated offshore emergency (Flin and Slaven 1996). The starting point for identifying a suitable psychometric instrument was to determine the personality characteristics and abilities deemed relevant to an offshore installation manager's (OIM's) crisis management ability. There were no published data, but an earlier survey of 134 practising OIMs (Flin and Slaven 1993) had asked "What characteristics or skills does an OIM need to cope with an emergency?". The most frequent answers were as follows:

- The ability to remain calm (56%).
- The ability to take decisions, particularly when under pressure (42%).
- Leadership (38%).

- Knowledge of the installation (33%) and the emergency procedures (28%).
- The ability to assess the overall situation (21%).

The resulting portrait is very similar to the profile in Table 2.2 and General Montgomery's maxim on leadership (men whose brains will remain clear when intensely frightened).

The search for a specific test of command characteristics to predict the "calm decision maker" was unproductive and it was not possible due to time constraints to use a test battery (a series of tests; for example, reasoning ability, personality, leadership style, anxiety level). Thus, it was decided to use a British managerial personality questionnaire, the Occupational Personality Questionnaire (OPQ) (Saville and Holdsworth 1992), which was already being used by some oil companies for OIM selection. The version used (Concept 5.2) is a self-report instrument with 258 questions, which provides scores on 30 dimensions of personality related to the world of work, including dimensions assessing preferred decision making approach (fast versus slow), propensity to worry, level of relaxedness, and preference for taking control. The objective of the study was to measure whether the OIMs' scores on any of the 30 personality dimensions would predict their emergency command ability. The OPQ was administered to a sample of 93 OIMs attending the Montrose Fire and Emergency Training Centre, which has an offshore command centre simulator. Ratings of each OIM's performance as commander during a simulated offshore emergency were obtained using a specially designed rating form with 16 scales based on the offshore oil industry's unit of competence "Controlling Emergencies" (see Flin and Slaven (1994), appendix B for the rating form and Table 2.4 for the standard of competence). At least two trainers rated the performance of each individual who played the role of the OIM in the simulator exercise, which lasted for approximately 45–60 minutes.

The personality scores were correlated with performance ratings and it was found that few dimensions of the OPQ predicted command performance level. Those dimensions that appeared to be of most interest were that the OIMs with higher performance ratings scored significantly higher on the "controlling" (likes to take charge), "outgoing" (sociable) and "decision making" (tends to make fast decisions) dimensions, and significantly lower on the "conceptual" (prefers abstract thinking) and "behavioural" (likes to analyse the behaviour of others) dimensions. (The last does not augur well for psychologists with ambitions in emergency command!) Scores on the "worrying" and "relaxed" dimensions did not, as expected, predict any aspect of command ability. Overall, the correlations were extremely modest and we concluded that this managerial personality questionnaire was likely to be of limited value for predicting managers' command decision making ability. It is acknowledged that the OPQ was not designed for this purpose and in addition, our command performance scale had not been pretested for reliability or validity and would require further development. Exploratory factor analysis of the performance ratings indicated that the scale had a two-factor structure, labelled communication skills and decision making. These two factors will be used to form a basis for the development of a future rating scale.

Commanders' Attitudes

Organizations such as NASA have devoted significant resources to their rigorous selection of commanders for space crew and air crew but, as already mentioned, they apparently have not managed to devise a definitive psychometric test of command ability. However, one NASA research study of commercial aircraft pilots showed that their performance might have more to do with attitudes than personality as measured by conventional instruments:

> "Personality characteristics, viewed as enduring components of the self, are considered an appropriate basis for pilot selection but, being resistant to change, are not perceived to be a fruitful target of training. Attitudes, in contrast, are less resistant to change and therefore may be altered through appropriate intervention."
>
> (Gregorich, Helmreich and Wilhelm 1990, p. 682)

From a study of team effectiveness on the flight deck, aviation psychologists developed the Cockpit Management Attitude Questionnaire (CMAQ) (Gregorich, 1990; Helmreich et al, 1984). This instrument is based on three attitude clusters: communication and coordination; command responsibility and recognition of personal limitations. Attitudes measured by the CMAQ were found to predict expert ratings of pilots' performance. More effective pilots recognized: (i) their personal limitations and diminished decision making in emergencies and encouraged other crew members to question decisions and actions; (ii) the need to be sensitive to the personal problems of other crew members that might affect operations and felt obligated to discuss personal limitations; and (iii) that their management style should vary depending upon the circumstances and the characteristics of the crew members (Helmreich et al. 1990). This type of research into flight deck commanders' attitudes and their impact on performance may have future applications for selection purposes but has not yet been developed in this way. However, the CMAQ (and adaptations of it) are increasingly being employed in team training, especially in the international airlines' Crew Resource Management training, nuclear control teams and emergency response teams (see Chapter 6 for details).

COMPETENCE ASSESSMENT IN INCIDENT COMMAND

The cornerstone of maintaining operational efficiency in many organizations is the use of regular competence assessment of key individuals or teams, either in response to a regulatory authority (e.g. the Civil Aviation Authority, the Nuclear Inspectorate) or as part of a standard training and monitoring programme. For example, commercial pilots are required to sit regular competence checks on a six-monthly basis in order to maintain their licences. For emergency command, there are clearly defined scenarios (such as engine out on take-off) and designated standards of response expected (see below). In organizations such as the merchant navy, the individual must undergo a series of tests and assessments in order to achieve the required qualification, a certificate of competency to command a ship, which must be updated every five years (Department of Transport 1988).

The starting point for any competence assurance system is the definition and documentation of the standards of competence required; in recent years this has been widely adopted for the British workforce. In the late 1980s, there was a government initiative to develop an improved system of national vocational qualifications (NVQs; SVQs in Scotland) based on universal standards of competence, which would be drawn up by industry-led organizations across all industrial sectors and occupational groups. Competence is the ability to perform consistently within an occupation to the standards expected in employment. Where there is an associated vocational qualification, the competence standards are used to assess performance in the workplace (Fletcher 1991). One important development that resulted from Lord Cullen's report (1990) with respect to offshore managers' ability to take command in emergencies was the introduction of formal competence assessment in emergency command. While this was not obligatory, the new safety case regime that was enacted after the *Piper Alpha* disaster made the installation operators responsible for ensuring the competence of offshore personnel in safety critical positions. When the oil industry began to produce a standard of competence for OIMs on "controlling emergencies" in 1991, it was somewhat surprising to discover that no relevant standards of competence for incident command were available from other UK organizations, such as the emergency services.

An offshore oil and gas industry working group of offshore installation managers was convened under their industry lead body (Offshore Petroleum Industry Training Organisation; OPITO), and this group developed a formal unit of competence on "controlling emergencies",

Table 2.4 OPITO Standard of Competence "Controlling Emergencies" for Offshore Managers. Reprinted with Permission of OPITO.

Element	Performance criteria
Evaluate situation and anticipate needs	a. Information from all appropriate sources is obtained, evaluated and confirmed as quickly as possible
	b. Valid interpretations of all evidence are made and valid decisions taken throughout the emergency
	c. Appropriate actions are ordered in the light of this evidence (this may include doing nothing)
	d. Potential outcomes of the emergency are reviewed against consequences and probabilities
	e. Resources to respond to the most appropriate outcomes are put in place as quickly as possible
	f. Emergency response teams are coordinated and directed in an effective manner
Maintain communications	a. All essential people and organizations are immediately informed of the emergency
	b. Reports of the situation as it develops are provided to installation staff at suitable intervals
	c. Appropriate communications are maintained during the emergency
	d. An accurate record of all events and of key communications is maintained
	e. Where possible, alternative means are put in place when necessary to maintain communications
Delegate authority to act	a. Valid decisions are taken on which activities should be delegated in the light of the circumstances of the moment
	b. Delegated activities are assigned to those most suited to deal with them in accordance with established procedures
	c. Functions are clear and fully comprehended by those to whom they are delegated. (This must include the necessity to report back)
Deal with stress in self and others	a. Symptoms of developing excessive stress in self and colleagues are recognized quickly
	b. Appropriate action is taken to ensure the continuance of the activities
	c. Action is taken to reduce the stress in oneself and whenever possible in colleagues

which defined the skills need by an OIM to manage an offshore emergency. This Unit has four elements (OPITO 1992; see Table 2.4):

The guidance notes advise that performance should be assessed in a minimum of three scenarios involving a prescribed range of initiating incidents (e.g. helicopter crash onto platform, gas explosion, drilling blow-out, accommodation fire). The OIMs, either with or without their emergency command teams, are observed during the scenarios (usually conducted in a simulator) by experienced offshore personnel and are assessed on the performance criteria. They are then endorsed as either "competent" or "not yet competent". The standard is not a formal qualification but it has been widely adopted as a general guideline by the major companies who have developed formal competence assessment methods for their incumbent and prospective offshore managers (e.g. Shell, BP, Total, British Gas, Mobil, Elf, Chevron). The OIM standard and guidance are now being updated, and a revised OPITO standard will be available in late 1996 (see Case Study 2.2).

While no incident command standards of competence were available in the early 1990s, other than that for offshore managers, the emergency services were, in fact, also working on the development of their own standards of competence. For example, the Fire Services Awarding Body (FSAB) has recently produced standards of competence for emergency fire services, which will lead to NVQs and SVQs. These concentrate on the functions carried out by firefighters and officers, and provide guidance for competence-based training. The standard on Supervision and Command (level 3) has 17 units of competence, six of which relate to command on the fireground (FSAB 1995):

1. Plan and implement the delivery of emergency fire and rescue services for an incident.
2. Direct emergency fire and rescue services to control and contain an incident.
3. Initiate and control measures to meet the health, safety and welfare needs of personnel within the emergency fire and rescue services area of control.
4. Gather and disseminate information pertaining to an incident.
5. Coordinate the completion of the operational phase of an incident.
6. Review the effectiveness of procedures following an incident.

Units 1, 2 and 3 are particularly concerned with command decision making at the scene of the fire, and they are shown in more detail with their elements of competence and performance criteria in Table 2.5. There is clear overlap between a number of the elements for the OIM and the

Table 2.5 *Emergency Fire Services Supervision and Command NVQ Level 3: Units 1–3 (of 17 Units) on Incident Command. Reproduced by permission of Fire Services Awarding Body.*

Unit of competence	Element of competence
1. Plan and implement the delivery of emergency fire and rescue services for an incident	1.1 Determine initial tactical options and brief firefighting crews 1.2 Maintain and use communication links with operational control for the receiving and giving of incident information 1.3 Gather and assess information to aid operational deployment of resources 1.4 Determine and secure resources to control and contain an incident
2. Direct emergency fire and rescue services to control and contain an incident	2.1 Establish an incident command structure 2.2 Deploy physical and human resources to control and contain an incident
3. Initiate and control measures to meet with the health, safety and welfare needs of personnel within the emergency fire and rescue services' area of control	3.1 Maintain the safety of personnel within the fire and rescue services' area of control 3.2 Liaise with key agencies to protect the well-being of the community and emergency services personnel 3.3 Deal sympathetically with victims at the scene of an incident 3.4 Dealing with situations involving the deceased

fireground commander, notably relating to information gathering, situation assessment, communication and resource allocation. (Level 4 units relate to strategic tactical command.)

As a result of the HSE improvement notices served on London Fire Brigade concerning command and control (see Chapter 1), the brigade decided to move ahead of the national fire service standards and to instigate the development of its own standards of competence for operations. The project team comprised five subteams of three officers, each subteam being responsible for developing certain areas of the functional map to the point where standards were produced. In the second phase, detailed role mapping took place for firefighter, crew commanders and watch commanders; on the basis of this work, the London Fire Brigade has now produced a full set of units of competence (LFCDA 1994; see Bonney 1995 for those relevant to incident command). A similar movement towards competence-based qualifications and training has taken place in a number of other countries. For instance, the Australian Fire Authorities Council (AFAC) first had competency standards recognized in 1992. Since then there has been continuing work to develop competencies for command and control, as well as nationally accredited courses. The relevant competency standards at levels 4, 5 and 6 are:

> "Level 4; Unit 3: Command/Control Activities at an Incident
> 3.1 Establish and maintain command and control of an incident
> 3.2 Establish communications and liaison
> 3.3 Monitor personnel to identify possible exposure to hazardous health related conditions
> Level 5; Unit 3: Command/Control Activities at a Major Incident
> 3.1 Establish and manage command and/or control of a major incident
> 3.2 Establish and manage communications and liaison at a major incident
> 3.3 Document incident information for reporting, analysis and evaluation
> Level 6; Unit 1: Manage and Coordinate Emergencies
> 1.1 Manage and coordinate emergencies
> 1.2 Liaise with other agencies and organisations"

The British police has also developed standards of competence, although there is no national UK framework, and these tend to be used for training purposes. Likewise, the prison service has had a working party establishing standards of competence for different grades, including incident command. In Australia, the police and ambulance service national competency standards are currently under development. There is also a new Australian standard of competence in emergency management for emergency planners, which has 13 units, including "develop emergency management policy" and "select emergency management strategies" (EMA 1995; Paul 1995).

Simulation-based Competence Assessments

A fundamental problem in competence assessment for emergency control is that real emergencies cannot be used, therefore role playing must be employed, either in simulators or in the work environment. Commercial airline pilots may be responsible for managing a serious emergency involving several hundred passengers when their aircraft is in flight, and to conform to Civil Aviation Authority regulations, airlines are required not only to train their pilots to certain standards but also to formally reassess their competence on a regular basis. This competence assessment covers not only pilots' technical ability to fly the plane but also their ability to maintain command during an emergency. Every six months the cockpit crews "fly" the simulator for their particular aircraft for a two-day assessment, which is carried out by more senior pilots. They deal with set piece emergencies, e.g. engine fire, incapacitation, decompression and bomb warning. In British Airways the scenarios are developed on a three-year cycle and are regularly updated using details of real incidents. On the first day there is a training element as well as some manoeuvres, which will be assessed. The second day involves a series of statutory tests in the simulator, which the pilot must pass to continue flying, e.g. competence to fly on instruments, dealing with an engine out on take-off.

While taking command in a crisis requires decision making under stressful conditions, the assessment itself will often create a useful level of anxiety, which will produce relevant psychological and physiological symptoms, albeit at a lower level than a life threatening emergency. The oil companies developing OIM were interested in how assessments simulate the stress of an emergency in order to assess commanders' decision making under pressure. According to flight crew assessors, it is not necessary to artificially induce an element of stress into their procedures because pilots already experience stress in the simulator during competence assessments because the continuation of their licence is dependent on a satisfactory performance. Nevertheless, assessors usually know how to introduce an element of stress into scenarios and to judge stress reactions where appropriate. The conventional techniques for increasing stress in simulator exercises are raising the difficulty of the scenario (e.g. equipment malfunctions), adding time pressure, introducing extra noise or heat or reducing lighting. Stress management has always been an important part of military training and competence assessment:

> "Officers in staff and command positions must now learn to deal with significant communication and information overloads, and this requires the capacity to sift the wheat from the chaff, the relevant from the irrelevant – often under conditions of considerable physical and mental stress."
>
> (Downes 1991, p. 6)

Those organizations employing simulation-based competence assessments (e.g. the military, commercial airlines) appreciate that performance in a simulator will not predict with 100% accuracy performance in a real-life incident, but there is a strong belief that this type of competence assessment does enable the organization to identify and "select out" those individuals who do not cope well in an emergency command situation. It is obviously vitally important that the competence assessments are carried out by experienced and highly trained individuals, to ensure the quality of the evaluation and also to maintain the credibility of the process for those being assessed. During or after the assessment, the assessee normally has an opportunity to explain or justify his or her actions. The assessment criteria, assessment method, and the selection and training of assessors are always formally documented. Video cameras are often used to record performance for later assessment or for feedback review.

In summary, where it is essential to ensure that an individual is competent to take command in an emergency, most organizations use competence assessments based on observed performance in a simulated emergency, either using high-fidelity simulators or on site. More than one scenario is typically used, and the scenarios have to be as realistic as possible.

CONCLUSION

There did appear to be general agreement across a heterogeneous sample of organizations as to the "right stuff" for incident command, both in terms of personality characteristics and managerial competencies (see p. 45). Techniques for selecting the right stuff were more variable, and validation data were not always available. For the organizations surveyed, promotion to command is usually a mid-career internal appointment. The selection decisions are made by senior officers or managers with relevant experience. The basis for the decision is the candidate's previous performance in the organization. Documentary evidence of performance record comes from staff reports, annual appraisals and personal recommendations by superior officers. Candidates are almost always interviewed and may be required to attend an assessment centre with interviews, psychometric tests and simulated job performance tests as part of the selection process.

The operational and technical demands for commanding officers differ across organizations due to specific task and operational requirements. Armed forces, crowds of civilians, passengers and industrial workers represent different command problems. Nevertheless, useful lessons can be learnt from studying the methods and principles employed. The psychological demands placed on the incident commander, whether a ship's captain, a police superintendent, a senior pilot or an OIM, are very similar in terms of the need to evaluate the situation, take decisions under stress, and implement and monitor an action plan through the emergency response team. These demands are neatly summarized by Mathis, McKiddy and Way (1982), reviewing management lessons for the police in the aftermath of the Hyatt Regency hotel collapse in Kansas:

> "The personality, experience, and training of an operations commander are the determining factors in how well he handles the responsibility of controlling the resources of a police agency during emergency operations ... He

must recognize the need to take command of the incident even though no precedent may have been set for his actions. He must remove himself from the chaos and emotionalism in a disaster and concentrate on problem solving ... He needs to be able to assess the situation and its implications and direct an appropriate organizational response."

(p. 49)

In the next chapter, techniques for simulating emergencies in order to train or to assess competence are examined in more detail.

CASE STUDY 2.1: TRAINING AND ASSESSING SUBMARINE COMMANDERS

This case is based on a conference paper presented by Commander David Charlton RN to the First Offshore Installation Management Conference, Aberdeen, April 1992.

According to Commander Charlton, the Submarine Command Course (SMCC; known as the Perishers course) probably represents the most demanding and stressful course undertaken by officers in the Royal Navy. It has a failure rate of 20–25% and will have a damaging effect on an officer's career prospects if he does not pass. Failure on the course results in immediate removal from operational submarine service, and subsequent promotion prospects in surface operations are less than encouraging. Selection for the Perishers course is based on regular reports from the candidate's Commanding Officer and the Captain of his Submarine Squadron. A typical candidate will be around 30 years of age with eight years' experience in submarines. Typically, six to eight officers are chosen for each course but they must pass the navigation Ship Command exam before they can begin. The 21-week course is held at HMS *Neptune* at Faslane in Scotland: it includes a five-week period at sea in a submarine, during which the students take the role of Duty Captain during a series of increasingly complex scenarios designed to test command skills. The course has four phases:

1. Attack and safety training
2. Command tactical training
3. Tactical training at sea
4. Final phase.

Attack and safety training is carried out in an onshore simulator designed for submarine command team training. The purpose of this is:

"to test an officer's ability to give positive leadership and to make quick, correct decisions under the stress imposed by various safety and tactical situations. It will encourage him to develop latent ability and allow an assessment to be made of his safety awareness and his command qualities.... He is required to make a number of complex calculations and estimations in his head, without recourse to computer assistance."

(Charlton 1992, p. 51)

Admiral Sir John Sandy Woodward, Commander-in-Chief of the Falklands Task Force, not only passed the course but returned several years later as a "teacher" responsible for selection. He recalls his own experience as a student:

> "Fundamentally the course was intended to push your luck and skill to the limit in very odd conditions. The key to a submariner's success is partly [self-confidence], plus the ability to hold a mental picture of the surface scene. It's not a very good analogy but imagine sticking your head out of a manhole in Piccadilly Circus, taking one quick swivelling look round, ducking back down into the sewer and then trying to remember what you've seen. The idea is to generate sufficiently accurate recall and timing to avoid a double-decker bus running over your head next time you pop through the manhole. Near-misses in the Perisher are a natural deliberate and frequent part of the game."
>
> (Woodward 1992, p. 42)

The next phase, command tactical training, is also carried out in the onshore simulator. Students are now expected to conduct more complicated attacks, and perform operations such as laying mines, photographic reconnaissance and intelligence gathering.

Tactical training at sea follows, where the students are expected to take the command role in a full range of submarine operations designed to test a broad range of command skills, such as command presence, safety awareness, management ability, technical knowledge, teamwork, controlled aggression and decision making under pressure. Having reached the required standard, students are pushed to their own personal operating limits, thus giving them confidence in their own "operating envelope".

At the end of this phase, the selection decisions are reached and the successful candidates progress to the final phase, which is a programme of general courses, including nuclear engineering, warfare, management, intelligence, administration and operations.

One important feature of the Submarine Command Course is its assessment of the potential commander's ability to take tactical decisions under stress, a topic that is discussed more fully in Chapter 4.

CASE STUDY 2.2: ASSESSING OFFSHORE INSTALLATION MANAGERS

This case is based on a conference paper by John Sinclair and David Cook (1994) of Mobil North Sea Ltd (MNSL).

MNSL currently operates two oil and gas production platforms in the North Sea, for which five OIMs and a number of deputy OIMs are required. MNSL has developed a comprehensive programme for both developing and assessing the OIMs in emergency command. This emergency command assessment involves the use of both MNSL and external independent assessors. This programme fits into an overall set of competence modules that the company is developing for its offshore staff. The training, development and assessment for OIMs and their deputies have been completed. This work fully satisfies the recommendations by Lord Cullen (1990) on OIM emergency training (see Chapter 1).

MNSL set out to satisfy both itself and the Cullen Report recommendations. The aim was to create an assessment process that would maximize the learning opportunities for individuals yet would be constructive and support-ive. The process could not be based on a pass/fail regime similar to the assessment used by the Royal Navy for its submarine commanders, where failure (historically around 25%) marks the end of an officer's career in submarines (see Case Study 2.1). However, similar elements of such training were considered by MNSL to be entirely appropriate. In addition, it was intended to develop emergency handling skills, build teams that would be capable of supporting the OIM even in the worst scenarios, and create a system that was not centred on a few charismatic personnel. Before starting the assessment process MNSL initiated the following four steps:

- Determine the assessment process
- Eliminate the fear of assessment/assessors
- Decide what to do with the results (particularly the less successful ones)
- Select/train the assessors

An OIM development model was produced by the MNSL Training Depart-ment, which was the first in a series of competence models for offshore personnel in critical positions. The model describes training and development activities for potential OIMs and provides for formal assessment in three key areas: (i) technical competency, (ii) managing safety and (iii) controlling emergencies. This competence model provided for an OIM being selected at an early stage through the career development system, and identified the key training and experience to be put in place prior to an OIM being assessed in emergency command and taking up position. The steps involved the simulta-neous development of technical, managerial and emergency training skills over a minimum of a six- to nine-month period. Some candidates had all of the necessary management/technical skills via previous assignments and/or work experience. The Emergency Preparedness training was conducted in three stages. The first was attendance at a basic emergency command skills course, typically for four to seven days. A written report was received on the candidate after this course. Subsequently, having performed at Fire Control/ Management of Emergency courses onshore and table top/minor training exercises offshore, the candidate was observed during a major offshore exercise. A written report on the candidate's performance identifying areas for improvement was produced. After further offshore table top and other training exercises offshore, the OIM attended an OIM Emergency Command Assessment session. The assessment of emergency command competencies is seen as a linear process, with evidence from each input used as a basis for assessment and for development action.

To fully understand the MNSL assessment process, it should be noted that in an emergency the OIM is based in an office, which forms the Emergency Control Centre (ECC); (see Figure 6.1 for layout). The OIM deputy and at least five other personnel are also in the ECC to support the OIM. The ECC provides the link to the outside world and takes the overview of the emergency. The Central Control Room (CCR) forms the link between the OIM and the scene of the incident. The OIM receives information by intercom from the CCR. During the assessment process two assessors were placed in the ECC. One was an external assessor and the second a Mobil (technical) assessor. The external assessor, a specialist in the command area, was responsible for providing:

- An independent and unbiased view of the command ability of the assessed individual.
- Expert command advice covering each element of the process, including debriefing.
- Assessment of information collection display and use (in real time).
- Assessment of information accuracy, relevance and interpretation.
- Comments and suggestions for improving the input and ability of other team members.
- Assessment of signs/control of stress.
- Evaluation of communications to the workforce, e.g. PA/Tannoy announcements, especially their timing, tone, frequency, duration and quality.
- Assessment of the use of time when under pressure.

The external assessors chosen by MNSL were former Royal Navy personnel with experience in training/assessing submarine commanders, from either the Offshore Command Training Organisation (OCTO) or Emergency Management Command and Control (EMC^2).

The Mobil assessor was responsible for assessing the OIMs':

- Grasp/understanding of the technical aspects of the scenario/installation.
- Use of appropriate documentation sources (e.g. emergency manuals etc.).
- Knowledge of MNSL emergency procedures.

- Knowledge of search and rescue (SAR) resources.
- Use of external resources (including Mobil onshore resources/contacts).

The technical assessors used by MNSL were ex-OIMs or personnel who had been members of the offshore management team. The technical assessor had received the appropriate command theory training to complement his experience and technical knowledge. The scenarios used for the assessments were developed by MNSL Loss Prevention engineers using credible scenarios from the relevant Safety Cases. Some of these scenarios contained lessons such as the consequence of overriding the protective (e.g. fire and gas and/or shutdown) systems. All assessments involved some scenarios that moved outside the "procedural envelope"; in other words, into areas where written procedures were no longer relevant, useful or appropriate. This is where the individual concerned was required to think from first principles, drawing on the experience of general command development work. There was a minimum of two abandonment scenarios per assessment. To make the assessment as realistic as possible, two areas were concentrated on: hardware, i.e. the assessment facility, manuals, equipment, alarms etc., and software, i.e. personnel and procedures. MNSL has used three different OIM assessment/ training facilities and is convinced that this process is not hardware dependent. The more hardware realism that can be obtained at realistic cost the better. However, greater benefit is obtained by using real staff as role players wherever possible, e.g. standby vessel captains, radio operators, fire team leaders, on-scene commanders, production operators, etc. Also, there was benefit by taking the whole of the ECC and CCR teams through the assessment (this was up to 20 people). This developed skills and effective teamwork among all emergency team members. In addition, to enhance realism, a realistic work programme and permits were issued each day prior to the start of the scenario developments. Typically MNSL ran up to eight scenarios over a two- or three-day period.

Each scenario was classified as either simple, intermediate or complex. A simple scenario was one that could not lead to abandonment; an intermediate one could possibly lead to abandonment but did not on this occasion; and a complex scenario was one that inevitably led to abandonment regardless of the OIM's action. Typical scenarios ran for between 30 and 60 minutes. These were followed by initial debriefs from both the CCR and ECC teams with their respective observers. This usually lasted for five minutes, concentrating primarily on the information displayed/presented at the conclusion of the scenario. This was followed by the OIM and his team having a debrief with both the ECC and CCR teams while the Mobil and external observers had an independent private review of the OIM's performance. Typically this lasted for 15–30 minutes. The next stage was a debrief with the OIM in private with the Mobil and external observers. In this session, any shortcomings and areas for improvement were discussed, highlighted and agreed with the OIM. Typically this took 30–40 minutes. Whatever the outcome, the OIM was encouraged to take all the ideas he had received from the observers and present them back to his team in a short briefing session prior to the start of the next scenario. This was the constructive part of the process, i.e. the external observers were never seen to belittle the OIM in front of his own team. The OIM was always being built up in front of his own team, which assisted in developing his command presence in future scenarios. In addition, coaching sessions on critical aspects such as abandonment were also given as required. For each scenario there was a written outline, initial incident conditions, initial weather conditions, the problem considerations, and fire and gas information. The technical assessors also had expected/possible actions/reactions for each development point in the scenario. This gave a factual basis on which to assess the OIM's technical performance.

MNSL is convinced that the best results will only be achieved when the MNSL technical assessor works closely with external assessors who have appropriate command knowledge, and where each respects the other's specialist skills. The experience of the external assessor to identify potential problems and solutions is fundamental. The external assessor provides areas for improvement, not only for the OIM but also for his team.

The OIM's performance was recorded on an assessment form developed using the OPITO guidelines for managing offshore installations (controlling emergencies) (see Table 2.4). The assessment documentation used by MNSL goes beyond that contained in the OPITO guidelines in that it contains advice to lead the assessor on how the process should proceed. Most importantly, it is not a "tick box" type regime. Detailed written text feedback is provided. MNSL used the scoring scheme it had developed for its Management System Improvement Plan. These were:

- Category 0: No evidence of the person responsible performing the activity.
- Category 1: Parts of the activity were performed as described in the guidance.
- Category 2: The activity was currently performed as described in the relevant guidance and was consistently implemented.
- Category 3: As Category 2, but in addition the person has improved the way the activity is performed – in short, an outstanding example, a new benchmark.

Each scenario was scored immediately and independently by each assessor upon completion. The overall resulting assessment produced a written development plan for each OIM and a judgement of competence. All personnel received a development plan on how they performed, with areas where they could improve. Finally, a written recommendation is made to judge the OIM "competent" or "not yet competent" in emergency command. This is signed and approved by the two line managers to whom the OIMs report. This is similar to the standard career development appraisal system. This reinforces that assessment, like safety, is a line responsibility. A number of additional benefits have derived from the assessment process. There are:

- Some initial assessment of other management team members and deputy OIMs.
- The introduction of scenarios that are theoretically possible but have never happened (i.e. living out the unthinkable, e.g. fire and explosion escalation scenarios, drilling into an adjacent well).
- Development of consistent actions by the OIM and his teams has been improved.
- Major lessons of the Safety Case are reinforced, in particular fire and explosion mitigation.

One of the other biggest areas for improvement has been in the pictorial display of information available to the OIM. This minimizes verbal communication, reduces noise in the ECC and reduces the probability of ambiguity. In the past MNSL had done a fine job of recording the log of events during incidents/exercises. Less attention had been paid to recording the necessary future actions, i.e. the things that might save you. An Action Tote has been developed in both the CCR and the ECC, which records the necessary future actions. These boards contain the estimated time by which an action must be completed to be effective. These have proved simple and highly effective. Integrated status boards have been optimized to display only the critical and pertinent information the OIM needs. One section of this board now contains a focus section. This allows the OIM's aim to be stated and written, and changed as the emergency develops. This has proved necessary and vital during abandonment preparation and abandonment scenarios, where there is a rapidly changing focus. The OIM needs to know that both the CCR, the scene of incident and all personnel at muster all understand his aim, i.e. preparations for abandonment or an actual abandonment etc. This OIM Emergency Assessment Programme has provided a necessary supplement to the MNSL appraisal system for OIMs. The standard appraisal system measures managerial and technical skills, and this process complements it and provides a measure of emergency command performance.

Summarizing, MNSL has satisfied both itself and the Cullen recommendations on OIM emergency training. MNSL has satisfied itself that the Beryl Alpha and Bravo managers have been put through a fair and thorough process, which has built their confidence and competence to maximize their performance during emergencies. There has been a step change in increased performance from the manager, the deputy managers and their teams since the process. The evidence for this is from the scoring system, the video recordings of assessments and, most importantly, from the feedback from the OIMs and their teams. It is thought that this process could be applied elsewhere to other managers who need to perform in an emergency. The process could be simplified/tailored for other emergency preparedness needs. (Reprinted with permission, MNSL).

3
Training the Incident Commander

"As far as the review team could gather their [Nominated Senior Officers] appointment was on the basis of rank, rather than any assessment of competence. They were given minimal training and there was no requirement that they should take part in an emergency exercise before being appointed. These arrangements were inadequate and fell short of practice on licensed nuclear and other high hazard sites."

(HSE 1994a, p. 157)

In some organizations it is difficult to separate the progression of training for command in general (essentially management training for those destined for senior positions) from incident command training for emergency command and control. The aim of this chapter is to review the methods of training for incident command, irrespective of whether this is taught as part of a more general programme of command (senior management) training, rather than as a specialist course. As explained previously, the terms "incident command" and "on-scene command" will be used interchangeably and in preference to "operational command", which has a more ambiguous definition.

Training for the role of incident commander in emergencies takes a number of different forms depending on the particular organization, its emergency response procedures and the seniority of the command position in question. Nevertheless, the guiding principles and objectives are very similar across organizations – the incident commander must be proficient in assessing the situation, implementing a plan of action according to operational procedures and monitoring the operation thereafter. He or she is responsible not only for the success of the operation, but also for the safety of all involved in the emergency. For obvious reasons, the precise content of training programmes differs across organizations, but the techniques employed for training incident commanders are reasonably consistent. Incident command training tends to be provided on the job in the form of exercises, drills or real incidents, with the trainee commander watching more senior commanders, then taking increasing responsibility. This is usually complemented by courses at professional training centres, such as the specialist colleges for officers from the armed forces and the emergency services. In the merchant navy, emergency response training for officers is undertaken by the nautical colleges (some of which have simulators) as well as in drills and simulated emergencies at sea (Elsensohn 1991; Le Marquand 1991). Typical training methods are described below. This is followed by a more detailed account of incident command training programmes in a series of five cases from the fire service, the police, the offshore oil industry, the nuclear power industry and the Royal Navy. The characteristics and skills of the ideal incident commander were discussed in the previous chapter. While there is no formula for developing these attributes, common training themes include leadership ability, decision making, coping with stress and team management. The theoretical foundations of the input on leadership are discussed in the final chapter.

INCIDENT COMMAND: TRAINING METHODS

"In the absence of actual experience in managing emergency operations, training becomes the only realistic alternative."

(Mathis, McKiddy and Way 1982, p. 49)

The most common training methods are exercises, simulations, case studies of major incidents, lectures (on leadership, principles of command, operational procedures), directed reading (the military favour biographies of famous commanders, accounts of battles and texts on command) and on-the-job learning. These are listed in Table 3.1, and discussed in more detail in the following subsections, with examples from different organizations.

Lectures, Case Studies and Background Reading

As in most other training programmes, a significant proportion of the course material is conveyed by lectures, often supported by pre-course background reading and handouts. Lectures are delivered not only by course tutors from the host organization but also by guest speakers from agencies that have particular expertise, universities and organizations with whom liaison will be required in a major incident. An important element on most emergency command development programmes is the use of case study analysis of previous incidents. This is used by the police on their Management of Disasters and Civil Emergencies (MODACE) courses, as

Table 3.1 *Methods of Training Incident Commanders.*

Training method	Comments
Background reading	This can be a directed reading list, a specific text (e.g. Nautical Institute 1986) or a specially prepared folder of course notes and supplementary articles (e.g. as used on the police MODACE courses)
Lectures	These are given by experienced incident commanders from the organization, and guest lecturers from other agencies or academics. Used on virtually all courses
Video films	Specialist training films or footage of disasters. Police forces and fire brigades produce their own films and the Emergency Planning College has a series on major incidents. The airlines use films of pilots' decision making in emergencies with re-enactments based on cockpit voice recordings
Syndicate exercises	These are small group exercises, typically used to formulate a plan or to discuss a case study
Case studies	Very widely used and generally regarded as an essential component of incident command training
Computer-based training	Used to provide individual tuition, for example to develop ship training knowledge or learn incident command procedures. The systems can also be networked to provide an interactive exercise
Table-top exercises	This is a generic term covering a range of different types of low-fidelity exercises. They can involve installation plot plans, models and role playing. Paper-feed exercises include incoming information and status updates, often generated by a computer program
Floor-plan exercises	A version of the table-top exercise but with models laid out on a larger scale plan on the floor. The police, the fire service, The Royal Navy and the coastguards all use these (The Fire Service College's latest model is the Oklahoma City bombing site.)
Simulators, "hot seat exercises"	Command training simulators can be high-fidelity technical simulators employed by surgical teams, the military and commercial airlines; realistic outdoor incident grounds are used by the police and the fire service and there are various types of command centre facilities, sometimes with computer control and video projection
Exercises (on site)	Most organizations carry out *in situ* training such as emergency response drills and exercises on their premises, e.g. nuclear installations and ships. Sometimes assessed by inspectors from a regulatory authority
Full scale inter-agency exercises	Designed for major incidents and disasters, typically involving high-hazard sites and multiple elements in the scenario. They involve the emergency services as well as local authority emergency planners and other organizations, such as receiving hospitals and the media

well as by the fire, ambulance and prison services, the nuclear industry and civil aviation, and naval officers in their incident command training. The case studies are often based on in-house reports and debriefs, or on journal articles (e.g. Kroon and Overdijk 1993; Mathis, McKiddy and Way 1982). There are also detailed reports in the public domain published by HMSO following public inquiries into disasters such as the Bradford fire (Popplewell 1985, 1986), the King's Cross fire (Fennell 1988), the Clapham rail crash (Hidden 1989), Hillsborough (Taylor 1989, 1990) and *Piper Alpha* (Cullen 1990). These reports are written clearly, with cogent summaries, quotations from witnesses, explicit diagrams and photographs. They typically contain a chapter on the response of the emergency services, and may deal specifically with command and control procedures. In cases where a public inquiry has not taken place, there may be a report from a Coroner's Inquest in England and Wales or a Fatal Accident Inquiry in Scotland (e.g. the *Ocean Odyssey* drilling rig blowout; Ireland 1991). Where an accident has been investigated by a particular government agency, there will be an Accident Report available (e.g. the Kegworth air crash; AAIB 1990). The Marine Accident Investigation Branch (MAIB) publishes not only reports of specific accidents (e.g. the *Marchioness* collision; MAIB 1991) but also regular summaries of shipping accidents (MAIB 1995), which do not name individuals or companies but which provide valuable teaching material. The trainers of commercial pilots use the Air Accident Investigation Branch (AAIB) reports as well as the confidential near-miss reports from the Confidential Human Factors Incident Reporting Programme (CHIRP) in the UK (Green 1990) and the Aviation Safety Reporting System (ASRS) in the USA (Chappell 1994). The HSE also publishes investigative reports, which sometimes deal with emergency response procedures, including emergency command (e.g. the Aldermaston report; HSE 1994b). The Royal Navy uses its internal Board of Inquiry reports as well as fleet case studies of peacetime emergencies or conflict events. The sharing of this type of information enables a better appreciation of the range of potential incidents that can occur, and if the case reports are sufficiently detailed, then important lessons relating to organizational and management issues can be conveyed during emergency command training. Significant lessons may also be learnt from the mistakes of other organizations facing similar command and control issues:

> "It's fortunate that major emergencies are infrequent occurrences in most communities. This fact, however, means that there are few natural opportunities in which to develop and refine management expertise. Hence, it is vitally important that we as a profession [the police] share our experiences and the lessons we have learned from the critical incidents we have dealt with in our communities."
>
> (Sarna 1984, p. 4)

One of the few published compendia of background reading for a command programme is the Nautical Institute's Command Diploma for chief officers, which has been obtained by several thousand individuals to date. The purpose of this award is to provide a scheme to improve the awareness and application of command expertise at sea. Part of this scheme involves the study of a specialist text, *The Nautical Institute on Command* (Nautical Institute 1986), which includes chapters on stress and decision making, training for command, fire and damage control, and lessons to be learnt from critical incidents. As mentioned in the first chapter, there are few general texts available on incident command, Brunacini's (1985) book on fireground command being a notable exception. Background reading materials I have seen on incident command courses usually include operational procedure manuals, government guidance (e.g. Home Office 1994), advice from specific agencies (e.g. AAIB 1992) and a mixture of articles, cuttings and lecturers' notes. In Australia, Queensland Police Service now has a full competency acquisition programme with study grades available in the Emergency Management module on incident management, disaster management and strategic emergency management (QPS 1994).

Emergency Exercises and Simulator Training

One of the foundation elements of incident command training is the use of simulated emergency exercises. These can be low fidelity such as table-top, plot-plan or paper-feed exercises, which involve participants discussing or role playing the evolution of an emergency scenario with directing staff providing status updates and new information as the scenario develops (Booth 1990). Such exercises provide a very economical method of testing contingency plans and practising coordination between different agencies during emergency response operations (see Dowell 1995 for an account of a table-top exercise with 30 participants managing a train crash). Floor-plan exercises and scale models are used by several agencies, including the fire service, coastguards and the police. For example, South Yorkshire Police have developed a portable model of a town, which they use in emergency management training, and Grampian Fire Brigade have a model of Aberdeen city centre, which provides a frame of reference for participants during inter-agency training.

To enhance the degree of realism, many organizations use simulated command centres in purpose-built or adapted suites with video recording and multi-channel communications, such as those used in the hostage negotiators courses organized for prison officers and police officers, or the industrial emergency command centre simulators.

Computer controlled simulations using video or virtual reality footage are becoming increasingly popular in several organizations, and these are discussed separately below. Very realistic outdoor training environments are provided in a number of training centres, including the Metropolitan Police public order training ground at Hounslow, London, which houses "Riot City", a mock town used to train riot control operations. The Fire Service College at Moreton-in-Marsh has a 550-acre campus containing a number of full-scale buildings that can be set alight, including industrial units, a house, a five-storey shopping complex, a 4000-tonne dry cargo ship with engine room, situated in a lake, a chemical plant, a motorway (complete with vehicle pile-up), a plane and a railway system. Exercises can also be staged at the scene of a hypothetical incident to illustrate the environmental and logistical problems that will be encountered. This is typically the procedure for the large-scale exercises involving all the emergency services, emergency planners, local authority departments and other agencies, rather than a specific training for incident commanders. Such exercises are expensive to stage but are an excellent method of giving a large number of participants practice and are useful for identifying weaknesses in emergency plans and response procedures.

For commanders working in a technical environment there are the high-fidelity simulators of flight decks, ships' bridges, plant control rooms and submarines, costing several million pounds to commission, build and install. The commercial airlines make use of aircraft cockpit simulators, which are used extensively in pilot training, requalification and competence assessment. The trainers can programme the simulator with different airports, weather conditions, technical problems and all manner of emergency conditions. (Having been very kindly allowed to "fly" a British Airways 747–400 simulator as part of this project, I can more than vouch for their realism. With no flying experience except as a passenger, it is the stuff of "the stewardess is flying the plane" nightmares.) The merchant navy also employs high-fidelity simulators for training and assessment, such as the ballast control simulators at Aberdeen College, and the ship's bridge simulators at the Marine Institute, St Johns, Newfoundland, and at the Maritime Operations Centre at Southampton Institute, Warsash, where there is also a Liquid Cargo Operations Simulator (LICOS), which is used for emergency training (Barnett 1991). The ship's bridge simulators at Southampton are full mission daylight/dusk nocturnal simulators, which have a 210° visual scene that can be programmed for a large number of geographical areas. They have an extensive library of ship types, ranging from small patrol craft to very large crude carriers. These simulators are used on a number of different training programmes, including the Bridge Resource Management courses (see Chapter 6).

Whichever level of simulation is used, from low to high fidelity, the emergency scenarios must be developed carefully by individuals with an intimate knowledge of possible major hazard events for the domain in question in order to ensure that they have credibility for participants and will deliver the desired learning objectives. Fisher (1978), discussing exercises for disasters and major incidents, states, "directing staff need to have a vivid imagination and previous experience of live operations in order to feed in the type of problem likely to be encountered" (p. 198). Scenarios typically incorporate features of previous incidents as well as potential management and communication problems. Across organizations, it was found that trainers managing simulated emergency scenarios had considerable experience in running such exercises and in judging the standards of performance required. They usually had command experience, and knew how to introduce and monitor levels of stress during the exercise. The methods used by the Royal Navy to exercise and assess warship commanders and their crews provide an excellent example of how to set up and assess complex emergency simulations. (See Case Studies 3.1–3.5). Moore (1988) gives a good description of the different kinds of exercises, simulations and case studies that have been found to be effective in police training for crisis management. Simulator training and realistic emergency exercises provide trainees with an insight into their own decision making and leadership skills, and into the reactions to stress that they are likely to experience in a real incident (sometimes called by military trainers the "personal operating envelope"). A sample of offshore managers who were interviewed following simulator training (Flin, Slaven and Stewart, 1996) reported that the advantages of managing simulated exercises were:

- Discovering how one responds and makes decisions under pressure.
- Practice in thinking of possible courses of action to deal with emergencies.
- Increase in self-confidence from having performed well.
- Opportunity to test the team structure and to identify strengths and weaknesses.
- An appreciation of the importance of communication during an incident.

Computer-based Simulations

Computer-based simulations for incident command range from basic tutoring systems, through interactive training programmes, to the full fidelity environments described above. For instance, in medicine, where there is increasing interest in training for decision making under stress, particularly in anaesthesiology, very sophisticated simulators are now being used for the training of crisis management, which range from full patient simulator facilities (Gaba 1994) to computer packages for interactive learning of crisis management (Schwid and O'Donnell 1992).

The emergency services are now using various types of computer-controlled simulation with video footage to train incident commanders. In 1991, the Scottish Police College, in conjunction with the National Computing Centre, began to use a multimedia interactive computer-based simulation suite (originally called VisTrain) for training superintendents in football crowd control. This system is now used regularly on courses for inspectors and more senior officers. Similar simulators have been adopted by other forces. Dr Jonathan Crego, technology training adviser at the Metropolitan Police in London, explained the background to the development of their simulator, Minerva, which was first used for training in 1992:

> "We have some sophisticated gaming and simulation in the Met. They were limited because it was clear it was an exercise. They lost the realism, the stress of being bombarded with an evolving incident that you can see, hear and touch. Where necessary, you must reproduce the stress under which people have to make decisions. This suite is an enabling tool through which you can provide that stress."
>
> (Quoted in Hilton 1992, p. 58)

The Minerva system is a fast-time command and control training simulator which uses a network of computers to present full motion digital video and computer graphics in order to exercise senior decision makers in crisis management (Figure 3.1). The first training programme used by the Metropolitan Police was for the management of sporting events, in particular football stadium and public order situations. New developments include a training programme that has been used for the Notting Hill Carnival (a three-day event in London, attracting up to one million people; see Crego 1995), and another version, currently under design, to train incident commanders for siege situations involving hostage negotiation (Crego and Powell 1994). According to Crego,

> "A key aim of Minerva is to build confidence by offering prospective Bronze, Silver and Gold commanders a chance to try out their decision-making and management skills within a simulation of a real event, where the outcome of their actions mirrors real life. As one chief inspector put it after taking part: 'What made it so challenging was that the way you chose to sort out problems affected how things turned out – just as they do on the street.'"
>
> (Crego 1995, p. 24)

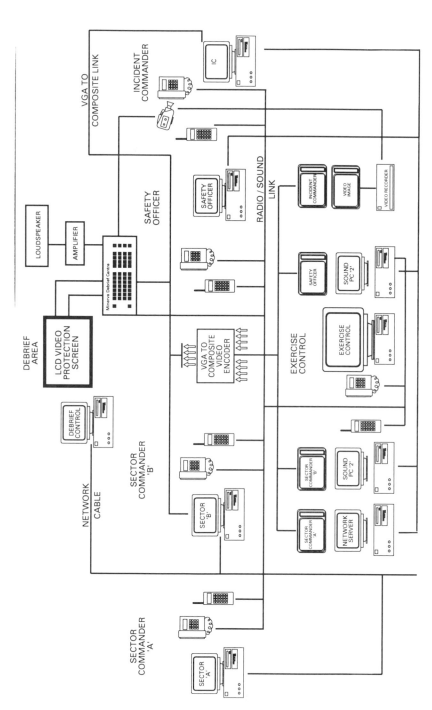

Figure 3.1 The Minerva Incident Command Simulator. Reproduced by permission of London Fire and Civil Defence Authority.

The Minerva and VisTrain public order exercises are run on a distributed team basis, with small groups of officers working together, taking the decisions of a semi-autonomous ground commander. Each group is allocated to a training "pod", which has a computer, with audio monitor and mouse, CD-ROM player, a multi-channel simulated radio, a telephone and a video phone. The teams are assigned different command roles, such as police ground commander, forward control unit or control, or are in charge of different areas of the location. They can communicate by phone and radio and must work together to deal with the simulated command problems as they unfold. All decisions and communications are recorded; the debrief stage is probably the most important component of the exercise. The Minerva package has now been adapted for the London Fire Brigade, which is using it to train officers in fireground command. The same type of system, known as C^3I (command, control, communication and intelligence), was installed in August 1995 at the Emergency Services College of Finland to train rescue leaders and their staff. This has a central control room, a tactical and action room, which can accommodate 24 observers as well as the rescue leader, and three smaller team rooms (Akesson 1995).

The Fire Service College also uses computer-based simulations to simulate the problems likely to be experienced by a fireground incident commander. The College's first system, ICCARUS, used multimedia hardware to display a complex warehouse fire, and the commander made decisions as the scenario unfolded (Powell et al. 1992; Simpson 1992). The new system, VECTOR, is based on a personal computer and can be adapted for other emergency services and for industrial commanders.

Computer-based systems to aid decision making are also available, although these are mainly for warfare commanders (Hutchins, in press), emergency planners (Belardo, Karwan and Wallace 1984) or emergency dispatchers (controllers) (Franklin and Hunt 1993). These can be used for training as well as under operational conditions. For example, researchers working with the Royal Netherlands Navy have developed a real-time damage control expert system, ANDES (Advanced Naval Damage Control Expert System), which can help damage control officers on frigates to develop their decision making skills (van Leeuwen 1993; Schraagen, in press). There are a number of non-military systems available, such as the European desktop system for crisis management and training called MEMbrain (Major Emergency Management), which can be tailored for nuclear plant emergencies, environmental disasters and other major crises. The system collects all relevant information from databases and on-line sensors, then presents simulations of possible crisis developments, as well as contingency and evacuation strategies (Drager and Furnes 1994). There are also software systems for managers who have to deal with the aftermath of an accident or commercial disaster. For example, CriSys runs on a desktop computer and provides pictures on a monitor screen, simulated radio broadcasts, incoming telephone calls and printouts of simulated reports by news agencies (O'Sullivan 1992).

Virtual reality (VR) simulations appear to offer great potential and are much talked about, but few organizations (with the exception of NASA, who commented on the expense of high quality VR) are using these in command training. The definition of VR also seems to have loosened in some quarters, with some laptop computer versions now being sold as VR. The full headset and glove VR technology can offer an impressive sense of reality and mental involvement, but while there are obvious applications for these systems in terms of realistic incident scene portrayal, incident commanders need to interact with their teams, and animate beings are much more difficult to simulate than landscapes or chemical plant environments.

Feedback in Training

Whatever type of exercise or simulation is used, it is generally accepted that the feedback stage of the training process is essential for increasing self-awareness and improving leadership skills in commanding officers. In Royal Navy exercises on warships, this is carried out by independent assessors as a "hot debrief" one hour after the exercise is completed, and the feedback is publicized to the entire crew and not just to senior officers. Feedback should be critical but constructive, designed to identify strengths as well as training needs within the emergency command structure. Where standards of competence for incident command are available, these are a useful template for informally assessing performance. It is important that senior commanding officers are occasionally asked to perform in "unseen" exercises so that their performance can be evaluated as well as that of the rest of the team.

This feedback element of training should be directed to improving the individual's appreciation of his or her own strengths and weaknesses when working under pressure. A NASA research psychologist explains:

> "The data on pilot attitudes clearly suggest areas where training can be beneficial ... These include decision making, interpersonal communication, leadership, and leader responsibilities, and personal characteristics and reactions. For example, with regard to personal reactions, a high percentage of pilots report that their decision making capabilities are unimpaired by high stress or fatigue – something that is patently untrue. Changing attitudes about personal limitations may well result in much more adaptive behavioral strategies and co-ordinated behavior in critical situations where maximum effectiveness is a life or death issue."
>
> (Helmreich 1987, p. 18)

Considerable skill and sensitivity is required to provide critical but constructive feedback, particularly using simulations. In the words of Moore (1985), the trainer:

> "needs to keep the views of the participants focused on the simulations itself. Throughout, the debriefing session requires very careful handling, the trainer taking care not to be destructive in commenting on the performance of individuals, nor indeed allowing anyone else to be destructive in their comments."
>
> (p. 15)

Crego and Powell (1994) emphasize the importance of the reflective review at the end of training sessions using the Minerva simulator with police officers. All of the participants assemble and can review any part of the session, which is then replayed on a large projection screen. They emphasize the need to maintain a safe, learning environment where officers can give and accept constructive criticism without feeling the need to be defensive:

> "The best sessions have occurred when we have let the officers in charge of the Silver [tactical] pod run the session.... During one of the reflective sessions, a particular Silver pod officer sat quietly with his head in his hands after reviewing a reasonably disastrous part of the crisis. He said 'I lost it here' and a Bronze [operational] pod officer said 'I don't think so. If we can see on the screen now what I saw, I think you'll find that I didn't pass on to you information I was getting on my screen.' When we reviewed the Bronze pod video it became clear that Silver had no option, as he wasn't given sufficient information from Bronze on the state of the crisis. The whole group learned important lessons on communication and the information requirements of Silver."
>
> (Crego and Powell 1994, p. 4)

Salas et al. (1995) caution that, because of the multiple levels that need to be addressed, performance feedback for team tasks is not entirely straightforward:

> "Feedback in a team environment should 1) enable each team member to perform his/her individual task, 2) demonstrate the contribution of an individual's performance to the performance of other members, and 3) demonstrate the contribution of an individual's performance to the performance of the team as a whole.... An unintended consequence of giving team level feedback without respect to the relationship of individual performance to the team performance is that incorrect behaviours may be reinforced. This in turn may result in no improvement and may wash out the impact of team feedback on both the individual and team overall."
>
> (Salas et al. 1995, p. 98)

See Powell et al. (1992) for a description of the debriefing process used with a fireground command training simulator.

Inter-Agency Training

The problems of inter-agency coordination and communication have been highlighted in major incidents, such as the King's Cross fire (Fennell 1988). This is addressed by the emphasis on common command structures as described in *Dealing with Disasters* (Home Office 1994) and by the development of joint agency training programmes, typically for major exercises or table-top scenarios. For example, Grampian Joint Emergencies Working Group runs a scale model and paper-feed scenario exercise involving participants from the local hospitals, local authority, military bases and the emergency services. Multidisciplinary teams discuss their operational responses and take decisions at each stage as the scenario develops. This provides an excellent opportunity for learning about other agencies' priorities and ways of working, as well as identifying potential communication problems. For example, in one exercise I witnessed, it transpired that the fire officers' interpretation of the term "well-developed fire" was different (in degree of severity) to that of the other players. In Australia an Inter-Service Incident Management System is used, which provides standardized training courses in incident management, designed to promote effective joint operations for several emergency response services.

INCIDENT COMMAND TRAINING: CASE STUDIES

In this section selected elements of the training programmes of the fire service, the police and the offshore oil industry are examined in some detail, with two additional examples drawn from the nuclear industry and damage control in the Royal Navy.

CASE STUDY 3.1: THE FIRE SERVICE

The British Fire Service has 56 000 serving officers and firefighters, organized into 63 regional fire brigades. The rank structure in ascending order is typically firefighter, leading firefighter, sub-officer, then station officer and divisional officer (assistant, III, II, I, senior), then assistant, deputy and chief officer (firemaster). There is only one point of entry to the lowest rank of firefighter, with no graduate entry or accelerated promotion system allowing direct appointment to the service at a higher level. Promotion through the system is dependent on examinations, performance appraisal and assessment centres, which allow access to the most senior command training courses.

Incident command training in the UK is provided by the fire brigades and by the progression training courses at the national Fire Service College at Moreton-in-Marsh, Gloucestershire. In ascending order of seniority, these programmes are the Crew Command Course, Watch Command Course, Junior Officer Advancement Course, Divisional Command Course and the Brigade Command Course. Selection for the final Brigade Command Course is on the basis of an extended interview (assessment centre), and successful completion of this course is generally required for appointment to the chief officer ranks. The first three courses carry out the majority of the incident command training to teach the exercise of authority on the fireground by fire service officers for the purpose of stabilizing emergency situations. These courses have recently been significantly revised. There is now a focus upon an operational command model centred around strategy, tactics and task. All training and subsequent assessments support the new fire service company standards (see Table 2.5).

The Crew Command Course

A firefighter will be required to act as on-scene commander from the level of crew commander when he or she is in charge of a single fire appliance and its crew. As first officer at the scene of a fire, the crew commander acts as incident commander until such time as the fire has been controlled or a more senior officer arrives. Therefore, an important component of incident command procedures in the fire service is this handing over of command, and in a large-scale incident (such as the King's Cross fire), the command role may be transferred several times.

This foundation command course is designed to aid the transition from a crew member to becoming the crew commander. It is carried out at the Fire Service College, where it is a three-week programme consisting of lectures, discussions, demonstrations, and fireground exercises. "In the majority of cases the crew commander works in the attack mode, dealing with crises as they arise.... in some cases the role of the crew commander is to lay the foundations upon which oncoming senior officers can build" (Murray 1993, p. 10). The key functions of the crew commander are identified as planning, briefing, controlling, supporting, informing, evaluating. These functions are generic to incident command, but in addition many technical and operational procedures are also taught, relating, for example, to different types of fire or use of breathing apparatus. Murray (1993) notes that:

"The aim of the course is to develop operational command abilities. Good command involves a gestalt of leadership, management, interpersonal and technical skills backed up by a sound basis of knowledge."

(p. 12)

The multiple roles of the crew commander are examined because, depending on the type of incident, the crew commander may have to function not only as incident commander but also as the equipment officer, the water officer, the control unit officer or the press officer. The course also emphasizes that the incident commander must be fully aware of both the responsibilities faced and the authority possessed to meet them. The crew commander's responsibilities can be regarded as legal (Fire Services Act, Health and Safety at Work etc. Act, hazardous substances legislation, environmental legislation), political (in relation to other agencies, the local authority etc.) and moral. This last category may have a universal application, as any incident commander may be faced with a moral dilemma, such as the judgement of degree of risk to firefighters when effecting a rescue. During the course, each student will be assessed (against competence standards) in the role of incident commander on at least three occasions.

The Watch Command Course

The watch commander's role when attending the incident is more complex than that of the crew commander, given the greater resources under his or her command, in terms of firefighters, appliances and equipment. Typically, the watch commander will manage an incident involving two or three appliances and their crews, and the commander will be operating in a tactical mode to the incident, assessing the situation, allocating resources and monitoring risks. At some events, such as an escalating incident or when resources are stretched, the command style may need to be more detached, maintaining a wider perspective and preparing to hand over responsibility to a more senior officer. The Fire Service College provides a nine-week course (including four weeks on fire safety) to train potential watch commanders, which involves two assessments of each individual.

Junior Officer Advancement Course

The leadership skills and technical training necessary to fulfil the position of Station Officer are taught on a nine-week course delivered in two parts. The second five-week stage (JOA2) is based on operational command, and covers the following topics: command role, procedural knowledge, operational planning, incident assessment, and command functions. The station commander is likely to be called to a larger or more complex incident involving four or five appliances and crews as well as support vehicles. The establishment of an organizational structure (for example, sectorization) to maintain control becomes increasingly important as the size of the incident develops. At this level, incident command has more of a strategic function and takes place in a specially equipped control unit set slightly back from the front of the event. The station commander will usually arrive at the incident by car after the initial response and he or she will be required to take over command from the more junior incident commander currently in charge.

Part of the training on this course involves two "hot seat" exercises, in which one of the 30 students is selected to act as the incident commander (Officer in Charge, OIC) in a control unit simulator to take charge of a complex fire (e.g. a large public building). Other students play the roles of support officers, while the remainder of the class watch on closed-circuit television, having been instructed to observe the OIC's performance in relation to the main command functions that were covered earlier in the course (organization, communications, incident plan, crew safety, logistics, liaison, post-incident). A detailed debrief session is run using video review and student feedback. Figure 3.2 shows the layout of the simulator facility.

The training exercise is designed to make the OIC step back into a supervisory role and take a wider view of the incident and its management. The OICs should by this point in the course appreciate that at any moment in time they can only attend to two or three of the command functions listed above, and therefore they must delegate responsibility in order to reduce the pressure on themselves.

Divisional Command Course

This is a nine-week programme for officers who will be progressing to the ranks of Divisional Officer. This is a middle management position, and officers of this rank will only be called to take command of the larger incidents:

> "Above 15 pumps the OIC is almost totally concerned with command and control logistics. The fire incident is now of such a size that the fireground itself will have been zoned, with firefighting in each zone under the command of a more junior officer. The Officer-in-Charge will now be involved in making sure adequate resources are available to zone commanders: coordinating back-up, liaising with other agencies such as police and ambulance; arranging for water supplies, safety, salvage; and managing the complex communications that all of this implies."
>
> (Powell et al. 1992, p. 111)

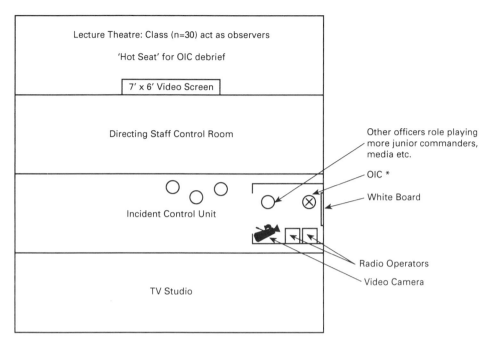

* OIC: *Officer in Charge*

Figure 3.2 *"Hot Seat" Exercise, Fire Service College, Junior Officer Advancement Course.*

This is essentially a management course, which includes operational command and specific incident command training concerning the control of major incidents and inter-agency liaison.

The Brigade Command Course

The Brigade Command Course is the senior management training programme in the fire service. It is of 16 weeks duration and includes an international project, where students make a detailed study of a specialist topic on a cross-cultural basis. The course qualifies officers to apply for chief officer posts and as such deals primarily with strategic management issues. Officers in charge at this level will only be called to the most serious and complex incidents, and in terms of incident command, they will tend to be in a strategic mode involving liaison with other agencies rather than a tactical role. In recent years a number of Brigade Command Course students have studied incident command for their international project, with a particular focus on decision making (Hendry 1994; Murray 1995), teamwork (Bonney 1995; Wynne 1995) and operational procedures (Dobson 1995).

CASE STUDY 3.2: POLICE OFFICERS

The British police forces have 153 000 serving officers and are organized on a regional basis. Like the fire service, there is a clearly defined rank structure, which rises from constable, through sergeant, inspector, chief inspector, superintendent, assistant chief constable, deputy chief constable to chief constable. There are both uniformed and plain-clothed officers, and they do not generally carry firearms, although some officers are specially trained and qualified to do so. Training is carried out at both force and national level. There is a Scottish Police College at Tulliallan and a Police Staff College at Bramshill in England, as well as individual force and regional training centres.

Incident command is only one of a number of duties that a police officer will be trained to perform. As mentioned earlier, a very junior constable may find herself or himself first on the scene of an escalating situation or even a major incident. As in the fire service, there is an operational–tactical–strategic command structure and as the scale of an incident increases, more senior officers will attend the scene. In the police service, however, they will not necessarily take over command. Incident command skills are taught using on-the-job training in individual forces and during training courses, which are part of the progression through the ranks (along with examinations and extended interviews (assessment centres)). Of most relevance to the theme of this volume is the training provided for middle ranking officers (from inspector), who are likely to find themselves as on-scene operational (Silver) commander at a major scheduled event or an unexpected incident. For instance, the course for newly promoted inspectors at the Scottish Police College includes sessions on major incidents and command decision making, which covers recognition-primed decisions (see Chapter 5), stress and teamwork under pressure. The students also receive training in public order incident management using the VisTrain crowd control simulator mentioned earlier.

There are a number of more specialized courses for officers who are likely to find themselves in the role of incident commander in a range of different situations, such as public order, sports crowds, firearms incidents, road traffic accidents and sieges. Under the Association of Chief Police Officers (ACPO in England and Wales; ACPOS in Scotland) guidance, certain types of incident command training are recommended for specific levels or types of command. Two examples are described here: the course on the management of major incidents and the hostage negotiators course.

The national course that provides training for command of major incidents is a one-week programme run at the Police Staff College, Bramshill, called "The Management of Disaster and Civil Emergency (MODACE) Course". This is for officers who may be required to act as Officer in Overall Command, Incident Officer, Senior Investigating Officer, Major Incident Control Room Coordinator or Incident Control Post Coordinator. These individuals are typically of the ranks of chief inspector or superintendent. The aim of this course is to define and develop the roles of senior police officers called upon to manage civil emergencies and disasters. The course consists of lectures from senior police officers, as well as guest lecturers, such as senior staff from the fire service, the ambulance service, the transport police, the AAIB or emergency planning departments. Talks are also given by experts discussing media relations, legal implications, casualty treatment, pathology, and dealing with survivors and relatives. Case studies of major emergencies are presented by police commanders. There is also syndicate work, such as paper-feed exercises, to allow students to practise their command and control skills. The course content is based on the police *Emergency Procedures Manual* (ACPO 1991), which provides national guidelines for emergency management. There is also a one-week MODACE course for more senior officers (ACPO ranks), which is designed for those at the Gold command level (e.g. assistant or deputy chief constables). This covers similar ground but at a strategic level.

The police also train officers for dealing with special types of incidents, such as public order, football crowd policing and hostage negotiation. The negotiators' course is a two-week training programme run at the Metropolitan Police College, Hendon and at the Scottish Police College at Tulliallan. Both courses involve lectures from senior police officers, experienced negotiators, psychiatrists and other experts, who cover operational procedures and key skills. They also present detailed case studies of hostage taking and hijack events, which are delivered by the police officers in charge or hostages who were involved. The most demanding and valuable aspect of this course is the simulated hostage taking scenarios, where the trainee negotiators have to communicate by phone or radio with an actor playing the role of the hostage taker. (The actor is typically a trained police negotiator, who will fully test the negotiation skills of the students.) The exercises are set up with a complete negotiation cell plus support officers, and an incident commander will take charge of the event. The incident commanders are typically superintendents who have attended a special one-day course in siege management, and they volunteer to participate in these exercises in order to rehearse their incident management skills. The exercises are conducted both indoors and outdoors and are recorded on videotape for personal review purposes. Each exercise is fully and critically debriefed by the course tutors and participating officers. See Fuselier (1991) for a detailed account of FBI procedures for hostage negotiation, and Greenstone (1995) for hostage negotiation team training in small police departments. Similar courses are run by the Prison Service Colleges for prison officers and governors who also require training in incident command and hostage negotiation.

CASE STUDY 3.3: OFFSHORE OIL INDUSTRY MANAGERS

As the job of an offshore manager is likely to be relatively unfamiliar to most readers, this section begins with a brief description of the emergency command requirement. The OIM position involves not only day-to-day responsibilities as the most senior manager on an offshore oil and gas platform, drilling rig or support vessel, but also the ability to take the role of incident commander should an emergency such as a fire or an explosion arise. Given the maritime and hydrocarbon hazards, an OIM must react quickly to deal with any such situation, but, unlike the manager of an onshore petrochemical or nuclear plant, he or she cannot call upon the emergency services for immediate assistance. In the short term, a crisis must be dealt with by the installation's own personnel, all of whom will have been trained in sea survival and fire fighting, and some will have undergone specialist training as fire team leaders, first aiders and lifeboat coxswain. On a large production platform there can be 200 or more personnel on board, with significantly more (up to 900) if construction or refurbishment work is taking place. The emergency evacuation of a British or Norwegian offshore installation is by no means a simple operation. The majority of platforms are located over 100 miles from land and are subject to the extreme weather conditions of the North Sea. Helicopter evacuation, which is the preferred option, can take several hours with a large crew since most of the infield helicopters only carry small numbers of passengers and the large search and rescue helicopters can take several hours to reach the more remote installations. Evacuation to the sea by totally enclosed lifeboats is a secondary option, but this can be difficult and dangerous in cold seas, where a swell of 20 to 30 feet is by no means uncommon. In severe winter weather it may well be the case that the best means of survival for a crew is to remain on board the installation, controlling the problem until evacuation is possible or the situation becomes untenable. One oil manager described the North Sea environment as "unique in its sustained nastiness" (Harvie 1994).

In an emergency, the OIM and the command team are expected to deal with the immediate situation and to take any action required to ensure the safety of personnel on board and the integrity of the installation. (See Figure 6.1 for a diagram of an emergency command centre team.) Actions may include:

- Shutting down production
- Ceasing drilling operations
- Mustering personnel
- Deploying firefighting or rescue teams
- Liaison with adjacent installations, onshore management, the coastguard, shipping and aviation
- Evacuation of non-essential personnel
- Total abandonment of the installation.

The training for this occupation came traditionally from previous work experience in other potentially hazardous environments, such as petrochemical plant management, or a naval career. Coming up "through the ranks" offshore exposed managers to gradually increasing levels of responsibility; in some cases, they had previously dealt with incidents offshore or had observed the managers who were responsible at the time. Specialist emergency training courses were gradually developed for the North Sea oil industry; for example, the four-day Management of Emergencies course at Montrose Fire and Emergency Training Centre and the coastguard search and rescue courses (Foster 1992, 1995). Following the *Piper Alpha* disaster in 1988, a new emphasis was placed on the training and competence assessment of these managers in relation to their emergency command abilities. A number of organizations now offer specialist courses, such as EMC^2 (Emergency Management Command and Control) or OCTO (Offshore Command Training Organisation), which draw on the expertise of former naval commanders (including, in the latter case, two admirals from the Falklands conflict) to provide intensive coaching and development of managers, using both outdoor training and emergency command centre simulator exercises. The oil companies also conduct regular training on their installations, from weekly lifeboat drills to full-scale exercises. Flin and Slaven (1994) provide details of the main training providers offering command training for offshore industrial mangers, and team training for offshore emergency command groups is discussed in Chapter 6.

The installation managers in the Norwegian offshore oil industry also receive intensive training in emergency command. One of the newest simulators is that of NUTEC in Bergen, Norway, which trains very large offshore teams in a purpose-built facility. This is based in a suite of rooms with full communication links, recording equipment and computer-controlled scenarios, in which not only the platform emergency response team participate, but also helicopter and ship captains who would be involved in a rescue operation. The simulator is built on the side of a fjord, and when the platform manager takes the decision to evacuate the installation, the crew have to leave the simulator and board a free-fall lifeboat, which they then have to launch. The last component injects a degree of realism found in few other industrial command simulators.

CASE STUDY 3.4: NUCLEAR INSTALLATION EMERGENCY MANAGERS

"In the event of an emergency four aspects of response have to be provided for. These are (a) the control of the accident at the site; (b) the assessment of actual and potential accident consequences, and alerting the relevant authorities and the public; (c) the introduction of countermeasures to mitigate the consequences as regards (i) individuals who could be affected in the short term; and (ii) longer term effects such as the contamination of food supplies, and adjoining waters; (d) the return to normal conditions."

(HSE 1994b, p. 1)

"The Nuclear Installations Inspectorate requires all employees at nuclear installations who could be involved in an emergency to be trained for their tasks and to be involved in regular exercises to ensure appropriate team performance."

(HSE 1994b, p. 28)

Nuclear power plants hold regular emergency exercises, known as shift exercises. In addition, there are larger exercises witnessed by the Nuclear Installation Inspectorate (NII), such as Site Exercises (Level 1), which concentrate on the operator's actions on and off site but may involve the emergency services and other external organizations. There are also Off-Site Exercises (Level 2) designed to test the function of the Off-Site Centre once every three years. These will also involve external agencies. The National Exercises (Level 3) also test the interaction of the various government departments and ministers at their headquarters, as well as the national emergency centres. These may last for more than a day, and one of the Level 2 exercises is chosen for this, once a year.

The emergency response organization is directed by an emergency manager (site emergency controller), who is located at the emergency control centre on site and is supported by a team of engineers, scientists and administrative staff. He or she is responsible for all aspects of the site operator's emergency organization in the early stages, including, where appropriate, notifying relevant off-site organizations, recommending actions for the protection of personnel on site and the public, and restoring the plant to a safe, stable condition. The training courses used for emergency managers in Scottish Nuclear's power stations have been developed over a number of years and essentially comprise the following three main elements (Burgoyne, personal communication, 1995):

1. Self-study packs/lecture-based courses: these are designed to cover reasonably foreseeable situations that could arise on the plant and the recommended courses of action to be taken. They also provide details on the company's emergency arrangements and, more specifically, the duties and responsibilities of each member of the emergency organization.

2. Seminars: these allow groups of emergency managers to discuss emergency scenarios and the appropriate response to them in a low stress environment.
3. Role play: all emergency managers are required to participate in regular emergency exercises (see above), which involve the full deployment of emergency resources responding to an emergency scenario in real time. These are often held in conjunction with representatives from external agencies (e.g. the emergency services). One exercise per year, per site is witnessed and assessed by the regulatory authority, the NII.

For a good description of the on-site and off-site emergency response arrangements at British Nuclear Fuels' Sellafield reprocessing plant, see Cammish and Richardson (1989).

CASE STUDY 3.5: ROYAL NAVY DAMAGE CONTROL OFFICERS

Although it was stated at the outset that this book will not focus on warfare commanders, there is nevertheless one particular group of military incident commanders whose role is equivalent to that of the civil emergencies on-scene commander. These are the officers in charge of damage control (more correctly, NBCD, Nuclear, Biological, Chemical and Damage) on board Royal Navy ships. As the nuclear, chemical and biological protection aspects of NBCD relate only to warfare situations, these will not be considered here. In a peacetime emergency or wartime action stations, this officer will be a department head (the marine engineering officer (MEO), usually, on frigates and destroyers, holding the rank of Lieutenant-Commander) who acts as the Action Stations NBCD officer. He or she is in charge of command and control with responsibility for firefighting, ship repair and casualty rescue, for any emergency situation, the most likely of which are fire and flooding. However, even the most junior engineering, supply and seamen officers are trained to take the command role in a damage control situation, because they take their turn acting as Officer of the Day and as such may be the most senior officer in charge (e.g. when the ship is in port with a reduced crew on board) when an emergency such as a fire occurs.

Training

The training of Royal Navy officers as incident commanders for damage control in an emergency is carried out at the Phoenix NBCD School, HMS *Excellent*, Portsmouth. There are two NBCD courses. The first is for junior officers who have already been at sea as midshipmen; they attend a one-week NBCD course prior to taking up their initial job at sea. There is a second one-week course for more experienced officers. The courses are formally assessed by written examination at the end of the week, and candidates also receive informal assessment and feedback during the programme. The more junior course consists of three days' training on damage control and two on nuclear, biological and chemical protection. The course content is based on the *Ship NBCD Manual* (MoD 1994a) and training takes the form of lectures, case studies, table-top exercises using ship plot plans, simulator exercises and computer-based training. The computer-based training is delivered in a purpose-built suite equipped with individual stations and a master control unit. Students either work individually on programmes to develop specific ship knowledge or more general incident management skills, or the stations can be networked to allow students to practise interactive decision making with other role players in the command and control structure.

Students are also trained in a Ship Control Centre simulator (of the hypothetical frigate HMS *Boadicea*), which allows them to role play the positions of Officer of the Day and other key positions during a simulated emergency, such as a harbour fire. Training school staff direct the scenario and also role play other personnel, such as civilian fire brigade officers, who will be called if a fire happens in port. Students are encouraged to work as a team and to use *aide-mémoire* sheets to ensure that they have followed appropriate procedures. Following each scenario a full debrief session takes place. The original simulator has now been replaced by a high-fidelity computer-controlled Ship Control Centre simulator. This has a main control room, which uses back-projected video images to customize the control panels and readouts for different classes of ship. The simulator uses the latest computerized decision aid (Damage Control Online Information Display System; DACOIDS), which provides regular status recording and prompt facilities. The more senior course employs a similar mix of training techniques, but this is attended by officers about to attain department head level who have key roles in the damage control organization, especially if the ship is at action stations. The courses are run separately for the different departments (e.g. supply officers, engineering officers). The simulator is also available for ships' command teams to use when ships are in port.

Assessed Exercises

Apart from regular daily and weekly exercises in emergency response, ships' crews are assessed in their command and control of emergencies by an independent team of expert assessors. This takes place at Flag Officer Sea Training (FOST), a Royal Navy organization based at Devonport, Plymouth, established to train (work-up) and maintain the operational efficiency of ships in the fleet. Several types of training and assessment are conducted by FOST:

- Preliminary safety training (two weeks): for ships that have just been commissioned or have come out of refit and are crewed by people who have not worked together at sea before.
- Basic operational sea training (six weeks): undertaken prior to joining the fleet as an operational unit.
- Continuation operational sea training (four weeks): carried out every 18 months. The continuation operational training includes a series of exercises (serials) carried out both at sea and in harbour, which increase in complexity as the work-up progresses. Performance of the ship's company, both as individuals and as teams, is assessed during these exercises by a small, highly qualified and experienced team of FOST staff NBCD instructors (nicknamed the "Wreckers"), who set up the exercises, observe them and then produce a detailed feedback report and overall rating.

See Atterbury (1992) for a more detailed description of FOST and its operation. Exercises at sea involve simulated conflict scenarios. For example, in one "serial" (scenario) the vessel is "buzzed" by fighter jet aircraft, resulting in simulated hits using real explosives (scare charges), which are followed by "fire", smoke (using smoke simulants) and "loss of several key systems". This seriously affects the ship's ability to maintain its "fight, move, float" capability and provides a formidable challenge to its command and control organization. Harbour fire incidents are also assessed, where ships in harbour on minimum manning levels, under the command of a more junior Officer of the Day, are faced with a simulated fire in an engine space.

The scenarios have been very carefully developed and are updated regularly. They are designed to test the overall command and control system and the competence of particular departments, e.g. damage control, weapons, engineering. The assessment team conduct a briefing with the senior officers on the day prior to the exercise. The assessors (a team of 6–16, depending on the size of the ship and the type of exercise) arrive on board 45 minutes prior to the exercise. The ship will already be at Action Stations if it is a wartime scenario. The scenario will run for 1.5–2 hours, during which time the assessors will manage the exercise, escalating events if appropriate, as well as observe the performance of key players and their teams. They may ask questions to determine why a particular course of action has been adopted, or "what if ..." type questions to test the range of an individual's knowledge.

The assessment of command and control performance is based on subjective judgements as well as on a number of objective criteria, which include:

- Time to achieve key objectives
- Whether initial reactions were in line with established procedures
- Completeness and accuracy of information recording, e.g. on incident boards

- Communication of plan of action, quality of team briefing
- Establishment of damage boundaries
- Performance of fire fighting teams
- Effectiveness of smoke control
- Effectiveness of command and control

On completion of the exercise the assessors sit down in private to compile their assessment reports. They work very closely as a team, writing up the incidents they have covered and discussing the performance and leadership of individuals in the command and control positions. Drawing on a consensus of opinion, the officer in charge prepares a report on the command and control aspects and an overall summary. Each of the principal staff officers covering the exercise gives his or her own assessments (e.g. weapons engineering, marine engineering, damage control). The time allocated for the writing up of the assessment is approximately one hour. As soon as this is finished, the three assessing officers give a structured "hot" debrief to the commanding officer and key personnel on the ship. This lasts for 15–20 minutes and will give a generalized and critical review of performance as well as the assessment rating. The detailed written report is also given at that time to the captain, and it is intended to be copied to the entire ship's crew.

The assessment process is taken very seriously and the resulting overall grade carries considerable weight with both the captain and the ship's company. The assessment grading is strict and it is rare for high grades to be achieved. Relative gradings between ships are discussed openly, and this element of competition clearly has a motivational benefit. Individual appraisal is provided on key personnel and also on personnel who have stood out, either positively or negatively, although this will only be filed onshore in exceptional cases. The final assessment is on a seven-point scale ranging from unsatisfactory to very good. The former requires a repeated assessment, and the latter is very rarely achieved.

The assessment procedures used at FOST are extremely impressive and have been validated by Falklands war veterans, who have commented that they were prepared and able to perform in battle conditions due to their training and the experiences of work-ups with FOST. Given the degree of responsibility placed on the assessment teams, it is obvious that these individuals have been carefully selected and trained for this appointment. Their credibility and professionalism are essential elements in the obvious success of this operation. Interestingly, the officer leading the assessment team (Lt. Cdr.) may be two ranks below the captain of the ship that is being assessed. There is a very strong emphasis on communication, teamworking and leadership skills in junior officers and NCOs, as well as in the senior officers.

The scenarios used in the assessment have been very carefully developed and are regularly updated, often on the basis of previous incidents, e.g. from

Falklands war and peacetime emergencies. They are certainly perceived as highly realistic by the ships' companies involved in the exercises. The feedback is carefully structured, notably critical, yet constructive, and is relayed very promptly to the ship's company. This is a fairly expensive operation to stage and to staff but there are demonstrable benefits of using independent teams of assessors to judge emergency response (damage control) capability in full-scale realistic exercises. Between visits to FOST, ships are given a structured training programme of exercises and drills which they must achieve on a self-umpired basis. These use specified levels of both frequency and quality standards. How well ships meet their training targets is part of the 'Management Information' fed back to shore authorities. These targets are taken very seriously and are passed to the very highest management levels within the government. FOST also employs two mobile training teams with eight staff, similar to the 'Wreckers'. These visit ships all around the world to help with internal training and also to provide an outside umpiring service for ships' NBCD exercises.

CONCLUSION

"The current move toward increased public accountability means that, whilst the [fire] service is respected for what it does, a more measurable degree of professionalism is being demanded. The ability of Incident Commanders is being scrutinised and it is important that the training provided for officers ensures that they can meet the demands placed upon them."

(Murray, 1994b, p. 67)

Incident command training across organizations employs the same kinds of techniques and methods to achieve similar ends. There are tremendous opportunities for these organizations to share information, but unfortunately there seems to be limited cross-transfer, perhaps due to the lack of an accessible forum where such issues can be discussed. The military and emergency services spend a great deal of time training for command and control in crises, and a number of commercial organizations that provide emergency command courses base their training on this expertise; for example, from the Royal Navy, the army or the fire service.

There is also an increasing number of post-graduate and post-experience courses in emergency planning or disaster management, some of which contain a module on incident command. For example, the Home Office Emergency Planning College at Easingwold runs courses and seminars, such as a three-day seminar on Incident Control and Emergency Centres Management. The Civil Emergency Management Centre at Hertfordshire University offers a postgraduate diploma/MSc in Civil Emergency Management, which has a module on command and control and legal requirements; Coventry University offers an undergraduate degree in International Disaster Engineering and Management; and the Disaster Prevention and Limitation Unit at Bradford University runs courses and seminars. The Disaster Preparedness Centre at Cranfield University offers research, training and consultancy, mainly to countries overseas who are vulnerable to disasters caused by natural hazards. Specialist organizations, such as the Emergency Planning Society, the Society of Industrial Emergency Planning Officers and the Institute of Civil Defence and Disaster Studies, may also be able to provide information or advice for training. Further afield, specialist centres can provide research publications, information and training courses; for example, in the USA, the Disaster Management Centre at the University of Delaware and the Institute of Emergency Administration and Planning at the University of North Texas. In Australia, Charles Sturt University has a bachelors degree programme in emergency management. National institutes of emergency management, such as the Swedish Defence Research Establishment (now part of the War College) and the Emergency Services Institute in Finland, can provide further information on courses and training methods.

The psychological skills that underpin effective command relate to stress management, decision making and teamwork, which are considered in the following chapters.

4
The Stress of Incident Command

"If you can keep your head, when all about you are losing theirs and blaming it on you ..."

(Kipling, *If—*)

"The officer in charge of a fire must never overlook the fact that his bearing will influence the crews working under him. He should at all times appear imperturbable, and any orders which he gives should be given clearly and simply, without shouting or signs of excitement."

(Home Office (Fire Department) 1981, p. 146)

Appearing imperturbable when you are in fear of your life or when you are required to take charge of a chaotic scene at a major incident, may be easier said than done. And yet, managing stress is a central element of emergency command and as such appears in the standards of competence on incident command in different occupations. This chapter examines the causes, effects and symptoms of stress from a psychological perspective. Drawing on relevant studies of stress and performance from military research, and from managers' and commanders' own accounts of their reactions in emergencies, a descriptive model of stress in emergencies will be used to identify optimal techniques for incident commanders to manage their own stress and that of their emergency response team members.

WHAT IS STRESS?

The word stress (probably from the Latin *stringere*, to draw tight) is the label now widely used to describe psychological distress and discomfort. If we consider work-related stress, it is important to distinguish between two types; using a medical analogy, these can be labelled chronic stress and acute stress. Chronic stress, usually called occupational stress, is related to conditions in the workplace and the individual's reaction to these, usually over a protracted period of time. The causes and effects of occupational stress have been studied since the late 1970s and are now receiving significant attention from the UK HSE, which commissioned a review of research (Cox 1993) and then published guidelines for employers (HSE 1995).

The other type of stress, which is the theme of this chapter, is acute stress, called emergency stress or critical incident stress. At its most extreme, this is where the individual is suddenly exposed to a threatening situation, such as a life endangering event or a traumatic scene, and experiences a pronounced physiological and psychological reaction, which has – in many situations – a highly adaptive, valuable effect. The "flight/fight" response, so called because of the need to flee or fight the threat, is produced when the brain perceives a threat in the immediate environment and signals the rest of the body to produce an energy surge to allow the person to quickly flee the situation or fight the aggressor. Any situation perceived by the individual to be very demanding or challenging can produce this effect, and most people will have experienced this in situations of fear or alarm, such as having a near miss when driving, flying in a plane that starts to produce peculiar engine noises, or having to give a talk to a large audience. Attending the scene of an emergency as an incident commander or as a member of the response team can be sufficiently demanding to produce the symptoms of this reaction, even if the individual's own life is not in immediate danger. The typical pattern of physiological effects is shown as a simplified diagram in Figure 4.1.

As Figure 4.1 shows, once the brain has detected a change in the environment which it interprets as highly threatening, it triggers the flight/fight reaction. The consequent release of hormones (e.g. adrenalin) into the bloodstream prepares the body for action by slowing down non-essential functions, such as digestion (hence dry mouth, butterflies in stomach), and gearing up the heart, lungs and muscles with extra power. Thus, the heart beats faster to pump more blood to the lungs for oxygenation, breathing rate quickens to increase oxygen intake and there is enhanced blood flow to the muscles. Sweating occurs to provide the necessary cooling during this process. This is an important, and on occasions life saving, pattern of response. People who report running faster than they have ever done before in order to rescue their child or to escape a fire, or who can manage to carry a casualty beyond expectations, are using the energy provided by this reaction. Rescuers who feel "high" in response to an emergency are experiencing the same effect, and there may be short-term positive effects on thinking skills and energy levels. Weisaeth (1987), discussing leaders in disaster situations, points out:

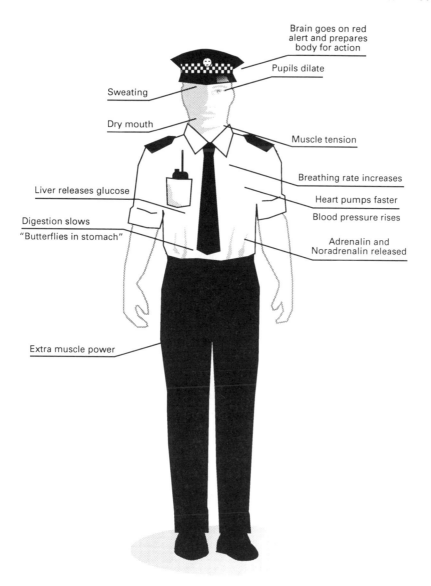

Figure 4.1 *The Emergency Stress Response (Flight/Fight Response).*

"it must be emphasised that a moderate degree of stress seems to have a positive effect on the ability of an individual to function. This applies to sensory processes, thought processes, decision-making and the ability to act."

(p. 8)

The downside is that this is an expensive state for the brain and body to maintain, and it can result in both short-term and longer term physical and psychological side effects.

If we look at the psychological process of stress, whether this be occupational stress or emergency stress, the psychological process is the same: at its simplest, stress occurs (and for the purposes of this chapter, the term stress will be taken to represent negative, unpleasant effects) when the perceived demands (stressors) exceed perceived resources to cope with these demands. Thus, the key element of this model is the individual's judgement of the degree of demand in the environment (danger, time pressure, responsibility) and whether his or her personal resources (knowledge, skills, support from others) can match these. The critical appraisal of demands and coping resources is based on a host of factors, such as previous experience, training and personality, thus resulting in distinct individual differences in the onset and extent of stress reactions. One incident commander faced with an emergency may feel calm, confident and totally in control, while another in the same circumstances could be uneasy, irritable and losing a grasp of the situation. This theoretical model can be portrayed as a balance mechanism, shown in Figure 4.2.

When the available resources are judged to equal or exceed the demands, then the individual feels in control and comfortable, and in this state moderate levels of demand may increase motivation and performance. When the demands outweigh the resources, then the stress response (distress) begins to occur, with a complex and interacting package of mental, physical and emotional effects. Cox (1993) offers a more precise definition:

> "The experience of stress is therefore defined by, first, the realisation that they are having difficulty coping with demands and threats to their well being, and, second, that coping is important and the difficulty in coping worries or depresses them."
>
> (p. 17)

Any attempt to manage or mitigate the stress reaction needs to be based on a proper understanding of the likely causes and effects of stress in a given situation, in this case, an emergency. The sections of this chapter deal in turn with the causes, buffers and effects of stress for the incident commander at the time of the emergency, as well as longer term effects and techniques for stress management. The impact of stress on decision making is examined in Chapter 5 and critical incident debriefing is considered in Chapter 6. (For a more detailed theoretical review, see Cox 1993; Stokes and Kite 1994; Wilson and Raphael 1993.)

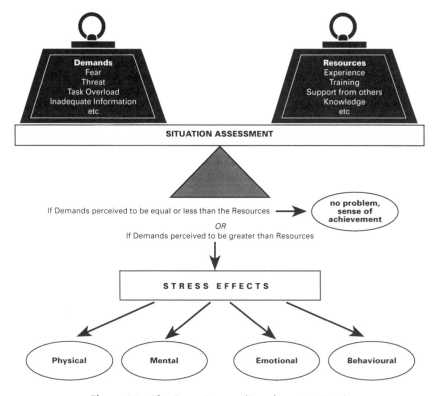

Figure 4.2   *The Stress Process (Based on Cox 1993).*

Despite the relevance of stress to emergency management, there appears to have been limited research into the influence of stress on the performance of emergency response personnel. There have been studies of stress in emergency response teams (Beaton et al. 1995; Duckworth 1986; Dunbar 1993; Durham, McCammon and Allison 1985; Mitchell 1988, Mitchell and Bray 1990; Paton 1991; Raphael et al. 1983), natural disaster relief workers (Paton 1992) and pilots (Stokes and Kite 1994); and the Centre for Disaster Psychiatry in Oslo has conducted investigations of rescuers in an oil rig disaster (Ersland, Weisaeth and Sund 1989) and firefighters (Hytten and Hasle 1989). There have also been studies of stress in disaster recovery teams who have to retrieve the bodies following catastrophic plane crashes such as the US Air crash at Pittsburgh in September 1994 (Bruder 1995) or oil platform disasters such as *Piper Alpha* (Alexander and Wells 1991). Some of these case studies consider the effects of stressors on performance and psychological well-being at the time of the event but mostly they deal with the longer term implications of emergency stress, typically in the form of post-traumatic stress disorder (PTSD) (Corneil 1995; Scott and Stradling 1992; Weaver 1995) rather than effects at the time of the incident. According to Elliott and Smith (1993):

> "Given the acute nature of many disasters, it is likely that the demands of the task will prevent many of the stressors' impact being felt until after the event. Concern has been expressed over the possible effects of such stressors in impairing the performance of the emergency services in subsequent crisis events, in a manner similar to battle fatigue among military personnel. Until recently, however, the phenomenon of stress related trauma among emergency personnel has been a much neglected area of study."
>
> (p. 35)

In fact, there has been even less work on stress effects on commanders in emergency response, with one or two notable exceptions, such as Weisaeth's (1987) chapter on leaders under stress (published in Norwegian) and Charlton's (1992) conference paper on stress in the training and selection of submarine commanders. Fredholm (1995), discussing operational command, proposes that "models ought to be developed concerning Fire Ground Commanders' and Staff personnels' handling of stress" (p. 29). Due to the dearth of published material on stress and performance in civilian rescue teams and their leaders, some of the following discussion is based on the research carried out by military psychologists, who have had a long-standing interest in the relationship between stress and performance (e.g. Cannon-Bowers, Salas and Grossman 1991; Driskell and Salas 1991; Klein 1996; Noy 1991; Orasanu and Backer 1996). In order to provide a unifying framework for this review, a descriptive model of the stress process in an emergency or major incident is presented. It is not an empirically derived model designed to chart precise causal relationships, but is simply intended to summarize the material to follow. As mentioned above, there are marked individual differences in reactions to being involved in an emergency, and whether exposure to a given set of stressors causes anxiety or other effects depends on the individual's judgement, which may be influenced by a number of intervening or buffering variables, hence the middle box, labelled "mediating factors".

CAUSES OF STRESS FOR COMMANDERS

The causes of stress (called stressors) listed below have been identified from published articles and interviews with commanders, both from the emergency services and from other occupations where this responsibility is part of the job, such as pilots, industrial managers and ships' captains.

There appears to be a great deal of consistency across reports from different professions and from military research regarding the principal causes of stress. Backer and Orasanu (1992) define stressors as variables that (i) produce a decrement in performance, (ii) a self-report of stress by the subject, or (iii) physiological change (p. 1). In a comprehensive review of the experiments on stressors that affect performance on cognitively complex tasks in military operations, they divided the causes of stress into three categories: (i) physical (fatigue, noise, time of day, temperature and altitude), (ii) psychological (danger, combat, workload, time pressure, information load, control, monotony, isolation and crowding), and (iii) social (interpersonal relations, group cohesion). See Orasanu and Backer (1996) for a discussion of physical and psychological factors in battle stress. Not all of these are relevant stress factors for emergency teams, but there is considerable overlap, as the studies of emergency response personnel indicate. Hodgkinson and Stewart (1991) identified three distinct event stressors for rescue and emergency service personnel, namely: (i) personal loss or injury, (ii) traumatic stimuli and (iii) mission failure. Hytten and Hasle (1989) found that the stressors for rescue personnel will vary for different types of disaster but that the main causes are: physical strain, exposure to danger, witnessing losses, having to make difficult choices, working under chaotic conditions, seeing and handling dead people and contact with the relatives.

Looking specifically at incident commanders, Kaempf (1992) reported that in the military and fireground environments, the stressors for decision makers have been shown to be time pressure, potential threat, workload, and environmental conditions such as noise and weather. Weisaeth (1987) highlighted the following causes of stress for leaders of rescue personnel in crisis situations:

- Serious threat to important values and goals, life, health, environment.
- Danger and fear for one's own life.
- Strain of responsibility.
- Fear of failure: catastrophic consequences of failing to solve the crisis.
- Having reduced ability to be effective: less control over consequences.
- Rapid changes requiring continuing assessments.
- Time pressure: which is not always accurate.
- Insecurity: regarding assessment of the situation and solutions.
- Little information – or information overload.
- Group pressure and the emergence of subgroups.

Drawing from the above studies, a comprehensive categorization of stressors is presented in Figure 4.3 and described below. These may not be applicable or of equal intensity to all incident commanders: for example,

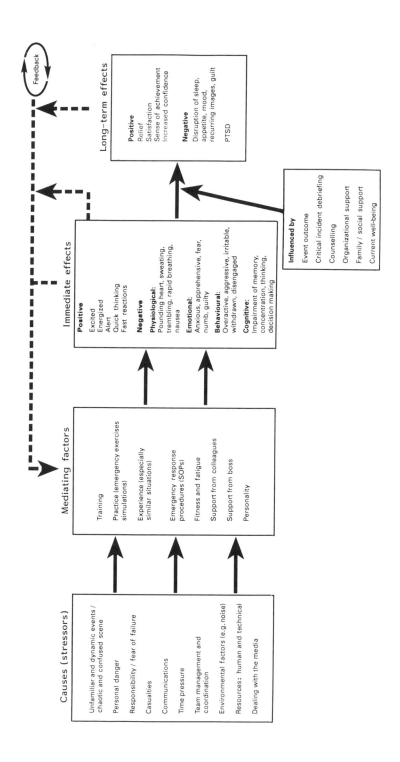

Figure 4.3 *Emergency Stress for the Incident Commander.*

one would expect emergency service commanders who deal with accidents and casualties on a regular basis to find fewer elements stressful than an industrial manager or a transport captain who is rarely exposed to the scene of a major emergency. On the other hand, a senior emergency services commander is likely to have to deal directly with the media on site at a major incident, a stressor that will not affect managers or commanders in more secure or remote locations. The magnitude or quality of the psychological and physical response to a given stressor may well be reduced by prior exposure to that element. This experiential distinction is considered in the next section as a mediating factor. It should also be noted that for the incident commander, the stress response may begin as soon as he or she is notified of the incident and begins to travel to the scene; however, the model does not deal specifically with before, during and after-event stressors, although it is appreciated that the pattern of stressors may change at different phases during a major incident or emergency.

Unfamiliar, Dynamic and Chaotic Events

By definition an emergency or crisis occurs suddenly and unpredictably; these incidents are characterized by their unfamiliarity, scale and speed of escalation. In a major incident the sheer magnitude and unexpected nature of the disaster can be one of the most stressful elements for emergency response personnel (Raphael et al. 1983). The police emergency procedures manual states:

> "Officers are most at risk from stress when confronting unfamiliar situations. Stress will undermine their confidence and their performance. Whilst there will be natural anxieties in the face of the unforeseen, experience indicates that the inadequate communication of information, lack of preparedness and training and lack of experience will significantly affect stress levels. In the event of a major disaster all these conditions are even more pronounced."
> (ACPO 1989, quoted in Home Office 1992, p. 30)

The challenge for the incident commander is to continually make sense of this unexpected and often dynamic situation in order to deploy the available resources most efficiently. When the problem is unfamiliar or where standard operating procedures do not fit (e.g. the United Airlines 232 plane crash; Haynes 1992), then the need for flexible and creative thinking constitutes an additional source of stress and mental demand. This type of problem can be stressful under normal conditions without the additional stressors present in a crisis or major incident.

Senior emergency services commanders I interviewed spoke of the initial scene of chaos and confusion following a major incident such as a plane crash, a major fire or an explosion as a prime stressor. On several occasions, Von Clausewitz's (1968) famous "fog of war" phrase was used to convey the sense of confusion and disorder that can be encountered on arrival at the scene. One senior police officer said that with experience, this scene of confusion would be anticipated along with the realization that in most cases, the scene can be brought under control reasonably quickly. The perception of chaos may sometimes be more apparent than real, in that, although not fully coordinated in the opening phase, very efficient rescue and control operations can be under way at this time.

Personal Danger

Where an individual believes that he or she is in personal danger of injury or death, this will typically produce a strong fear reaction. Reports of Second World War operations have shown that in some theatres of action, there was one battle stress casualty for every soldier wounded in action. However, combat stress (known as shell shock during the First World War) is caused by a combination of stressors (fatigue, isolation etc.), and the specific threat of being killed or wounded in action – although a key stressor in war – is only part of the problem (Driskell and Salas 1991a; Noy 1991; Orasanu and Backer 1996; Solomon 1993). There are also studies of self-imposed danger, such as parachuting and diving, which examine the behavioural and emotional stress effects caused by fear (Idzikowski and Baddeley 1983). Emergency service personnel do report experiencing stress due to fear of personal danger (Hytten and Hasle 1989; Durham, McCammon and Allison 1985), and although they are trained to avoid becoming casualties themselves, the personal risks are very high in some disaster and rescue environments.

An incident commander is only likely to be in personal danger when taking command from within the zone of hazard; for example, an airline pilot, a police support unit inspector, a ship's captain, a naval damage control officer or an industrial manager may all have to function when their own life is in jeopardy. In contrast, emergency services commanders, while they may be exposed to a level of risk, normally operate outside the immediate danger zone. When the commander is under personal risk, this can result in a level of fear that is likely to affect performance. However, interviews with oil industry managers who had been in charge of an offshore emergency (Flin and Slaven 1994) indicated that they were often so preoccupied with the required management and decision making tasks that they did not have time to think about personal risk until after the emergency was over. It appears that incident commanders are often more worried about personal danger to their staff or those for whom they are responsible (and have a "duty of care") than of risk to themselves.

Responsibility/Fear of Failure

All rescue personnel are likely to feel a heightened sense of duty when responding at an emergency, but this is even more so for incident commanders who hold the formal responsibility for the success or failure of the operation and who may be held accountable at a later date (e.g. the police commanders at Hillsborough). Managers and commanders are acutely aware that they are answerable for their actions. The incident commander is directly in the spotlight from the emergency response teams, more senior managers, their peers, the media and the public:

> "Members of the public expect the police to take charge and manage emergency situations, whether personal or general. Police officers accept this expectation and any inability to cope adequately with a crisis, however severe, may give rise to feelings of guilt and having failed personally and professionally."
>
> (ACPO 1989, quoted in Home Office 1992, p. 30)

The sense of responsibility may trigger concerns such as: "Will I be able to cope?", "Can I manage this?", "Do I have control of this situation?" – but the person in charge is unlikely to share these worries with others. As with fear of danger, some incident commanders interviewed said that they were not aware of worrying about fear of failure until they had a quiet moment to review their actions. An experienced ambulance service commander said one cause of stress for him at major incidents was realizing that it was going to be necessary to change his plan (e.g. due to changing site conditions), given his awareness of the difficulty that this can create once teams and their equipment have already been deployed. This problem is exacerbated when there are casualties and when rescue personnel are having to work in dangerous conditions. Hansen (1995), assistant fire chief and deputy commander in charge of rescue and recovery following the bombing (with 168 fatalities) of the Federal Building in Oklahoma City in April 1995, describes his feelings about taking a difficult decision shortly after the initial blast when the rescue effort had just got under way inside the collapsed building:

> "we got our second terrible jolt of the morning – reports of another bomb. Immediately, a flash of panic raced through our minds: if this disaster were indeed the result of a bomb then filling the building with firefighters and police might be part of a well-orchestrated sinister plot. Given the structure's weakened condition, a subsequent blast could be more deadly than the first.

I felt my gut get tight. We knew we had rescuers deep inside the building, and it was going to take time to get them out. We never lost concern for the surviving victims, but with a hundred rescuers now inside, this threat dramatically increased the chances for additional loss of life. So within minutes of the notification we ordered everybody out. The decision to pull out people was made quickly. In truth there was no choice to make. The first rule for those responding to an emergency is not to become victims themselves."

(Hansen 1995, p. 18)

Weisaeth (1987) suggests that the strain of responsibility can cause the leader to "abdicate" either by over-delegating or by making himself impossible to contact; alternatively, overwhelming feelings of responsibility can make the leader have a sense of indispensability, refusing to leave the scene in order to rest or sleep, thus creating a new stress load due to fatigue.

Casualties

Even though the incident commanders are unlikely to be directly involved in rescue operations, the sight of dead, maimed or badly injured bodies is generally regarded as a key stress factor for most individuals involved in emergency response (Ursano and McCarroll 1994). One police officer involved in a major disaster said, "I felt panic, because the bodies were coming in so fast that I couldn't clear my mind and couldn't lose the feeling that at any moment I might see a member of my own family" (Home Office 1992). Hodgkinson and Stewart (1991) state that "traumatic stimuli abound in disaster situations – a number of badly damaged human bodies may be distressing for even the hardiest of emergency service personnel" (p. 175), and they add that particular types of incident, such as a mass transportation accident, "may involve impact at speed which results in severe damage to bodies, a factor which increases the stresses on recovery teams" (p. 49). Raphael et al. (1983), in their study of stress at an Australian train crash, commented that 12 of their sample (of 77 rescue personnel) found "the sight and smell of mutilated dead bodies to be the most stressful. They expressed feelings of shock at the terrible injuries they saw. Another group (11) were affected most by the anguish of relatives and the suffering of the injured" (p. 13). Hytten and Hasle (1989), in their report on Norwegian firefighters who dealt with a hotel fire with 14 fatalities, found that "finding injured or deceased guests" was one of the highest stressors. In another study of firefighters who were asked what sorts of incident bothered them most, 98% listed dead or injured children as the most distressing feature, with multiple casualty incidents, deaths, high rise fires and threat of injury or death also mentioned (Dyregrov 1989; see also

Elliott and Smith 1993; Lindstrom and Lundin 1982; O'Brien 1995; Paton 1991). Even experienced ambulance personnel find injured children and fatalities stressful aspects of their job (Glendon and Glendon 1992; James 1988), as do police officers (Joyce 1989). The incident commander may also be affected by the knowledge of casualties and the presence of distressed relatives, even if he or she is not in direct contact with them.

Communications

One of the major stressors is the management of communications concerning the current status of events and the implementation of emergency response actions: "Communications problems are considered the most common operational snag in the majority of departments, effecting the firefighters' ability to start, coordinate and complete effective operations" (Brunacini 1985, p. 54). The typical problem for the commander is that insufficient information is available to form a proper situation assessment, and the incoming situation reports are inadequate, inaccurate or incomplete. This is particularly apparent in major incidents and disasters (Quarantelli 1995; Williams and Rayner 1956), where all of the normal communication channels may be disrupted. Paradoxically, too much information also creates a problem for the incident commander and information overload is a known stressor (Orasanu and Backer 1996). In the case of an overload, the members of the incident command team can become confused with reports, requests, infiltered updates and irrelevant messages. However, commanders I interviewed said that on balance they would prefer to have too much rather than too little information. Public inquiry reports sometimes reveal that emergency command teams had disregarded, mislaid or misinterpreted key information. Weisaeth (1987) also notes that "After many crisis situations it has been shown that the group handling the crisis had information which they did not manage to use" (p. 10).

The potential for overload is heightened for teams operating in emergencies in warfare operations rooms (see Klein 1996), plant control rooms (Roth in press; Roth, Mumaw and Lewis 1994), emergency operations centres (Scanlon 1994) and emergency communications centres (Rhodenizer, Peppler-Swope and Bowers 1996), where, in addition to the usual telecommunications, there may be banks of computer screen displays fed by sophisticated technical monitoring systems. Similarly, in a large-scale accident with several incident command and control centres, the management of communications becomes more critical, with an increased likelihood of conflicting reports (e.g. numbers of missing persons or casualties) and the risk of losing track of information (Auf der

Heide 1989). The reliance on information recording, (computers, audio taping, whiteboard marking, note taking and log writing) becomes paramount, especially if the command posts have to be moved during the incident. Further communication problems include teams operating on different radio frequencies and equipment malfunctions, such as battery failures in personal radios, poor radio reception because of the location or unexpected interference (e.g. media helicopters). Walton (1988), an FBI officer, advises that "thought should be given at the very beginning of the crisis for backup communication. In an emergency, the radios almost unfailingly malfunction" (p. 24). Computers crashing can present a further unwelcome problem. Candidate submarine commanders are tested on their ability to continue decision making when their computer systems fail (Charlton 1992) – a cartoon on the wall at their naval base shows an officer sweating profusely, with six stopwatches hanging from his neck. Training simulations for incident commanders (irrespective of profession) almost always recreate communication problems because these are a perennial source of stress for the key decision maker.

Time Pressure

Many incidents are characterized by time pressure, where the commander has to make decisions very quickly in order to save life and to prevent the escalation of the problem. This appears to be generally regarded as a stress factor for commanders (Weisaeth 1987) and their teams (Hytten and Hasle 1989), and may be particularly acute in the opening stages of an incident. Brunacini (1985) advises commanders that, "Most of the time on the fireground the first five minutes are worth the next five hours". Orasanu and Backer (1996) define time stress as "the ratio of time to perform required tasks by the time available" (p. 100), and they review specific performance effects resulting from this stressor. The time pressure may take the form of a limited window of opportunity to make key decisions (such as an aircraft with limited fuel), and judgement of the available time will be critical (Orasanu and Fischer, in press). In an escalating emergency the commander's options may become more limited if critical actions are not implemented within a certain time period. Both laboratory and field studies show clearly that a sense of time pressure increases demand on the commander, and consequently can cause stress. In fact, applying time pressure is one of the standard manipulations for inducing stress in simulator training (Charlton 1991, 1992); underestimation of available time is likely to increase the impact of this stressor (Weisaeth 1987). Commanders may also have to resist the temptation to rush into action and to avoid overreacting to perceived time pressure; a number of aircraft accidents have demonstrated that even experienced pilots can make this kind of misjudgement (Stokes and Kite 1994). Williams and Rayner (1956) neatly describe this stressor, in relation to medical teams at disasters, as "a compelling urgency to act and a tendency to think that every act must be performed as rapidly as possible" (p. 661). Similarly, Weisaeth (1987) states that one of the commander's leadership skills is to be able to feel pressure and stress without having to take immediate action. The importance of time judgement for command decision making is examined in Chapter 5.

Team Management and Coordination

This set of stress factors relates to the demands caused by the management of the command team, the interface between commanders of the same service, and the liaison between commanders from different organizations. In some emergencies, the inability of other key players to deal with stress may put pressure on the commander. The negative reactions of others to a dangerous situation (including over-enthusiasm) may heighten the commander's own responses. Team coordination appears to be a critical factor in effective emergency response, and team training needs to be conducted in realistic pressure situations to give commanders exposure to management problems. Walton (1988) warns that as a crisis gains momentum the number of people in the command post will grow: "Generally speaking, the smaller the command post in terms of operational personnel, the better the command post" (p. 24). In addition, there may be coordination and liaison problems between commanders within a given organization, especially when officers are handing over command every time a more senior member of their service arrives on the scene, or if the incident is split over two or more sites. As the examples in Chapter 1 illustrated, liaison between commanders from different services and organizations may not always function as smoothly in the heat of a real incident as it does in an exercise. See Auf der Heide (1989) for a discussion of coordination problems at disasters and the need for common incident command systems (Irwin 1989). The Home Office (1994) guidelines for command and control at major incidents are specifically intended to address this problem. The impact of these coordination factors is likely to be minimized by careful emergency planning and team training.

Environmental Factors

A range of environmental factors, such as noise, heat and poor visibility, may cause additional stress. Studies of stress in military personnel usually examine environmental causes of stress due to the hostile conditions they may be working in, such as excessive heat or cold, altitude and isolation (Orasanu and Backer 1996; Driskell and Salas 1991a; Noy 1991), and they also investigate exposure to stressors over extended periods of time – days or weeks – which are much longer that the typical exposure of emergency response teams to civilian or industrial emergencies (although possibly relevant to a large-scale disaster response, e.g. flooding, forest fires). Excessive noise is a feature in explosions, fires, gas leaks, large football crowds and rock concerts; not only is the noise itself a stressor (Moore and von Gierke 1991; Smith and Jones 1992), but it also hampers communication, making the incident commander's job even more difficult. One offshore manager said that he was shocked by the noise of escaping high pressure gas in an emergency, and that he and his crew "could not hear themselves think" (Flin and Slaven 1994).

Resources: Human and Technical

A key task for the commander is resource estimation, particularly for the emergency services attending a major incident, who also need to maintain cover for all the routine car crashes, fires and heart attacks that will continue to require an emergency response at the same time. Where the incident is widely spread, e.g. a plane or train crash, then the distribution of limited resources becomes even trickier for the incident commander. The resource problem can be compounded by equipment failures, particularly when these affect communications or rescue operations. Fredholm (1995) argues that the balance of resources to the demands of the emergency is the key determining factor in the difficulty of the commander's decision making. Perhaps surprisingly, an excess of resources can also present the incident commander with a serious management and logistics problem because the incident ground becomes congested with personnel and machinery (Brunacini 1985). Williams and Rayner (1956) pointed out that the huge public response that follows notification of a major incident can bring mixed blessings for resource control.

Dealing with the Media

One factor that is perceived to be a stressor by senior emergency services commanders is dealing with the media at a disaster or large-scale emergency. When a major incident occurs the press and broadcast journalists will be at the scene of the event within the first hour, and will often expect to be able to interview a senior commander dealing with the event.

While all of the emergency services have major incident procedures that are designed to cope with this – such as officers dedicated to media duties, who can provide update briefings – this will not always satisfy the demands of the media on site. While senior officers are given media training and usually have significant experience dealing with journalists, a disaster will attract the international media and managing their requirements can provide another difficult demand for the incident commander. There are a number of useful books on dealing with the media, although these tend to focus on corporate crises rather than civil emergencies (Algar 1992; Barton 1993; Berge 1990; Regester 1989).

Stressors for Emergency Response Teams

The model in Figure 4.3 would apply in the main to all emergency response personnel, but there may be other factors to take into account (see Lewis 1994; Mitchell and Bray 1990; Raphael 1986). For example, an individual's role in an emergency can be a critical mediating factor in his or her stress reaction. The commander may be so absorbed in the management of the event that he or she experiences less immediate stress than more junior personnel. Ironically, it may be those present who are least involved in the immediate rescue, such as side-line or off-site personnel, who experience a more marked stress reaction than those who are involved and feel themselves to be in personal danger (Raphael et al. 1983). This is because those attending a disaster want to be involved, and they can feel useless and frustrated if they cannot use their skills and energy to help (Paton 1991). Therefore, it is important for incident commanders, where possible, to acknowledge the importance of all those involved; for example, officers directing traffic or controlling outer cordons are performing a critical and life saving task (e.g. by allowing movement of ambulances) although they may feel that they have made less of a contribution than their colleagues working at the front line of an incident. "Even those recovering the bodies need to be told they are doing a good job, and everybody needs to be thanked and their efforts acknowledged, even if it is just for making the tea" (Home Office 1992, p. 11).

A related cause of stress for rescue crews or personnel on site is the waiting time. Hytten and Hasle (1989), in their study of firefighters who had dealt with a major incident resulting in multiple fatalities, found that time pressure and waiting time were the most stressful aspects (after dead and injured occupants). There are many examples of this. For example, ambulance service personnel often have to stand and wait while the fire service retrieves injured victims. Likewise, firefighters may have to delay their operations while ambulance crews stabilize trapped casualties.

Emergency service personnel may be called as back-up to a major incident and then have to wait, doing nothing, for several hours because it transpires that they are not immediately required. On an offshore oil installation or a ship, the crew who are not in the emergency response teams may be called to an emergency muster at lifeboat stations and will have to wait there until the emergency is contained or an evacuation takes place. Perception of time will elongate for those waiting to respond. The emergency situation will also have energized these individuals for immediate action and they will find the inactivity and waiting to be frustrating and tiring. This effect is unlikely to be experienced by incident commanders, but they should remember that waiting and doing nothing may be stressful, and may ultimately affect the behaviour of those who become involved at a later stage.

Conclusion (Causes)

Emergency stress (as with combat stress; see Weather, Litz and Keane 1995), represents an amalgam of stressors and it is difficult to pinpoint precise causes and effects, given the multiple stress elements present in most major incidents. In terms of stress management, some of these factors are immutable (e.g. casualties) but others may be lessened by good organization and training (e.g. communication, resource allocation). The extent to which an incident commander is affected by exposure to any or all of the above stressors will depend on a number of intervening or mediating factors, which act as buffers. Many of these factors are discussed in more detail in other chapters, therefore only a brief description is provided in the following section.

MEDIATING (BUFFER) FACTORS

The main categories of mediating factors, which will increase or decrease the impact of a given stressor on the incident commander, are shown in Figure 4.3. The mediating factors influence the individual's perception of both the stressors (threats) in the situation and his or her ability to cope with them. For example, in studies of fear and performance in dangerous environments, such as diving, parachuting and combat, Idzikowski and Baddeley (1983) found that, "individuals' perceptions of the dangerousness of the situations will vary depending on such factors as previous battle experience, how long the combatant has been active since his last leave, and intelligence" (p. 130). Again, there is almost no relevant research that has specifically studied incident commanders, so the factors listed have been identified from previous research with both emergency services and military personnel, and my own interviews with incident commanders. The influence of the mediating factors can increase or decrease the stress reaction and consequently can provide valuable indicators for appropriate stress management.

Training, Experience and Practice

Weisaeth (1987), in his description of stress in leaders of rescue personnel, states:

> "the most important single factor determining how one reacts and manages in a catastrophe situation, is the level of training and experience one has in coping with physically dangerous situations."
>
> (p. 1)

There is little doubt that this is the critical mediating factor for stress in incident commanders, irrespective of profession or type of emergency. Prior exposure to the conditions of an emergency, through experience or simulation, not only develops the commander's decision making and team management skills, which will make the real thing easier to tackle, but also improves the commander's knowledge of what he or she finds most stressful and how this can be controlled. Charlton (1992), discussing the importance of personal stress awareness in submarine commanders, explained:

> "Given that a student is able to cope with the 'pass level' of stress, subjecting him to increased levels will enable him to appreciate and understand his own response pattern and thereby identify the warning signs that he is approaching his personal limit. Knowledge of the effects of stress enables the individual to take positive steps to avoid the stressors or to reduce them to limit their impact, thereby defusing a potentially dangerous situation."
>
> (p. 57)

Lagadec (1991) interviewed a number of managers and politicians who had responsibility during or after a crisis for his book *States of Emergency*. Only one of these was an incident commander, a police chief, Douglas Burrows, who was in charge of the train crash and chemical fire in 1979 at Mississauga, Canada, with a subsequent evacuation of 217 000 residents. When asked whether the sudden shift into a situation of this scale was a psychological shock for the person in charge, Burrows replied:

> "As a police chief or senior officer you have very broad responsibilities which can include saving lives. But that's just part of your job, so you do it.

The public expects it of you. For the average person, such situations might cause a lot of stress, but of course in our case the conditioning helps. From the time you begin your police training, you come into contact with stressful situations. In contrast, you may have people in responsible political positions who haven't any prior experience in handling serious incidents – they may even break up under stress, knowing that thousands of lives depend on their decisions. As far as our officers are concerned, we come to know them over the years, so the ones we know couldn't handle the stress of major decision making, we keep in lesser roles. But of course, it doesn't work that way with government officials."

(Lagadec 1991, p. 69)

As Burrows explains, emergency services commanders will have had significant experience in dealing with accidents, incidents and emergencies, although very few of them will have been the officer in charge of a major incident or disaster, due to the relative rarity of these events. Furthermore, the most senior officers called to take over command of such an event will probably have had less recent incident command practice than the middle ranking commander being relieved. (Brunacini (1985) mentions the "Let's put it out before the Chief gets here and screws it up" syndrome, p. 8.) Murray (1994a), also discussing fireground command, says:

"Thankfully, larger and more serious incidents occur less frequently than smaller, routine ones. For the more senior incident commander this results in less opportunities to develop further experience. However, at the same time, at more serious incidents the consequences of error increase."

(p. 21)

Unlike emergency services personnel, most designated incident commanders, such as industrial managers, ships' captains and commercial pilots, will not have had any prior experience of a full-scale emergency, and it is therefore essential that they are provided with simulated exposure to the full range of stressors using exercises and training events. This is endorsed by Driskell and Salas (1991a), who emphasize:

"From a training and simulation point of view, one critical component in maintaining personnel performance in a stress environment is to provide practice and the exercise of critical tasks under operational conditions similar to those likely to be encountered in the real environment."

(p. 188)

(See Chapter 3 for examples of training under stressful conditions for incident commanders.)

One further point is to note the feedback arrows shown in Figure 4.3. These indicate that while the experience of a previous incident or simulation that was well managed will have a positive effect on the commander's confidence and future performance, a badly managed incident or an unpleasant experience may well have a detrimental influence on future ability to cope with stress. This is one reason why simulator experiences and debriefing need to be handled with considerable sensitivity in order to produce the appropriate training outcome.

Standard Emergency Response Procedures

One important facet of many stress management systems is the need to have some sense of one's control over events. For the emergency commander, whose job is to take decisions that will control the situation, the use of standard response (or operating) procedures (mentioned in Chapter 1) will assist in providing a feeling of control in an ambiguous and demanding environment. They are widely used in technical environments, such as aviation and industry, and they can prevent a commander "stalling" in the critical opening phase of a high pressure incident (Skriver and Flin 1996). A sense of being able to cope, of being able to implement some initial actions, will reduce the commander's stress reaction, just as having no idea of what to do and having to engage in creative thinking under pressure is likely to produce an enhanced stress response due to the increased mental demand. Commanders who have thought through (mentally rehearsed) their emergency response plans should find it easier to implement these actions when operating under stress. One offshore manager said that his advice to an inexperienced manager who had to deal with an offshore emergency would be, "Keep calm or you lose it straight away. You must have performed contingency plans in your own mind, i.e. thought out possible scenarios and responses before incidents occur" (Flin and Slaven 1994, p. 26). So, while the prime function of standard response procedures is to assist in decision making and team coordination, it should be noted that they may also help to mitigate the effects of stress for those in command positions.

Fitness and Fatigue

The commander's general level of mental and physical fitness will influence his or her ability to deal with stress in an emergency. Pilots are trained to monitor their physical well-being and to declare any physical symptoms that could affect their performance. The negative effects of fatigue on performance are well documented, particularly in relation to sustained military operations (Noy 1991). In most civil emergencies, the operation will not remain in an intensive response phase for more than 24 hours, and while those involved will be very tired (and may have been called out having just completed a full shift), they will not be expected to continue functioning for days without sleep. However, in some natural disaster recovery situations or criminal incidents, such as a hostage taking, sieges or hijacks, the operation may run for days or longer. In these cases the incident commanders should be sensitive to the problems that sleep loss will have on their own thinking skills and that of their teams (e.g. hostage negotiators). Those officers working shifts as incident commanders may not sleep well, if at all, during their rest period. In military guidelines, a minimum of four hours sleep, preferably between the hours of midnight and 6 a.m. is recommended. Senior commanders often find it difficult to relinquish control of an operation but they are generally trained that their effective functioning will be impaired by fatigue and that they may jeopardize the mission if they do not take adequate rest. It is also necessary for them to demonstrate to more junior colleagues that this is essential, and they should remain vigilant for signs of excessive tiredness in key personnel, because this may result in unnecessary mistakes or even injuries (Mitchell and Bray 1990).

Fatigue as a known mediator or stressor is also used in simulated emergencies to test trainee commanders' decision making under pressure. Charlton (1992), who was responsible for selecting commanders, said:

"Submarine commanding officers must be able to make potential life or death decisions at any time of the day or night. It is therefore vitally important that the Perisher student is able to experience the effect of tiredness upon his decision-making process. The ability to make a correct judgement as though instinctively can only be gained through practice and the thorough knowledge of one's own limitations.... The simplest way to test an individual's mental and physical stamina is to require him to make complex decisions when tired, thus the better a student is able to perform after a significant lack of sleep, the more likely he is to make correct command decisions. The stress level induced by sleep deprivation may be enhanced by the individual's self-doubts as to how he will perform under such circumstances."

(p. 53)

In terms of psychological fitness, an ongoing personal problem that is creating worry and anxiety may diminish the cognitive resources and emotional resilience of the most experienced commander and cause failure under increased pressure. The question of mental fitness for duty is a sensitive issue; while managers, captains or commanders may be reluctant to admit the risk of a personal worry affecting their command ability, they should be aware of the possible consequences (and their subsequent accountability if their organization has a disclosure policy on fitness for duty). Ultimately, the organization has a responsibility in terms of its culture and support systems, so that any individual in a safety critical or responsible position should feel comfortable in disclosing the presence of a personal worry (not necessarily the details) and, if appropriate, being relieved or excused command, without this being regarded as a failure. Interestingly, the one situation where this is accepted is bereavement. However, there are many other domestic and personal situations that can result in equally debilitating "grief" reactions, which can be concealed and managed under routine operations but which may interfere with performance under stress.

Support from Colleagues

In almost all models of occupational stress, social support (from colleagues, family and friends) appears as a mediating variable. That is, individuals appear to be able to cope with stressors better if they have the support of others with whom they can share problems or workload, or simply relax and unwind. In an acute stress environment, this support comes from one's fellow team members who are sharing the unpleasant experience. Studies of military stress show that support from one's team or unit is a key factor in the mitigation of combat stress (Noy 1991) and that group cohesion may improve performance under demanding conditions (Orasanu and Backer 1996). The military make extensive use of "buddy–buddy" systems to enhance emotional support under battle conditions, and the emergency services rely heavily on teamwork in their operational approach, which buffers the exposure to stressors for the personnel involved.

In contrast, the incident commander will be unlikely to have any of his or her own peer group at the scene of the event, and will be in a more isolated position as the most senior member in charge. Command training typically encourages the suppression of any signs of anxiety, and the leader becomes the focus of attention in many high-pressure situations. A Royal Navy "battle stress" video (HMS *Dryad*, 1987) includes advice from Falklands War commanders, who agreed that command is stressful. They were conscious that their crews had to draw strength from them, that they were in the limelight and had to set an example. One of them said that when things go badly, eyes tend to turn to the Captain to see if he is going into a decline: "panic spreads very fast if the Captain is doing the wall of death". Support can be drawn from the immediate command team, the off-site control centre, aides and in some cases equally senior commanders from other agencies, but the "loneliness of command" is well documented in both managerial and military writing.

An excellent example of a commander receiving stress-reducing support from a distant control centre comes from the United Airlines 232 air accident. In the words of the captain:

> "If you have a serious problem like we did, and you need the kind of help that does not add to the tension level, a voice like Bauchman's [the air traffic controller] certainly was an influence on us and helped us remain composed. The only time that Kevin's voice ever cracked was when he found out that we were in position to land on runway 22 instead of runway 31 and he had emergency equipment sitting in the middle of our intended landing area – and only had two minutes to get it out of the way before we arrived. He raised his voice just slightly and then it fell back into his calm, soothing, here it is voice. When I had the opportunity later to compliment Bauchman on his coolness throughout the tense situation, he told me, to my surprise, that he had transferred to Sioux City because he found his previous duty station too stressful."
>
> (Haynes 1992, p. 10)

Support from the Boss

As mentioned above, a key factor in the ability of military teams to withstand combat stress is the degree of trust and regard they have for their leader (Noy 1991). While commanders need to be aware of their significant influence on the stress levels of their teams, they also need to realize that their relationship with their own immediate boss may be a factor that can enhance or diminish the stress of the command role. In the emergency services, a superior officer may arrive during the event to take over command or may remain in contact via radio or telephone. In other situations, such as an industrial incident, the more senior manager may be in direct communication at the time of the event and may subsequently be responsible for reviewing the on-scene commander's performance. Relevant questions include:

- If the commander has a bad relationship with the boss, will this affect his or her performance?
- Do senior commanders always agree on the optimal strategy?
- To what extent does the commander value his or her superior's advice?
- Is there a penalty for disregarding advice given by a more senior member of staff who is not at the scene of the incident?
- If the emergency response does not go to plan, how much support and loyalty can the incident commander expect to receive from his or her superior?

Fiedler, an American psychologist who has spent 40 years researching leadership, regards what he calls "boss stress" as a prime cause of poor managerial performance (Fiedler, Potter and McGuire 1992), while Hogan, Curphy and Hogan (1994), in a discussion of inept leadership, state that 60–70% of American employees report that the worst or most stressful aspect of their jobs is their immediate supervisor. This issue has not been studied directly with incident commanders, but – given its impact in other managerial domains – it would be surprising if it did not bolster or threaten the commander's confidence in an emergency or major incident, and thus it has been included as a mediating factor.

Personality

There is little doubt that individuals show distinct differences in their sensitivity to and interpretation of stressors, and personal thresholds for stress responses show high variability and may change over time. Therefore, personality has been included as one of the mediating factors, although as a variable it offers fewer options for stress management, beyond the obvious one (discussed in Chapter 2) of selecting the "right stuff" for emergency command, or at least avoiding the "wrong stuff". In terms of the former, which is "selecting-in" individuals with the appropriate characteristics for stress resilience, the identification of these has not proved fruitful. Driskell and Salas (1991a) reviewed this literature and concluded that research to date has not revealed any particular personality variables that can predict response to military stress, although there is some evidence that the trait of "adjustment" might be worthy of investigation. As mentioned earlier, Elliott and Smith (1993) suggested that the personality measure of "hardiness" might be useful. Driskell and Salas point out that this type of measure relates more to ability to deal with everyday life stressors, rather than the acute stress of a military or emergency setting. Smith (1989) reviewed selection methods for high risk and stressful occupations, including pilots, police and firefighters, but apart from "emotional stability", there did not appear to be any consistent set of personality traits identified. Likewise, in a very comprehensive review of personality and stress in pilots, Stokes and Kite (1994) were only able to find a number of promising avenues for future research rather than any consensus data on a stress resilient profile.

Is it any easier to identify (and "select-out" individuals who display) the characteristics that predict an inability to cope with stress? Apart from mental illness or impairment, the answer again seems to be negative, hence the very long and rigorous selection procedures based on observations of performance in stressful situations for jobs where this is critical, such as pilots, astronauts and submarine commanders. There is military interest in screening out personnel who are likely to suffer combat stress reactions (CSR) (traditionally misjudged as cowardice or lack of moral fibre). Noy (1991) refers to an American screening programme introduced during the Second World War because of the expense of evacuating psychiatric casualties: "As it turned out, the screening did not reduce the rate of CSR. Furthermore, when later the so-called predisposed were sent to combat, they functioned as well and as long as others and received as many decorations" (p. 514). He goes on to review more recent work, and concludes that while it is difficult to pinpoint the personality characteristics that will predict the incidence of CSR, there may be traits that partly determine speed of recovery from its symptoms. In sum, the few relevant studies of personality and ability to function well under acute stress conditions have not yielded a definitive set of predictive personality traits. Psychologists continue to believe that personality is a mediating factor, and, in the words of Hilton and Dolgin (1991), who reached a similar conclusion relating to the role of personality in the selection of military pilots, "It is possible that psychology may have been pursuing the right stuff but with the wrong scales" (p. 95).

Conclusion (Buffers)

The above discussion reviewed some of the factors that influence individuals' interpretation of stressors and their judgement of their ability to cope with these, thus increasing or decreasing the level of the stress reaction (effects) they are likely to experience. Training and experience not only provide an opportunity to develop decision making and team management skills, but they also give commanders a higher degree of self-awareness of which stressors they are likely to be affected by and how to deal with their reactions. In the next section, the typical effects of stress and how these are manifested as symptoms at the time of the emergency are considered.

EFFECTS AND SYMPTOMS OF STRESS DURING THE INCIDENT

The bulk of the literature on stress effects reported by emergency response personnel and other rescuers deals with their longer term reactions to having been exposed to a stressful situation rather than the effects at the time of the event. This section concentrates on the latter, because what is of prime interest here is the possible influence of stress on the commander's ability to function as a leader. (The effects of stress on decision making are reviewed in Chapter 5.) Again, there is a dearth of available data as these effects are almost impossible to measure in the "heat of battle": Reports that are available are based on observations, personal accounts or self-report questionnaires administered after the event. The incident commander also needs to be aware of the signs and symptoms of stress in others because he or she may well be responsible for managing any problems caused by stress in the rest of the emergency response team or in victims being rescued.

It is important to preface this section by emphasizing that exposure to stressors does not necessarily produce negative effects, particularly in personnel who have had prior exposure to these circumstances. There may also be immediate positive effects such as increased motivation and energy, faster reactions, clearer thinking and improved memory retrieval in response to the stimulation of a sudden challenge from the environment (Charlton 1992; Orasanu and Backer 1996; Weisaeth 1987). Referring back to Figure 4.2, it is only once the perceived level of challenge begins to exceed the individual's judged ability to cope with the stressors that the symptoms of distress become predominant. Most researchers have been interested in how exposure to a potentially stressful situation will degrade the performance of leaders, troops or rescue personnel, thus the weight of emphasis is on these negative effects. No attempt has been made to link particular stressors (e.g. time, danger, responsibility) with specific physiological or psychological reactions because in a major incident multiple stressors will be present simultaneously. As Figures 4.2 and 4.3 illustrate, the effects occur as an interdependent package of reactions, which can be categorized as physiological, emotional, behavioural and cognitive. For example, a report on stress for police officers responding to disasters states, "Some common physical signs of stress are flushing, sweating, irritability or itching, aggression, inefficiency, over zealousness, loss of confidence or of interest, or any combination of these factors" (Home Office 1992, p. 31). Moreover, these symptoms have knock-on effects on each other, so that realizing that your heart is pounding or your hands are sweating may make you feel even more anxious, which further impairs your concentration or your temper. Charlton (1992), recounting his observations of candidate submarine commanders, neatly makes the point that the normal physiological responses to stressors can make the student's anxiety worse:

> "a dry mouth, pounding heart, sweating, trembling hands increase the misery and stress and leads to a downward spiral. The descent is accelerated by his awareness that others know he is afraid, that they know he knows they know – which only makes him worry more, hence the downward spiral."
>
> (p. 54)

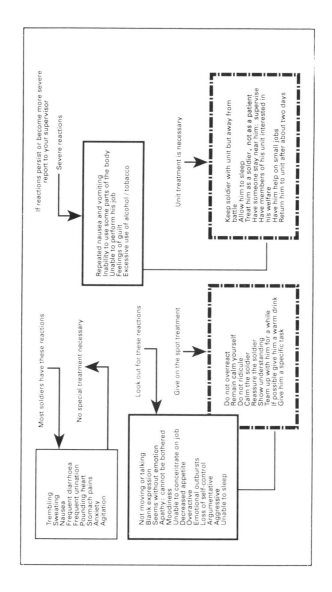

Figure 4.4 *Effects of Stress in Battle. Reprinted with the permission of the Army Personnel Research Establishment (now DRA Centre for Human Sciences), Farnborough, UK.*

See Hodgkinson and Stewart (1991, p. 176) for a detailed listing of the symptoms that may be experienced by disaster workers in rescue and recovery operations.

Physiological Effects

The physical responses to stressors are related to the flight/fight response mentioned earlier, and include increased heart rate, rapid breathing (hyperventilation), trembling, muscle tension, sweating, faintness and irritation of the digestive system ("butterflies in the tummy", frequent urination, diarrhoea, nausea, stomach pain). These effects are very well documented for a range of acute stress situations, real and contrived, and they are certainly experienced in combat (see Figure 4.4; Solomon 1993) and in emergency response (Hodgkinson and Stewart 1991). These effects are part of a natural reaction, and if they are anticipated and treated as a normal response rather than an illness, then they are likely to have less impact on the individual's overall emotional state (Noy 1991). They can also be controlled to some extent by specific stress reduction techniques, based on breathing exercises and muscle relaxation. The ubiquitous advice to reduce anxiety by "taking a deep breath" has a calming effect, which helps to counteract the physical stress response.

Emotional Effects

A wide range of emotional responses can occur as part of the stress response, ranging from positive feelings of excitement or alertness through apprehension and anxiety, to a loss of emotional control, where the individual becomes aggressive or visibly distressed (e.g. crying). Possible reactions include surprise, euphoria, anger, sadness, fear, horror, hopelessness, helplessness and depression. Lindstrom and Lundin (1982), in a study of emergency service personnel who attended a major fire, reported the following reactions during the fire: non-comprehension of the situation, guilt, a sense of chaos, helplessness and a loss of emotional control. Noy (1991), discussing combat stress, says that there is a tendency for emotions to be exaggerated in a polarized manner. Ersland, Weisaeth and Sund (1989) studied the emotional responses of both professional and non-professional rescue personnel at the *Alexander Keilland* oil rig capsize in the North Sea. They found that that both groups (but especially the non-professionals) frequently reported that they had experienced mild or severe emotional stress reactions during the rescue work, such as anxiety, irritation, uncertainty and discouragement. In a study of 57 firefighters and 58 non-professional firefighters who assisted at a major fire, Hytten and Hasle (1989) found that half this group reported moderate to strong stress responses during the rescue action, of which anxiety was the most common reaction.

There are also cases where a scene of carnage at a disaster site may make a rescuer feel completely devoid of emotion: "There were so many bodies, the mind became numbed. The first was the worst; after a time they ceased to be people and became just shells" (police officer, quoted in Home Office 1992). In mass casualty situations both rescue and medical personnel may experience a sense of guilt that they are not able to do more for the casualties. According to Williams and Rayner (1956), these feelings can be both debilitating and disruptive. The emotional effects an individual is experiencing may be concealed (up to a point), and better indicators of stress are the resulting changes in behaviour, which are more easily observed.

Offshore installation managers who had handled an emergency on their platform or rig said that they felt confident and just got on with the job in hand. There was little time for self-reflection, although they were aware that they had become the focus of the crew's attention, who were watching the OIM's reactions more than listening to what was said. In terms of emotional response, many of the OIMs said that they felt calm, possibly due to the rapid pace of events and the amount of concentration required for decision making. Several of them said that they only became aware of their emotions once the immediate danger had been removed. One said that his crisis management advice to other OIMs would be: "Don't get flustered, not to lose your calm. Realise implications and consequences. Think ahead and don't be afraid to make fast decisions" (Flin and Slaven 1994, p. 26).

Behavioural Effects

There is not a finite list of behavioural effects related to stress, as the defining feature is a change in the individual's normal behaviour pattern. Thus, a level of activity that is normal for one individual may be unusually high or low for another, and in their case be symptomatic of a stress effect. Nevertheless, the following behaviour patterns have been documented, which may be seen as variants of the "flight–fight–freeze" triad; for example, avoidance, over-zealousness or rigidity. What appears to be likely is that the pattern and direction of response will be fairly consistent for a given individual, hence the value of allowing commanders to experience their own pattern of response in training. Because these behaviour changes may be subtle (but may be clues that a key team member is not performing his or her job properly), then the better the leader's knowledge of each team member, the more likely it is that these changes will be noticed (which raises the question of who is monitoring the commander for signs of stress). Extreme and florid behavioural reactions are uncommon, even in combat stress. Stress-induced behaviour changes include hyperactivity, anger, argumentativeness, irritability, jumpiness, aggressiveness, swearing, shouting or emotional outbursts. At the other extreme, the individual may become withdrawn, detached, apathetic and disengaged from surrounding activities; this type of change may be more difficult to spot when team members are preoccupied with their own responsibilities. Again, experience seems to play a buffering role in the incidence of such effects. Ersland, Weisaeth and Sund (1989) found that non-professional rescue workers reported hyperactivity and restlessness to a significantly higher degree than professional rescue personnel. Hytten and Hasle (1989) found that about a third or more of their firefighters (not all professionals) reported moderate levels of restlessness, overactivity, high spirits and irritability, but only 10% believed that their stress reactions had disturbed them in carrying out their rescue tasks.

There is a need for incident commanders to be aware of the wide range of emotional and behavioural reactions that may be observed at a time of stress, some of which may appear to be inappropriate, such as laughter. Black (or gallows) humour is employed as a coping strategy by many professionals exposed to stress, including medical staff (Keller and Koenig 1989; Rosenberg 1991), police officers (Jackson 1995; Joyce 1989) and firefighters (Taylor and Shevels 1995). There have been instances of senior officers overreacting on overhearing such comments; a report from a police workshop on disasters has advised that:

> "Police management, in order to make the most effective use of the human resources available to them and to minimise the negative effects on officers exposed to major disaster work, need to be fully aware of the complex nature of psychological reactions."
>
> (Home Office 1992, p. 13)

Cognitive Effects

While incident commanders are unlikely to be immune to any of the effects outlined above, the effects of stress on their thinking and decision making ability are of particular interest. Charlton (1992), who was responsible for the selection of future submarine commanders, referred to the "flight, fight or freeze" response manifested as problems in decision making, "tunnel vision", misdirected aggression, withdrawal, and the "butterfly syndrome", "where the individual flits from one aspect of the problem to another, without method, solution or priority" (Charlton 1992, p. 54). He also mentions self-delusion, where the student commander denies the existence or magnitude of a problem (reported also for pilots; Stokes and Kite 1994), regression to more basic skills, and inability to prioritize. Weisaeth (1987), discussing the enhanced cognitive demands for leaders under stress, describes reduced concentration, narrowing of perception, fixation, inability to perceive simultaneous problems, distraction, difficulty in prioritizing and distorted time perception. Likewise, the psychologists Dorner and Pfeifer (1993) studying strategic thinking under stress, observed "a tendency to counterbalance a sinking feeling of competence by spectacular (but ineffective) decisions" (p. 1358). Not all researchers agree that the decision making of experienced incident commanders will be degraded by exposure to acute stressors. Klein (1996) argues that the type of decision strategy employed by experts under pressure may actually be reasonably stress proof. This issue is dealt with in more detail in Chapter 5, which examines decision making.

If one looks at other members of the emergency response team, then a wide range of cognitive performance decrements have been reported. Hodgkinson and Stewart (1991) mention disorientation, mental confusion, difficulties in naming objects (e.g. important equipment) and in simple calculations (e.g. body counts), and a loss of objectivity. Williams and Rayner (1956) observed the following reactions in medical disaster personnel: (i) taking action more rapidly than necessary, (ii) intense concentration on the task at hand to the exclusion of all else, (iii) reliance on familiar responses, even when these are ineffective or inappropriate and (iv) difficulty in thinking ahead. Similar effects have also been reported for pilots in high stress situations (Stokes and Kite 1994). Ersland, Weisaeth and Sund (1989) found that the ability to plan before acting was the most frequently disturbed under stress: this was reported by 48% of non-professionals and 30% of professionals in their sample of marine rescue personnel. Very few of their sample of 24 professional rescue crew and 101 non-professionals felt that their ability to judge risk, to cooperate or to function as a leader had been affected; however, around 20% of the sample felt that their ability to make decisions had been at least moderately affected.

There has been extensive research both in and out of the laboratory on the effects of specific stressors on task performance, such as vigilance, reaction time, monitoring, signal detection (see Driskell and Salas 1996) and on the execution of complex cognitive tasks in military operations (Orasanu and Backer 1996) and flight decks (Stokes and Kite 1994). Both experimental studies and self-reports have revealed possible deficits in short-term or working memory, narrowing of perceptual focus, problems in logical reasoning, increased error rates and lapses in attention.

Harrington and Gaddy (1993) catalogued stress-induced behaviours in nuclear power plant control room crews during simulated accidents; these included misreading instruments, pacing in front of a panel in a state of confusion, focusing on a lower priority problem, not hearing dissonant information, although acknowledging it, and rechecking or redoing tasks for no technical reason when other actions were required. The effects of stress on team performance in military (Burgess et al. 1992) and flight deck teams (Stokes and Kite 1994) have received considerable research interest and are discussed in Chapter 6, which deals with team management.

Effects on Survivors of Major Incidents

For effective management of a rescue operation or the training of response teams, commanders also need to understand the potential reactions of victims – who are likely to suffer considerable stress, due to their injuries, near death experience or simply their total unfamiliarity with an accident environment – during and after the incident. For those interested, there are research studies (e.g. Joseph et al. 1994, on survivors of the *Herald of Free Enterprise* disaster; Weisaeth 1989, 1994, on 123 Norwegian industrial workers exposed to a disastrous factory explosion), personal accounts (Dudgeon 1991), and several readable texts on the subject (e.g. Gibson 1991; Hodgkinson and Stewart 1991). In addition, there are psychological studies of crowd behaviour in relation to fires (Canter 1990; Donald and Canter 1992), football grounds (Canter, Comber and Uzzell 1989), and evacuation from aircraft (Muir 1994), stations (Proulx 1993, Proulx and Sime 1991) or mines (Vaught and Wiehagen 1991) which disprove certain notions of panic (Fischer 1994) and identify optimal leadership and communication behaviours (Sugiman and Misumi 1988).

Conclusion (Effects)

The effects of stress on the incident commander at the time of the event will depend on the level of the stressors and the extent to which they have been "buffered" by mediating factors. While exposure to the demanding conditions of a major incident may produce some performance enhancing effects, a range of negative reactions have been consistently reported for personnel working in acute stress conditions. These include physiological, emotional, behavioural and cognitive changes, which can affect the performance of commanders and their teams during the emergency, rescue or recovery operations. The next section gives a brief overview of the longer term stress reactions that can cause more serious problems for a minority of emergency response personnel.

EFFECTS OF STRESS AFTER THE EVENT AND PTSD

While there is only a very limited literature on the stress effects for commanders and response personnel at the time of an emergency, significantly more has been written on the subject of stress effects immediately after the event and in the longer term. This may simply be because this is easier to measure, or because of increasing public and professional interest in the effects (and litigative redress) of trauma on victims, helpers and survivors. Again, hardly anything has been published on the specific reactions of those in command positions, and the available data deal with rescue personnel in general. These reports of after effects typically show a range of physical, emotional, behavioural and cognitive reactions:

"I went off duty at 6 pm and got drunk. That was my stress management. I got home about 3 am and just wept. And I've not wept for years. I was in a daze for three or four days."
(Police officer after a major incident, quoted in Home Office 1992)

"as an ADO I would be called out of bed and drive on my own to an incident. Once I'd finished I'd drive home again in the early hours and have a cup of tea. I'd brood over the events and feel quite depressed. Sometimes I'd end up in tears."
(Fire service officer quoted in Elliott and Smith 1993, p. 40)

A common reaction for both experienced incident commanders and veteran emergency response personnel is that they can continue to cope with the stressors at the scene of the event while they are busy and preoccupied with accomplishing their duties. It is only when they "have time to think" about the danger or tragedy they have been exposed to that any significant stress reaction occurs, as the above quotations illustrate. Similarly, Lindstrom and Lundin (1982), in their study of rescue personnel who attended a hotel fire in Sweden, reported that emotional reactions to the disaster ranged from an early onset of effects at the disaster site for some people, to a number who reported "superman"-type behaviour while in uniform, but began to experience an emotional reaction when they took off their uniforms. Hodgkinson and Stewart (1991) believe that:

"Leaders are often those who are most affected. They feel a natural sense of responsibility for those they manage, and may feel an intense, often rationally unfounded sense of responsibility for the damage that has occurred – 'If I hadn't sent them in there to do that at that moment, no one would have been hurt.' They will also feel responsible for the group's recovery. It is also likely that the leader will feel lonely and isolated. Leadership peers are often highly competitive, unsupportive and critical of each other.... Many leaders also find it hard to recruit support from their staff because they have to appear strong at all times."

(p. 128)

The common negative symptoms experienced after the emergency response has been completed include fatigue, exhaustion, sadness, guilt, recurring images, intrusive thoughts, inability to sleep, loss of appetite, reduced interest in everyday events, diminished concentration, depression and loss of confidence (Hodgkinson and Stewart 1991; Weaver 1995a). These reactions are well documented for emergency response personnel, particularly when there are casualties (Duckworth 1986; Durham, McCammon and Allison 1985; Ersland, Weisaeth and Sund 1989; Hytten and Hasle 1989; James 1992; McFarlane 1988; Mitchell and Bray 1990; Paton 1991; Raphael et al 1983; Raphael 1986). It should be emphasized that they will not be experienced to the same degree by each person, and a successful emergency response can also result in very positive feelings of job satisfaction, accomplishment, pride and achievement, as well as improved knowledge and skills for the commanders and their teams (Moran and Colless 1995).

For the majority of individuals suffering from negative effects, these symptoms will begin to subside as normal feelings and functioning return. Where the symptoms persist or are particularly acute, then this may be a sign of what is called post-traumatic stress disorder (PTSD), a syndrome that is medically recognized as a mental disorder (American Psychiatric Association 1994). The criteria for a diagnosis of PTSD are:

1. Experience of highly traumatic and unusual event.
2. Re-experiencing the event (e.g. dreams, intrusive recollections).
3. Persistent avoidance of things associated with the trauma or numbing, with reduced responsiveness to one's environment.
4. The presence of two or more symptoms of increased arousal that were not evident before the trauma (e.g. hyperalertness, sleep disturbance, survival guilt, impaired memory and concentration, intensification of symptoms on being reminded of the event).

Symptoms of anxiety and depression are also commonly reported in conjunction with these factors. In a study of PTSD in 50 junior fire service officers, Taylor (1994) found that over 80% had experienced one or more PTSD symptoms, and approximately a third had experienced these symptoms for months or years. (Only 5% of this group had sought help for these symptoms.) Five senior officers were also interviewed, two of whom said that they had suffered from PTSD, while a third was convinced that he would eventually succumb due to the cumulative effects of attending traumatic incidents. (See Taylor and Shevels 1995, for a brief report; see Corneil 1995 for a larger study of PTSD in American fire officers.) The subject of PTSD and its management have been discussed extensively elsewhere, and the interested reader is referred to Hodgkinson and Stewart (1991), Scott and Stradling (1992), van der Kolk, McFarlane and Weisaeth (1996) and Wilson and Raphael (1993) for further information.

The incidence and strength of these longer term reactions will again be buffered by mediating factors, such as the event outcome (failure or success), experience, personality and social support from the organization, colleagues, friends and family. The Department of Health (1991) report by the working party on disasters states:

> "Following our consultations, we have no cause to doubt that there is good evidence that early intervention which is pro-active and includes elements of debriefing and supportive counselling prevents chronic stress."
>
> (p. 5)

Ersland, Weisaeth and Sund (1989) found that 88% of rescuers in their study had a need to share their feelings with others. It is now realized that good critical incident debriefing techniques, where the commanders and crews discuss and review the management of events, can help to minimize negative reactions, as well as functioning as an excellent learning opportunity (see below). This is used for several occupations, including police officers (Bohl 1995; Mashburn 1993), military personnel (Shalev 1994) and oil industry staff (Johnson and Hansen 1994). The provision of mental health counselling, either on site or available afterwards (Duckworth 1986) has been shown to be beneficial in assisting even the most experienced emergency response personnel to deal with their personal reactions to traumatic and demanding events:

> "Peter Wright, South Yorkshire chief constable, has released the first full details of the traumatic effect the Hillsborough disaster had on his officers. In a report to his police authority he said 58 officers subsequently went on sick leave, mainly because of shock and stress. More than a year in working days had been lost as a result.... But Mr Wright says: 'Any effects that the disaster had upon the health of the force appear to be short-lived. It is thought that this is due to the efforts of the welfare officer and our consultant counsellor, who started their work within hours of the tragedy occurring.'"
>
> (*Police Review*, 1989, p. 2312)

Taylor and Shevels (1995), discussing PTSD in fire service officers, recommend both peer group support and professional counselling, pointing out that some fire brigades already have formal counselling schemes. Captain Haynes (1992), who succeeded in landing the stricken United Airlines 232 plane, said afterwards:

"Prior to my emergency, I did not pay much attention to the subject of post traumatic stress which Vietnam, Korean War and World War II veterans experienced. I certainly do now – it is a very serious problem. The after-the-fact stress of a trauma is going to occur; it can rear its ugly head any day, and in this particular case in Sioux City the response group brought in the post trauma unit right away, so its personnel could begin their operations at the scene of the accident."

(Haynes 1992, p. 10)

The question of subsequent litigation in relation to PTSD has become a significant consideration, particularly for the emergency services. Following the King's Cross underground fire, one of the firefighters was awarded £147000 on a PTSD claim (*Guardian*, 5 November 1993), and a ticket collector was awarded £375000 (*Health and Safety at Work*, January 1995). In law, the incident commander has a duty of care to his or her staff, but the issue of exposure to stressors that may result in a subsequent PTSD claim raises some very thorny legal problems for the emergency services in particular. Following the *Piper Alpha* disaster, there were a number of successful PTSD claims against Occidental from those onboard an adjacent firefighting vessel which was being used as an accommodation barge, and the master of the vessel was required to appear as a witness in the High Court to be examined on this very issue. In our increasingly litigious society, this is a problem for incident commanders that is not going to go away, and organizations need to address the question of responsibility, duty of care and possible negligence claims before their incident commanders find themselves being cross-examined in the witness box (Brown and Campbell 1994; see also Chapter 7).

MANAGING STRESS

This final section offers an overview of possible approaches to stress management for incident commanders and their teams. These have been subdivided into:

1. Cure: (i) identifying and (ii) treating cases of stress reactions that have occurred.
2. Prevention: (i) training and (ii) management to minimize unwanted stress reactions and their effects on performance.

The cure approach essentially involves dealing with the negative effects of stress, whereas prevention focuses on the mediating factors that can buffer exposure to the stressors and diminish their apparent threat to the individual.

Cure: Identifying Stress in Oneself or Others

A rather obvious starting point in stress management is to diagnose that a debilitating stress reaction is being experienced by oneself or by other team members. By all accounts, incident commanders are often so preoccupied dealing with the management of the situation that they pay little attention to their own stress reactions. But self-awareness is critical, and battle stress was certainly in the mind of Admiral Woodward (1992), the Falklands Battle Group Commander, as he recounted in his memoirs:

> "Quite a few individuals had by now cracked up.... It is quite hard to know what to do about men who are obviously suffering from stress. Of course the real cases, where a man is obviously not able to do his job are easy: they must be sent home by whatever means available. But there are others for whom trauma is not sudden or obvious, men who do not betray the classical obvious symptom of just not absorbing any new information. These are men who just go on doing that for which their brain has been programmed and can, by self-protective means, hide for a very long time the real truth that, in any emergency they will fail to react.... The transmission centres of their brains had simply jammed – just shut down because of mental trauma. I resolved to remain watchful and observant for such behaviour in myself, just I was trying to remain watchful and observant towards the stress cases among the ships."
>
> (p. 208)

As Woodward was all too aware, part of the incident commander's responsibility is the mental health of the emergency response teams, and appropriate sensitivity to their stress levels is therefore required:

> "Supervisors should monitor the performance of their officers and be alert for symptoms of stress in an individual. Officers whose behaviour or performance deteriorates should be relieved or withdrawn in the interests of themselves and their colleagues."
>
> (Home Office 1992, p. 31)

It is important that incident commanders realize (as Admiral Woodward did) that they are not immune to the effects of stress, and that in the unlikely event that these become debilitating, colleagues, possibly alerted by a more junior team member, are trained to take the necessary action of removing or sidelining the commander:

"Where, in the opinion of his subordinates, a supervisor is himself exhibiting symptoms of stress to the detriment of his performance it should be brought to the attention of another supervisor."

(Home Office 1992, p. 31)

Cure: Treatment of Clinical Cases

In the rare case of an individual exhibiting a complete breakdown of normal functioning, he or she should, if possible, be taken from the site for psychiatric treatment. Nowadays in combat zones only those with acute psychiatric symptoms are medically evacuated. Personnel exhibiting the signs of battle stress are not labelled as patients; instead, the current treatment philosophy is to move them back from the battle ground but to keep them with their units and give them rest, employing the "buddy system" to maintain social support. Reports suggest that soldiers treated in this way can be returned much more rapidly to active duty, with fewer long-term effects (Noy 1991). A summary of such treatment methods for combat stress is shown in Figure 4.4 (see also Bass 1992, who used this model for a discussion of stress in managers). This would also appear to be a sensible approach for incident commanders to adopt for any member of their staff who shows symptoms of stress that are causing distress or may be interfering with performance. The individual should be switched to a non-essential task and kept under observation, but should be treated as if he or she were having a normal reaction and if possible kept with the crew. Hodgkinson and Stewart (1991, p. 185) advise that in such cases, "a process of 'gearing down' is helpful, where stressed individuals may be moved from the centre of the incident to the periphery, and if appropriate, be allowed to rest. During this process some ventilation of feelings and reactions can be achieved". Armstrong et al. (1995) give a useful description of multiple stressor debriefing (MSD) with Red Cross emergency workers following the East Bay Hills firestorm of 1991 in California, which destroyed more than 3500 dwellings and resulted in 25 fatalities.

A Home Office workshop in 1991 on the psychological problems experienced by police officers attending disasters concluded that welfare, morale and stress issues pertaining to both senior and junior officers tended to be overlooked during disasters and were only considered after the event. They recommended that a special team under the command of a senior officer should be present at a disaster to deal only with the stress and welfare of the responding officers: "Welfare personnel at the scene can ease the burden on commanders and supervisors who are fully committed with the operational tasks" (Home Office 1992, p. 14). This provision of disaster mental health specialists, such as professionals who are volunteers with the American Red Cross, is now used in the United States. For instance, at the United Airlines plane crash at Pittsburgh in 1994, psychologists and psychiatric social workers attended both the crash site (Bruder 1995) and the temporary morgue (Weaver 1995b) to provide on-site support for the staff and volunteers involved in the recovery and identification of corpses and body parts of the 132 victims (see Mitchell 1988; Hodgkinson and Stewart 1991, for other examples). Hodgkinson and Stewart (1991) found that some emergency services managers are resistant to this type of professional support, believing that any serious discussion of feelings and vulnerabilities could release a "Pandora's Box", which "might open the floodgates and inaugurate a culture dramatically the reverse of the normal macho image" (Hodgkinson and Stewart 1991, p. 187). Since then, there has been a perceptible reduction in the level of resistance, but there is more than a grain of truth in the Pandora's box view. By all accounts, this kind of on-site mental health support requires very careful personnel selection and considerable skill. The counsellors have to realize that rescue and recovery personnel cope with horrific conditions such as mass casualties by using psychological defence mechanisms, sometimes described as a "trauma membrane" (Lindy 1985). Bruder (1995) describes this as:

> "an abruptly and rigidly erected set of defences that serve to protect the victim and in this case the recovery worker from experiencing the overwhelming anxiety that would accompany a full recognition of what one has been through or is going through. It is the psychological equivalent of setting one's jaw as you plunge forward into completing a particularly revolting but necessary task. The full range of psychological defences are employed suddenly in the creation of the trauma membrane with denial and repression at the forefront along with intellectualization, projection and reaction formation. All of these were in evidence amongst the recovery workers we had contact with at the command post [the United Airlines 232 air disaster in 1994]"
>
> (p. 8)

Therefore, mental health personnel, particularly those working on site in recovery operations, must be careful not to damage these important protective defence mechanisms by intrusive or inappropriate counselling techniques.

Prevention: Training

The importance of training for stress-proofing personnel has already been emphasized above and in Chapter 3, particularly with regard to realistic exercises and simulator sessions. Weisaeth (1987) says that "Being prepared for rescue work through practical exercises appears to cut the occurrence of disturbing physical reactions by more than half" (p. 13). Practical experience seems to help emergency response personnel to "digest" disaster experiences (Hytten and Hasle 1989). It also helps them to deal with stress at the time of the incident:

> "The activities which firemen are required to perform can be frightening.... Unless the fireman has experienced the fears to which these conditions give rise and has learnt to control them, there is a risk that he will get into difficulties in the hazardous circumstances of the fire ground and will himself need to be rescued."
>
> (HSE 1984, p. 5)

Training of the required emergency response procedures, even to the point of overlearning, is used in the military (Orasanu and Backer 1996), in aviation (Stokes and Kite 1994) and in the emergency services (Elliott and Smith 1993; Rolfe and Taylor 1989) to ensure effective performance under stress conditions, although the problem of creating appropriate levels of stress in this training is frequently aired (Driskell and Salas 1991a). In addition, the use of case studies and presentations by experienced personnel can establish a more realistic expectation of what can actually be accomplished at a major disaster, thus reducing the likelihood of subsequent guilt and failure emotions (Paton 1991). Inzana et al. (1996) have found that US Navy personnel who received preparatory information on stress effects and their management before performing under high stress conditions reported less anxiety, were more confident and made fewer errors that those who were not given this briefing.

In recent years there has been increasing emphasis on a second kind of training, that is, specific instruction on the causes and effects of stress as well as techniques for coping with stress reactions. One such method is called "Stress Inoculation Training" (Meichenbaum 1985). It has phases of conceptualization, skill acquisition and practice (e.g. breathing control, muscle relaxation, visual imagery), and application of the skills in exercises. Trainees learn that they do not react directly to stressor events but only through their interpretation (as shown in Figure 4.2), thus permitting alternative conceptualization of both the stressors and their personal coping resources. This technique has been used with a wide range of occupations, including oil industry personnel undergoing firefighting and freefall lifeboat training (Hytten, Jensen and Skauli 1990). Studies of the effectiveness have shown somewhat mixed results, but a recent meta-analysis concluded that overall the technique appears to be beneficial in reducing anxiety and enhancing performance under stress (Saunders et al., 1996). The fundamental principle of providing those likely to be exposed to high level stressors with some basic stress management training appears to be a good idea, and this is certainly done with pilots and industrial emergency response personnel on their Crew Resource Management (CRM) courses (Flin 1995b; see also Chapter 6).

Prevention: Management

There are general management techniques that will help to tackle the impending load on the site commander. For example, American fireground chief Brunacini (1985) advises delegation:

> "You must develop the ability to divide an overall problem into its parts and then delegate authority. This reduces the number of subordinates you will have to deal with, makes for easier control, and reduces the stress placed on you. It also reduces the stress on your officers by limiting their responsibility to the assigned aspects of the operation."
>
> (p. 8)

Predetermined incident command structures are designed to achieve the appropriate organizational hierarchy, with team members trained to adopt the appropriate roles with flexibility in the case of escalation. In the aviation industry, particular attention has been paid in recent years to the importance of teamwork in emergencies and their CRM training, mentioned above, is designed to foster enhanced team coordination under pressure, which helps individual team members perform better in stressful environments (Orasanu and Backer 1996).

Critical incident stress debriefing (Mitchell 1988), mentioned above, can play an important role in stress management after the event (Everly and Mitchell 1995; Gibson 1991; Lewis 1994; Mitchell and Bray 1990). This is designed to assist the participants to reconstruct a complete and detailed narrative of the event. By doing this, they are able to see it as a whole and put it into some kind of perspective. It is recommended that this sort of debrief should not be started until at least 48 hours after the incident (Manolias, personal communication, 1996). Immediately after the event, it is a good idea to get people together informally to share feelings and to let off stream; the operational debrief can contribute to this "defusing process". In essence, this is:

> "a structured meeting for those involved in the rescue and immediate support, where as a group they can retell their experience, discuss their feelings, share what they have learned from the experience in terms of their own response and ways of coping, and learn about normal reactions to stress. This is best done within 24 hours of the event, or as soon as possible. It may also be done informally, in a social setting, or in one to one sessions."
>
> (Department of Health 1991)

Besides providing a forum to exchange feelings and responses, it may be an opportunity for the commander to explain the rationale for decisions that the team found difficult to accept. Dyregrov (1989) cites the case of a fire chief who ordered his men to stay out of the freezing water of the Potomac River in Washington, after an Air Florida plane had crashed into it with a number of survivors. His crew were apparently angry and frustrated at this decision. However, during the debriefing he explained that he was aware of the smell of jet fuel and that two of his men had died of asphyxiation in a similar incident, thus he felt the risks were unacceptable.

Individual coping strategies that can be used during or after the event are very important; sharing these within a group or crew may offer valuable tips for less experienced team members. These may be physical, such as deep breathing or simple muscle relaxation exercises (which are surprisingly effective), behavioural, such as walking away from the scene for a few minutes, or cognitive, such as reassuring oneself that this sort of situation has been coped with before. Durham, McCammon and Allison (1985) found that the most frequent coping behaviours used by emergency response personnel were reminding oneself that things could be worse (57%) and trying to keep a realistic perspective on the situation (53%).

CONCLUSION

This chapter has reviewed the psychological research into the causes, buffers and effects of stress for the incident commander and emergency response personnel. There is a need for more research into the impact of stress on site commanders, and how experienced commanders manage to deal with their reactions in stressful situations demanding high level performance. In the main, emergency response crews appear to deal very effectively with exposure to dangerous and traumatic situations, and a better understanding of their coping skills would benefit less experienced emergency response personnel, such as industrial managers and their response teams. The final word is given to Jon Hansen, incident commander at the Oklahoma bomb site:

"We understand that remaining calm when confronted with chaos is critical to our effectiveness. Escalating our heart rates will only drain us of the energy we'll require seconds later. We cannot allow our hearts and minds to yield to the panic around us."

(Hansen 1995, p. 94)

5
Command Decision Making

"On arrival at the scene of a fire, officers are bombarded with a mass of visual and other information relating to the incident, its progress and its context. On a shorttime scale, often under great pressure, the Officer in Charge must grasp the situation, understand the problems being faced, prioritise fire service actions on the basis of reasonable strategy, deploy available resources, know when to ask for reinforcements and what these should be."

(Simpson 1992, p. 42)

"The failure of the OIMs to cope with the problems they faced on the night of the disaster clearly demonstrates that conventional selection and training of OIMs is no guarantee of ability to cope if the man himself is not able in the end to take critical decisions and lead those under his command in a time of extreme stress."

(Cullen 1990, para. 20.59)

The decision making skill of the on-scene commander appears to be one of the most essential components of effective command and control in emergency response: "Experience has shown that an effective response depends on timely receipt of accurate and complete information and on sound decisions and appropriate actions set in train at the outset" (Home Office 1994, p. 6). As discussed in the first chapter, managers' and commanders' decisions are coming under increasing scrutiny following major incidents: "A Scotland Yard inquiry into the riot at the Trafalgar Square anti-poll tax rally last March has found that slow decision making by police chiefs and a breakdown in communications contributed to the violence" (*The Sunday Times*, 3 March 1991). The foregoing review of the selection criteria, selection methods, training and competence assessment of incident commanders showed that their decision making is regarded as a critical skill for successful incident management. But while the subject of leadership has generated a voluminous literature over the centuries, it has only been very recently that research psychologists have begun to investigate leaders' decision making in demanding, time-pressured situations such as a major incident scenario.

In this chapter, traditional models of decision making and their potential application to commanders' decision making in emergencies are considered. This is followed by the introduction of a new school of thinking, naturalistic decision making (NDM) research (Klein et al. 1993; Zsambok and Klein, in press), which is particularly concerned with decision making in complex real-world settings. The dominant NDM model, called recognition-primed decision making (RPD) (Klein 1989, in press) is described, as well as a taxonomy of emergency decision making (Orasanu and Fischer, in press). These are then used as a framework against which to review other studies of emergency decision making, from fireground, medical, military and industrial professionals. Finally, the impact of stress on the decision making of experienced commanders is examined.

TRADITIONAL DECISION MAKING THEORIES

The traditional decision making literature from mathematics, statistics, economics and operations research is very extensive but it offers little of relevance to the emergency manager, because it tends to be derived from studies of specified problems (often artificial in nature), inexperienced decision makers and low stake payoffs. Moreover, it is rarely concerned with ambiguous dynamic situations, life threatening odds or high time pressure, all important features of a serious emergency or a major incident. If we turn to the traditional psychological literature on decision making, with some notable exceptions (e.g. Janis 1989, 1992), it tells us almost nothing of emergency decision makers, because so much of it is based on undergraduates performing trivial tasks in laboratories. Another possible source of data is the management decision making research, but this is concerned with individuals making strategic decisions when they have several hours or days to think about the options, carefully evaluating each one in turn against their business objectives using decision analysis methods. These provide a range of explanatory frameworks, which may have value for managers' or consumers' decision making, such as subjective expected utility (SEU), multi-attribute utility theory (MAUT) or Bayesian statistics (see Goodwin and Wright 1991; Lipshitz 1994; Noorderhaven 1995; Wright 1984), where the decision maker is encouraged to emulate a normative (or in mathematical terms, ideal) strategy of decision making. At its simplest form this usually incorporates the following stages:

1. Identify the problem.
2. Generate a set of options for solving the problem/choice alternatives.

3. Evaluate these options concurrently using one of a number of strategies, such as weighting and comparing the relevant features of the options.
4. Choose and implement the preferred option.

For example, when choosing a car there may be five models that are potentially suitable. How do you decide which to buy? Each model has a number of features, some of which are more important to you than others. So you rate each feature in terms of its importance to you (subjective utility) and assess which of the models offers the best combination of these attributes. There are different strategies, some more exhaustive than others, for carrying out the feature evaluation and comparison. In theory, this type of approach should allow you to make the "best" decision, provided that you have the mental energy, unlimited time and all of the relevant information to carry out the decision analysis. This is typically the method of decision making in which incident commanders are trained. But we know from our everyday experience that when we are in a familiar situation, we take many decisions almost automatically on the basis of our experience. We do not consciously generate and evaluate options, we simply know the right thing to do. This may be called intuition or "gut feel", but in fact to achieve these judgements some very sophisticated mental activity is taking place. So we can compare these two basic types of decision making, the slower, analytic option comparison and the faster, intuitive judgement. Which style do commanders use when deciding what to do at the scene of an incident?

NATURALISTIC DECISION MAKING

Since the mid-1980s, there has been increasing interest by applied psychologists in naturalistic decision making (NDM) that takes place in complex real-world settings with the following four key features: (i) dynamic and continually changing conditions, (ii) real-time reactions to these changes, (iii) ill-defined goals and ill-structured tasks, and (iv) knowledgeable people (Klein et al. 1993, p. vii). These researchers typically study experts' decision making in dynamic environments such as flight decks, military operations, firegrounds, hospital trauma centres/intensive care units and high hazard industries, for example nuclear plant control rooms. The first meeting of researchers who were studying naturalistic decision making took place in 1989 at Dayton, Ohio under the sponsorship of the US Army Research Institute. Their deliberations were published as a book, *Decision Making in Action*, edited by Klein et al. (1993). A second, larger conference of 150 researchers, now including more European psychologists, was held in Dayton in June 1994, organized by Klein Associates; the book *Naturalistic Decision Making*, edited by Caroline Zsambok and Gary Klein (in press), presents a series of position papers resulting from that meeting. This NDM research has enormous significance for the understanding of how commanders and their teams make decisions at the scene of an incident, because it offers descriptions of what expert commanders actually do when taking operational decisions in emergencies.

Klein (1991) outlined ten factors characterizing decision making in naturalistic settings (see Orasanu and Connolly 1993 for more detail):

1. Ill-defined goals and ill-structured tasks.
2. Uncertainty, ambiguity and missing data.
3. Shifting and competing goals.
4. Dynamic and continually changing conditions.
5. Action feedback loops (real-time reactions to changed conditions).
6. Time stress.
7. High stakes.
8. Multiple players (team factors).
9. Organizational goals and norms.
10. Experienced decision makers.

The major incidents described in Chapter 1 all share these characteristics. In typical NDM environments (e.g. flight decks, trauma units, warship command centres, major incident sites, control rooms and firegrounds), information comes from many sources, is often incomplete, can be ambiguous, and is prone to rapid change. In an emergency, the incident commander and his or her team are working in a high-stress, high-risk, time-pressured setting, and the lives of those affected by the emergency (including their own rescue personnel) may be dependent on their decisions. How, then, do they decide the correct courses of action?

In the view of the NDM researchers (see Klein et al. 1993; Zsambok and Klein, in press), traditional, normative models of decision making, which focus on the process of option generation and simultaneous evaluation to choose a course of action, do not frequently apply in NDM settings. There are a number of slightly different theoretical approaches within the NDM fraternity to studying decision making but they all share an interest in dynamic high-pressure domains where experts are aiming for satisfactory rather than optimal decisions due to time and risk constraints. Lipshitz and Ben Shaul (1996) point out that a common feature of NDM models is that they have a situation assessment (or recognition) process and a reasoning (serial matching of situations with actions) process and that these take place in an ongoing cycle of thinking and acting. As Orasanu and Connolly (1993) explained, "people think a little, act a little and then evaluate the outcomes and think and act some more" (p. 19), or as Frederico (1995) says, "In naturalistic settings, thinking and acting are interleaved not separated" (p. 106). Thus, the focus is not on a single decision point or a choice dilemma; rather, the decision maker has to implement solutions to a series of interrelated problems extremely rapidly. The dominant NDM theory, which has been used to study a range of incident commanders, is recognition-primed decision making (Klein 1993).

RECOGNITION-PRIMED DECISION MAKING

Dr Gary Klein is the chairman and chief scientist of Klein Associates, Ohio, which conducts research into decision making by attempting to "get inside the head" of decision makers operating in many different domains. Klein's approach stemmed from his dissatisfaction with the applicability of traditional models of decision making to real-life situations, particularly when the decisions could be lifesaving. He was interested in operational environments where experienced decision makers had to determine a course of action under conditions of high stakes, time pressures, dynamic settings, uncertainty, ambiguous information and multiple players. Klein's research began in the mid-1980s with a study of urban fireground commanders (Klein, Calderwood and Clinton-Cirocco 1985) who had to make decisions such as whether to initiate search and rescue, whether to begin an offensive attack or concentrate on defensive precautions and how to deploy their resources. They found that the fireground commanders' accounts of their decision making did not fit into any conventional decision-tree framework. Klein tells the story of receiving a research contract to study decision making and then interviewing his first fireground commander, who had just successfully managed an incident. When he asked the commander to describe the decisions he had just made, to Klein's disappointment, the commander told him that he was not aware of having made any decisions, instead he had just taken the appropriate command and control actions to extinguish the fire. Klein says at this point he could imagine his contract disappearing into thin air, but was sufficiently intrigued by the commander's claim that he did not make decisions, to continue the study:

> "The fireground commanders argued that they were not 'making choices', 'considering alternatives', or 'assessing probabilities'. They saw themselves as acting and reacting on the basis of prior experience; they were generating, monitoring, and modifying plans to meet the needs of the situations. Rarely did the fireground commanders contrast even two options. We could see no way in which the concept of optimal choice might be applied. Moreover, it appeared that a search for an optimal choice could stall the fireground

commanders long enough to lose control of the operation altogether. The fireground commanders were more interested in finding actions that were workable, timely, and cost-effective."

(Klein 1993, p. 139)

During post-incident interviews using a technique they developed called the critical decision method (Klein, Calderwood and McGregor 1989), Klein and colleagues found that the commanders could describe other possible courses of action but they maintained that during the incident they had not spent any time deliberating about the advantages or disadvantages of these different options. It appeared that these incident commanders had concentrated on assessing and classifying the situation in front of them. Once they recognized that they were dealing with a particular type of event, they usually also knew the typical response to tackle it. They would then quickly evaluate the feasibility of that course of action, imagining how they would implement it, to check whether anything important might go wrong. If they envisaged any problems, then the plan might be modified, but only if they rejected it would they consider another strategy. Klein Associates have also studied other decision makers faced with similar demand characteristics (e.g. tank platoon captains, naval warfare commanders, intensive care nurses) and have found the same pattern of results (Klein 1993). On the basis of these findings, they developed a template of this strategy, called the recognition-primed decision model (Klein 1995). This describes how experienced decision makers can rapidly decide on the appropriate course of action in a high-pressure situation.

The model has evolved into three basic formats, as shown in Figure 5.1. In the simplest version, shown as Level 1, the decision maker recognizes the type of situation, knows the appropriate response and implements it. If the situation is more complex and/or the decision maker cannot so easily classify the type of problem faced, then, as in Level 2, there may be a more pronounced diagnosis (situation assessment) phase. This can involve a simple feature match, where the decision maker thinks of several interpretations of the situation and uses key features to determine which interpretation provides the best match with the available cues. Alternatively, the decision maker may have to combine these features to construct a plausible explanation for the situation. This is called story building, an idea that was derived from legal research into juror decision making (Pennington and Hastie 1993). Where the appropriate response is unambiguously associated with the situation assessment, it is implemented as indicated in the Level 1 model. In cases where the decision maker is less sure of the option, then the RPD model Level 3 version indicates that before an action is implemented there is a brief mental evaluation to check

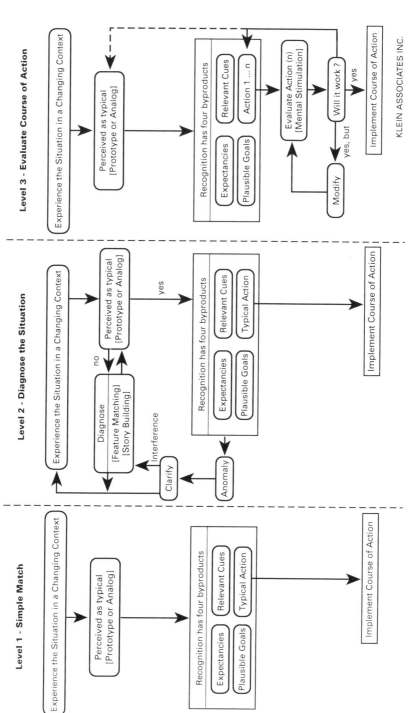

Figure 5.1 *The Recognition-Primed Decision Model (Klein 1995). Reprinted with permission of Klein Associates.*

whether there are likely to be any problems (Klein and Crandell 1995). This is called "mental simulation" or "preplaying" the course of action (an "action replay" in reverse); if it is deemed problematic, then an attempt will be made to modify or adapt it before it is rejected. At that point the commander would re-examine the situation to generate a second course of action. To the decision maker, the NDM type strategies (such as RPD) feel like an intuitive response rather than an analytic comparison or rational choice of alternative options. Key features of the RPD model are as follows (Klein 1993):

- Focus on situation assessment.
- Aim is to satisfice, not optimize.
- For experienced decision makers, the first option is usually workable.
- Serial generation and evaluation of options.
- Check option will work using mental simulation.
- Focus on elaborating and improving option.
- Decision maker is primed to act.

At present, this appears to be one of the best models available to apply to the emergency situation, whether the environment is civilian or military; onshore or offshore; aviation, industrial or medical. In the original work with fireground commanders, 80% of their decisions were of the RPD type, and in subsequent studies with fireground commanders and tank platoon leaders, at least 40% of their decisions were found to involve RPD strategies (see Klein 1993). Further support for the RPD strategy being used in a military setting came from a study of 14 US naval officers from AEGIS cruisers (commanding officers and tactical action officers). All subjects were interviewed for two hours to determine their style of decision making during a non-routine incident involving anti-air warfare in low-intensity conflicts (Kaempf et al. 1992). The officers recalled ten incidents from operational settings and four from training exercises; the resulting analyses of their decision processes showed that they were using an RPD strategy for 95% of their actions. That is, the officers relied on situational recognition resulting in the recall of one appropriate action, rather than a deliberate comparison of alternative courses of action (Klein et al., in press, gives details of the study).

In the USA, the RPD model is being widely adopted; it is being used at the National Fire Academy as well as in a number of military, medical, aviation and industrial settings (see Zsambok and Klein, in press, for details). The RPD model and associated research techniques have begun to generate a degree of interest in the UK, most notably by the Defence Research Agency (Pascual and Henderson, in press), the police (Stewart 1995) and the fire service (Kaempf and Militello 1992; Stewart 1996). In fact, Murray (1994b) has suggested that the RPD model is a more valuable approach to developing understanding of decision making on the fireground than the traditional analytic frameworks: "The analytical approach to decision making has its uses as an ideal normative model but it is not descriptive of 'real world' decisions at emergency incidents" (p. 68).

EMERGENCY DECISION MAKING

While the RPD model is currently attracting significant interest and research activity and it undoubtedly has high face validity for practitioners, there are a number of other approaches within the NDM community. These researchers are striving to describe the types and relative effectiveness of decision strategies employed by experts in natural, if demanding, circumstances. For instance, Rasmussen (1983, 1993), a Danish psychologist who is one of the most eminent researchers in this field, proposes that decisions in real-life work contexts such as control rooms or medical diagnosis can be categorized as skill-based (almost automatic, e.g. driving), rule-based (following rules or procedures) or knowledge-based (creative). Klein's RPD model shares a number of the characteristics of the rule-based and knowledge-based decisions. The models and approaches described below have been selected on the basis of their general applicability from a number of different work environments – flight decks, firegrounds, hospitals, battlefields and offshore oil platforms. The focus here is on the incident commander as the decision maker, although in all of these environments, the commanders function as part of a team. Team performance and decision making are discussed separately in Chapter 6.

Decision Making on the Flight Deck

While a flight deck is a very technical and specialized environment, there are useful pointers from the findings of aviation psychologists that can aid our understanding of command decision making under pressure. The NASA psychologists have some of the very best data on human performance in emergencies from their flight simulators, cockpit voice recordings from accidents, and their Aviation Safety Reporting System (ASRS) – a no-jeopardy confidential incident reporting system for pilots (Chappell 1994). Drawing on Rasmussen's concept of rule-based and knowledge-based decisions and Klein's RPD model, NASA psychologist Judith Orasanu (1995b) has developed a new taxonomy of pilots' decision strategies, which is founded on two components – situation assessment and selecting a response (course of action). Her categorization is based on the types of decisions identified in detailed recordings and observations of decision making in flight deck simulators; accident reports implicating crew factors (with cockpit voice recordings); and a set of ASRS incident reports involving problem solving and decision making factors (see Orasanu and Fischer, in press). From this analysis, the following six types of rule-based and knowledge-based decisions can be discriminated:

1. Go/no-go decisions. These are based on prescribed actions for a given set of conditions. For example, certain problems appearing while a plane is travelling down the runway would immediately lead to an aborted take-off. (A police commander taking a shoot/no shoot decision could be operating at a similar speed of irreversible decision making.)
2. Condition–action rules. Here the crew have to recognize the problem as a predefined condition and implement a standard response. If x then y. This is closest to Klein's recognition-primed decisions, although in aviation these decisions are prescriptive and are likely to be included in aircraft or company flight manuals. The pilot has to know the rule and decide if conditions merit applying it.
3. Choice problems. In this case there is no fixed rule, several options are available (e.g. divert airports) and the crew must choose one of them, in the light of situational constraints (e.g. fuel, weather, runway length), current objectives and possible consequences.
4. Scheduling problems. Several tasks must be accomplished within a limited time period, using limited resources, and the crew have to decide who will do what and when.
5. Procedural management. The situation is ambiguous but there are indications that make the crew believe that it is of high risk. In this event, the crew follow standard generic procedures coupled with their own knowledge and experience to make the situation safe, often with the aim of landing at the nearest airport.
6. Creative problem solving. This is the most demanding decision category, although of rare occurrence. The crew may or may not be clear as to the nature of the problem but in either case, there is no standard procedure or guideline to deal with the conditions. In this situation they have to invent a new solution (while keeping the plane aloft). The most famous example of this kind of creative decision making is the United Airlines 232 accident, where the crew used asymmetric thrust on two engines to steer the plane after they lost the third engine and their hydraulic power (Haynes 1992; see Chapter 1).

These different decision strategies (with courses of action) are displayed in her latest model of pilot decision making, shown in Figure 5.2. In order to determine the relative frequency of the six decision strategies, Orasanu, Fischer and Tarrel (1993) analysed 94 ASRS reports from pilots and found that of 240 decisions in reported incidents, 54% were single-option rule-based – either go/no go (14%) or condition–action (40%), where the pilot has a standard operating procedure for responding in a given situation (similar to RPD) – 36% involved choices and the remaining 10% were scheduling, procedural management or creative problem solving. Orasanu and Fischer (in press) have concluded that there is not one best decision making approach; rather, it appears that effective crews tailor their decision strategies to the features of the situation. Aviation accident reports also show that poor situation assessment was a more common problem than poor decision making which was based on an adequate diagnosis (Orasanu, Dismukes and Fischer 1993). So, as in Klein's RPD model, the situation assessment is critical, and emphasis is added to two key variables in the assessment phase: judgements of available time and level of risk. Fischer, Orasanu and Wich (1995) have found that when pilots were asked to assess an incident scenario based on a real event, the key dimensions in their decision making were judgements of risk, time pressure, the ambiguity of the situation and the response options. (See also Jensen 1995, for an extended analysis of pilot judgement and decision making.)

Situation awareness and assessment have been receiving serious scientific interest as a foundation for effective decision making, initially in aviation but now more widely (Endsley 1995, in press; Orasanu 1995a). This process concerns problem recognition and diagnosis, as well as continued monitoring of the environment, and it will be familiar to many commanders but under different labels. For example, in Brunacini's (1985) book on fireground command, he describes a basic fireground management function called size-up: "Size-up is a systematic process consisting of the rapid, yet deliberate, consideration of all critical fireground factors and leads to the development of a rational attack plan based on these factors" (p. 38).

Grimwood (1992), writing on firefighting tactics, gives a good example of situation assessment:

"It is important for the firefighter to train his mind to 'tune-in and observe' essential features as he responds to every fire call. As the fire vehicle turns into the street to start looking for that hydrant, read the crowd psychology up ahead – are they trying to tell you something?, perhaps the fire is at the rear, are they panicking? Get an early glimpse of the structure from a distance, where possible, and scan all visible faces on the road for signs of fire. What is the roof access like? What type of structure is it? Is the construction

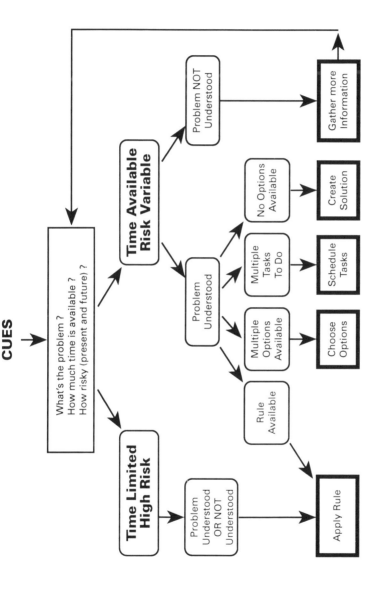

Figure 5.2 Pilot Decision Process Model. The Upper Rectangle Represents the Situation Assessment Component, the Lower Rectangles Represent the Course of Action Component, and the Rounded Squares Represent Conditions and Affordances (Orasanu 1995b). Reprinted with permission of the Human Factors and Ergonomics Society.

likely to present any unusual hazards? Is there a 'haze' in the air that may suggest smoke is issuing out of view? Your nose will soon tell you! ... your senses are finely tuning themselves ready for action.... The more information you can absorb at this stage, the more effective you will be when it comes to taking any necessary rapid action.... All this should be taken in during the time it takes to step off the pumper and walk into the building. The firefighter should do all of these things without thinking. They should be second nature."

(p. 241)

In a number of the major incidents described in the opening chapter, the problem lay more with situation awareness than with the absence of appropriate procedures. For example, at the Hillsborough stadium, the problem was initially interpreted as crowd disorder and for crucial minutes was treated accordingly, with the police not allowing the fans on to the football field. At the Bradford football stadium fire, the problem was correctly diagnosed as fire but the potential speed of escalation and the magnitude of the blaze were not anticipated, thus the available time was probably overestimated and the level of risk underestimated. In these cases, the definition of the problem, the time calculation and the level of risk were key components of the decision making process.

My discussions with industrial managers and emergency commanders suggests that Orasanu's model may have more general application beyond the flight deck. To take an industrial example, the offshore manager in an emergency has a set of rules (actions) specified for particular circumstances (e.g. blowout, shallow gas, fire). These are laid out in their emergency procedures manuals and practised in training (Dickson 1992; Haines 1995). The procedure may be of the go/no go type such as shutting down production, whereas other problems would require a choice of action or some element of task scheduling. Industrial emergencies are often multifaceted and require to be managed by cycles of decision making, where different types of strategy may be required for different problems. As we have seen in the *Piper Alpha* disaster, or the Three Mile Island nuclear reactor incident (Perrow 1984), there are rare occasions where high hazard plant managers may also face a crisis with totally unanticipated elements and have to engage in creative decision making. Fireground commanders and police commanders have indicated that this taxonomy may also be an appropriate categorization for the types of decisions taken by incident officers. The emergency services are almost always working on unfamiliar sites but they too have standard procedures where, in a given set of circumstances, certain actions are taken, sometimes involving a choice (e.g. where to set up a forward control point or an outer cordon), or the scheduling of tasks using limited resources. They often encounter ambiguous problems for which they have to apply standard procedures, as well as situations for which no rules fit and they must think creatively to come up with a solution. The next section concerns fire service officers and the research to date on fireground commanders' decision making.

Decision Making on the Fireground

There have been a number of studies of decision making by fireground commanders in addition to the work of Klein, Calderwood and Clinton-Cirocco (1985), which led to the development of the RPD model. A new project assessing the application of the RPD model to fire officers in London Fire Brigade is briefly outlined, followed by three other models of decision making; one from a British fire officer (Murray 1994a, b), one from a Swedish fire officer turned researcher (Fredholm 1995) and a third from French fire officers (Pandele 1994a). Swedish psychologist Berndt Brehmer (1996) has also studied fireground decision making, and his ideas on dynamic and distributed decision making are summarized at the end of this section.

Decision Making on the London Incident Ground

Charlie Hendry, a senior divisional officer with London Fire Brigade, and Eugene Burke, the brigade's occupational psychologist, recently carried out a study of command decision making (Burke and Hendry 1995; see Stewart 1996, for a brief account). They interviewed seven experienced London Fire Brigade incident commanders using the critical decision method (Klein, Calderwood and McGregor 1989). Each interview lasted for approximately three hours. Their objective was to gather information on decision making knowledge which could be incorporated into a simulator-based assessment technique. The officers were briefed to think about a recent incident that they had found to be particularly demanding or challenging, and which required a number of critical decisions. They were then asked to recount the incident, to sketch its location and to provide approximate times when events occurred. Using this "time-line", significant events were then probed to identify key decision points. These decision points could be a conscious act to control the incident (e.g. establishing a plan of action), a response to a certain event (e.g. people trapped) or a change in the incident (e.g. fire spread).

The types of decisions identified (69 in total) were then classified into three basic types, with the relative percentages shown in brackets:

- Standard: either taught explicitly or so common that other officers would agree as to the alternatives (38%).
- Typical: modifications to standard operating knowledge to meet the requirements of the situation (43%).
- Constructed: no standard solution available; typically involves creative problem solving (19%).

Burke and Hendry also assessed the number of options that the officer considered at each decision point, and found that only one course of action (i.e. no alternatives) was considered at 81% of the decision points, and for the remaining decisions (19%) only one alternative course of action was considered. In no case was more than one alternative thought about. Using their time log, they also established that the mean rate of events was one every 1.75 minutes, while the mean rate of decision points was one every 3 minutes. They commented, "As well as describing the frequency with which the incident commander is hit with information, these statistics also serve to emphasise the information processing workload under which incident commanders have to operate" (p. 4). They note that many features of fireground decision making revealed in their data are in line with Klein's RPD model; for example, the consideration of a single course of action, based on experience and restricted by time pressure. Further similarities are:

- "Mental simulation and visualisation play a key function in surfacing the final action plan.
- Simulation and visualisation are widely used in considering what tactic(s) might be best suited to various situations as part of a commander's personal skill maintenance routines (i.e. I already had a plan because I had thought about a fire in that building before) and in crew discussions of incidents.
- Standard procedures usually only come into effect once an action plan has been formulated or the incident has been resolved."
  (Burke and Hendry 1995, p. 6)

This is the first British attempt to study fireground incident command decision making within the NDM framework, and Burke and Hendry's results suggest that Klein's approach may be a promising method of revealing the implicit knowledge and decision making skills of expert fire commanders which can then be incorporated into selection, training and simulations. London Fire Brigade has recently developed a functional model of incident command, building on its competence standards and naturalistic models of decision making, such as RPD (Burke et al. 1996).

Control Model of Operational Command

Brian Murray (1994a), a divisional officer with Warwickshire Fire and Rescue Service, has also been studying operational command and decision making in fireground commanders, noting that:

> "In the past, the Fire Service has tended to use the traditional decision making model:
>
> • identifying the problem;
> • analysing it;
> • developing possible solutions;
> • selecting the best solution; and
> • converting the best decision into effective action.
>
> Evidence is now available which suggests that in operational situations this model is not wholly appropriate."
>
> (p. 22)

From his own experience as a fireground commander, a special study of operational command conducted for the Fire Service College (Murray 1993), and ideas from Klein (see above) and Brehmer (1992), he has proposed a three-component dynamic model of operational command on the fireground (Figure 5.3).

The three elements of the model are (i) assess the situation, (ii) decide what to do and (iii) implement decisions. The first component is an assessment process, which functions on a series of inputs. These can be subdivided into external inputs from the emergency situation and resources, and internal inputs, labelled knowledge of fire science/special risks, past experience and evaluating skills. There is also an additional input from a comparator module, which is called the desired state in accordance with responsibilities (effectively a goal). This is very similar to the situation assessment stage shown in the models of Klein and Orasanu. Interestingly, Murray, as a practising fire officer, shows resources as a key input, and not only does Brunacini (1985) also attest to the importance of this judgement but it is the basis of Fredholm's fireground command model discussed below. Unlike pilots, fire commanders have considerable resources at their disposal and their judgement of risk level determines the number of resources they will call to the scene. This is actually quite a fine judgement because (i) these resources are not unlimited, and calling appliances means they are unavailable or delayed for other emergency calls; however (ii) not requesting sufficient additional resources will hamper the operation, if the fire escalates, but (iii) too many personnel or appliances can cause coordination and control problems.

The products or outputs of the situation assessment are (i) the commander's overall perception of the existing situation and (ii) a forecast or

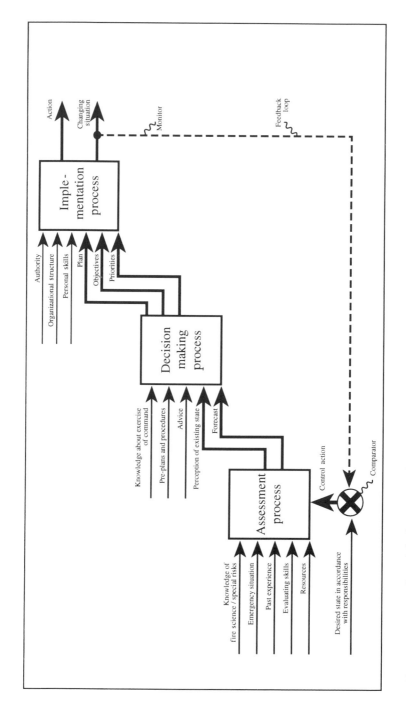

Figure 5.3 Control Model of Operational Command (Murray 1994b). Reproduced by permission of Fire Professional Magazine, ESC Publications Ltd.

prediction about how the incident will develop. These are fed into the second phase of the decision judgement along with knowledge of command responsibilities, standard procedures, previously prepared plans and advice from others. On the basis of this combined knowledge and new information, the decision is reached as to the plan of action, with specified objectives and priorities. Before the plan is implemented, several other factors may have an influence on the precise actions ordered; these are shown as the commander's authority, personal qualities and the organizational structure. Firegrounds are dynamic environments and actions will produce reactions, which provide the commander with new information that can be used to continually reassess the situation and amend the operational plan in line with current objectives.

Murray's model does not state explicitly when and where RPD or concurrent option evaluation might take place, but he does acknowledge the relevance of Klein's model and its emphasis on reaching a satisfactory resolution rather than aiming for an optimal or ideal solution. Brunacini (1985) also believes that "The very worst fireground plan is no plan (the next worst is two plans)" (p. 243). Murray (1994a) suggests that his model may be useful for pinpointing exactly what knowledge is required to assist the commander, which in turn can aid the design of training interventions. He is now carrying out research to test his model and improve the definition of the initial input variables by investigating how fire officers make situation assessments in the minutes after they arrive at the scene of the fire, with a particular focus on how expert commanders make their judgements as compared to novices.

Situational/Resource Model of Decision Making

A third approach to the study of fireground commanders' decision making has been developed by Fredholm (1991, 1995), who has been analysing the problems of establishing effective command and control at major fires and rescue operations in Sweden. He argues that there is a need for a better distinction between the decision making style needed when in direct command and control in the damage area, which he calls "concrete intuitive thinking", and the overall command and control (of priorities, goals, resources, liaison etc.), which he believes demands a more analytic style of decision making required for large-scale incidents. He presents a taxonomy of four typical operational and tactical problems:

1. Limited situation, strong resources, e.g. a car or apartment fire. It is less important to reach an optimal solution because there is a minimal chance of failure.

2. Limited situation, critical resources, e.g. apartment fire likely to spread. Immediate resources must be used optimally in the initial stage to meet the demands of the fire before losing control.
3. Limited situation, weak resources, e.g. barn fire. Available resources can only be used to secure the fire boundaries that are evident to the commander.
4. Unlimited situation, weak resources, e.g. complex accident with gas leak. A large-scale incident for which resources are inadequate. The scale and dynamics of the situation are very difficult to assess.

Situations 2 and 4 make the greatest demands on the commander's decision making skill because there is little margin for error. The limited situations 1–3 can be managed by direct command and control using what he calls the more intuitive, concrete decision making. This is usually at a junior level of command, with an emphasis on technical competence, and the aim is to think fast in order to achieve a rapid response. With reference to Klein's work, Fredholm (1995) explains, "Intuitive decision making is rather spontaneous and depending on feelings, which are based on and recognitions" (p. 26). At higher levels of command in charge of the larger scale event (situation 4), Fredholm believes that a more analytical, synthetic style of thinking is required because the problems are of greater temporal and spatial complexity in a dynamic, chaotic situation. He argues that fireground commanders have less experience of this more classical style of decision making, and that more research is needed to study key aspects of decision making, such as situation assessment, goal formation and mental modelling, required for unlimited situations (major incidents). (The inquiry into the Brightside Lane fire (HSE 1985a) mentioned in Chapter 1 raised exactly this question of the degree of experience commanders had with incidents of this magnitude.) Senior police officers (such as Assistant Chief Constables) who will act as strategic (or Gold) commanders may also find themselves having to use this analytic, forecasting style of thinking in order to build a mental model in a control centre remote from the scene. Again, in accord with Fredholm's suggestion, the emphasis in their previous training for incident management may have been on the faster, more intuitive style of decision making required of the operational (Bronze) or tactical (Silver) commander. In addition, where there are several levels of command at an incident, team communication and coordination also need to be addressed, such as maintaining a shared understanding of the situation across the command levels. This is considered in the following chapter.

There are similarities between Fredholm's ideas from fireground command and Orasanu's findings from the flight deck. Both are arguing for a contingency approach where the decision style should be matched to the situation. This implies that decision makers should be able to diagnose the situation and have a repertoire of styles (or at least two) at their disposal. In both cases, they argue that the optimizing analytic style can be appropriate under certain emergency conditions. Orasanu suggests that when time and risk permit, then pilots can try to reach an optimal rather than just a satisfactory decision, thus a more analytical style becomes appropriate; e.g. choose the best divert airport from the available options. Fredholm believes that for large-scale incidents an analytic style is more appropriate; the situation is not going to be resolved in minutes, it will be a longer operation over an extended site. The senior commander needs to take the time to build a mental model of the problem space before proper command and control can be achieved. (Quarantelli (1995), who has long argued that conventional command and control models are inappropriate for the management of large-scale disasters, is probably making a similar point, although he does not explicitly discuss cognitive processes; see also Brehmer (1991b), who says that as we move up the hierarchy of an emergency management system the decisions become qualitatively different.) For the limited situations, described above, the hazard has already been realized but may be manageable; those first on the scene must implement their decisions very quickly to achieve rescue and damage limitation. In this case (as with a high time-pressure problem in flight) the preferred strategy is to engage in the much faster intuitive or recognition-primed type decision making, which will achieve a satisfactory (if not optimal) solution.

Method of Tactical Reasoning

A fourth model of command decision making comes from France, where a system called the method of tactical reasoning (MTR) was developed by senior fire officers. Commandant Pandele (1994a, b), an instructor at the French Fire Academy, has described the system in detail (in French), but a brief account in English has been written by Samurcay and Rogalski (1991), psychologists who have carried out several studies into the use of this system. The MTR approach is taught to fire service officers as a decision making aid, and it is intended to provide a common paradigm for incident management:

> "with the aim of rationalizing situation analysis and optimization in decision making. It was a transposition of the military method for tactical reasoning. This method expresses common processes for elaborating and choosing strategies for the class of emergency problems."
>
> (Samurcay and Rogalski 1991, p. 289)

The stages of MTR are as follows:

1. Search for information: topography, people concerned, actual and predicted meteorological conditions, astrological conditions (date, daylight), resources, incident type.
2. Analysis and anticipation of the information (current and future state).
3. Identification of tasks to be accomplished in order to reach the objective (or goal).
4. Management of real and anticipated time, and the means of operating.
5. Elaboration of one, two or even three ideas for manoeuvre (equivalent to the "intention" of the sector leader) (Pandele 1994a).

The actual choice of option or manoeuvre is not regarded as part of the MTR. There are detailed instructions and forms that can be completed for each stage of the process, and in essence the method is based on the classical decision making process. As Samurcay and Rogalski (1991) explain, the procedure essentially encapsulates the stages of (i) information processing, (ii) option generation and (iii) optimization – defining a set of choice criteria and evaluating their values for proposed solutions. For their research, they have diagrammed in the MTR model using Rasmussen's (1986) symbolic representation of operations and states of knowledge (see Figure 5.4).

As can be seen from Figure 5.4, the sequence shares a number of elements with the models presented above, most notably the initial situation assessment, anticipation and goal identification steps, but thereafter it shows a classical decision approach of option generation and comparison. Samurcay and Rogalski's research into fire officers' use of MTR method has been designed to provide an insight into the cognitive processes employed in complex problem solving, an area in which they note the dearth of empirical investigations. In one study (Samurcay and Rogalski 1988) they analysed the cognitive difficulties officers experienced when using MTR as a tool in decision making. A group of 110 officers attending the National French Fire Academy, who held responsible positions in operational command, were trained in MTR using a general introduction, followed by case studies and a desktop simulation. Various observations and assessments were collected, including a training questionnaire and performance on a case study and simulation. They found that there was a tendency for trainees to take shortcuts in defining solutions, leading them to underestimate important parameters of the incidents. "Moreover, the process of optimization was often very rough: a tendency was to choose one criterion instead of combining the pertinent criteria (unidimensional instead of multidimensional optimization)" (Samurcay and Rogalski 1988, p. 147). This appears to be a form of inadequate situation assessment, identified as a typical problem in other domains, such as aviation.

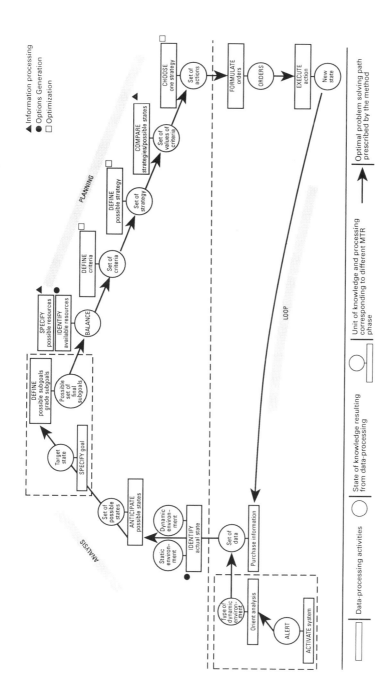

Figure 5.4 Phases of the Method of Tactical Reasoning (Samurcay and Rogalski 1991). Reproduced by permission of John Wiley & Sons Ltd, Chichester.

What is interesting about the MTR model is that it is basically a normative form of decision making, as described at the start of the chapter. But this is precisely what we now think that American (Klein, Calderwood and Clinton-Cirocco 1985) and British (Burke and Hendry 1995) fireground commanders *do not* do in fast-moving incidents. Murray (1994b) comments:

> "The analytic approach is used in the Fire Service training, the most notable example being the 'Method for Tactical Reasoning' (MTR) as used by the French Fire Service. However the applicability of such analytic process models for stressful emergency situations is not established.... The analytical approach to decision making has its uses as an ideal normative model but it is not descriptive of 'real world' decisions at emergency incidents."
>
> (p. 68)

Is this, then, a cultural difference? Why would French fire officers take decisions in a different way from their British and American counterparts? Setting aside obvious national differences in firefighting tactics and organizational structures, the psychological processes taking place between the ears of incident commanders are likely to be very similar perceptual, memory and thinking operations for a given incident type. The answer may be found in a later observation by Samurcay and Rogalski (1991):

> "At the end of the training session (around 28 full hours) the trainees did not appear really convinced about the utility of MTR as an aid in decision making for operational situations with a fast 'tempo'. For many of them MTR was considered useful as a guideline for reasoning and communicating, as a tool in foreseeing or in long and complex operations (with a slow 'tempo')."
>
> (p. 293)

In fact, this seems to echo the point Fredholm was making with regard to the need for analytic decision making (rather than intuitive RPD-type) for major incidents. Perhaps the analytic style of MTR is particularly applicable for the larger scale incident, the "unlimited situation" in Fredholm's terms, such as a heavy snowstorm in a city, a forest fire or a nuclear incident. This seems to be a method of decision making suited to the strategic commander who needs to consider the longer term resource implications, including the political, economic and public relations aspects, as well as the immediate operational problem.

Dynamic Decision Making

One of the most salient features of a fireground commander's decision task is the speed of fire development. Brehmer (1996) is particularly interested in this type of dynamic decision task, which he believes has four important characteristics: a series of decisions, which are interdependent, a problem that changes autonomously and as a result of the decision maker's actions, and a real time scenario. He gives the following example:

> "Consider the decision problems facing a fire chief faced with the task of extinguishing forest fires. He receives information about fires from a spotter plane, and on the basis of this information, he then sends out commands to his fire fighting units. These units then report back to him about their activities and locations as well as about the fire. The fire chief then uses this information to issue new commands until the fire has been extinguished."
>
> (p. 19)

Brehmer and his colleagues have developed a computer program (NEWFIRE) based on a forest fire scenario, which incorporates the four elements of dynamic decision making described above. The decision maker takes the role of the fire chief and, using the grid map of the area shown on the computer screen, has to make a series of decisions about the deployment of fire fighting resources with the goal of extinguishing the fire and protecting a control base. The commander's actions are subject to feedback delays, that is, time delay in actions being implemented or in the commander receiving status update information. Brehmer's studies have shown that decision makers frequently do not take such feedback delays into account; for example, they send out too few firefighting units because they do not anticipate that the fire will have spread by the time they receive the status report. He argues that the decision maker needs to have a good "mental model" of the task in order to control a dynamic event, such as a forest fire, and his research has enabled him to identify several problems of model formation: dealing with complexity, balancing competing goals, feedback delays and taking into account possible side effects of actions. Brehmer (1996) uses control theory to encapsulate the dynamic decision process: "the decision maker must have clear goals, he must be able to ascertain the state of the system that he seeks to control, he must be able to change the system, and he must have a model of the system" (p. 29).

When the decision maker is under stress, Brehmer argues that three "pathologies of decision making" can occur. He calls these (i) thematic vagabonding, when the decision maker shifts from goal to goal, (ii) encystment, when the decision maker focuses on only one goal that appears feasible, and, as in (i), fails to consider all relevant goals, and (iii) a refusal to make any decisions. Dorner and Pfeifer (1993) examined decision making under stress (white noise) using a version of the FIRE program and found that subjects working in the stress condition appeared to alter their decision making style to cope with the interference from the noise.

They appeared to adopt an analytic style of decision making using a "more sketchy" (lower resolution) situation analysis. They acknowledged the dangers of generalizing from a computer task to real-world dynamic emergencies; nevertheless, this type of research can suggest aspects of decision making that can be tested in more realistic simulations.

Decision Making in Medical Emergencies

At first glance, decision making in medical emergencies might seem to be out of place in a book on incident command. But in fact this domain shares a number of psychological similarities with crises that occur in other situations, as far as decision making, leadership and team working are concerned:

> "When a crisis does present itself – a patient suffers an unexpected cardiac arrest or a surgical catastrophe occurs – it is obvious to everyone who works in an operating room that some anesthetists cope better than others. These anesthetists take more steps to prevent a crisis, and they are better prepared when they occur. They are the ones who bring order from chaos. They take command and they know what to do and how to ensure that it gets done."
> (Gaba, Fish and Howard 1994, p. 1)

Researchers in this field, particularly anaesthetists, have become very interested in the NDM approach and they have developed naturalistic decision making models for their own crises management training (their use of simulator training is discussed in Chapter 3 and their team training in Chapter 6). While anaesthetic crises are rare, they are not unknown (the job – like that of a pilot – is said to be characterized by "hours of boredom, moments of terror"), and, because of the relative infrequency of adverse events, anaesthetists receive very limited exposure to emergency decision making situations. One of the leading investigators in this field is David Gaba (1992), an anaesthesiology professor at Stanford Medical School, who has adopted an NDM approach for his research into crisis management. He claims that the classical medical decision method, which involves a careful testing of hypotheses against the available evidence followed by a systematic analysis of all possible options for treating the problem, is a powerful approach, but that it does not work well when the evidence is scant or ambiguous:

> "In complex dynamic domains like anesthesia many problems require quick action to prevent a rapid cascade to a catastrophic adverse outcome. For these problems deriving a solution through formal deductive reasoning from 'first principles' is too slow. In complex dynamic domains the initial responses of experts to the majority of events stem from pre-compiled 'rules'

or 'response plans' for dealing with a recognized event. This is referred to as recognition-primed decision making because once the event is identified the response is well known. In the anesthesia domain these responses usually are acquired through personal experience alone, although a few that involve major catastrophes (e.g. Advanced Cardiac Life Support) have been explicitly codified and taught systematically. Experienced anesthetists have been observed to mentally rearrange, recompile, and rehearse these responses based on the patient's condition, the surgical procedure, and the problems to be expected. Ideally precompiled responses are retrieved appropriately and executed rapidly. When the exact nature of the problem is not apparent a set of generic responses appropriate for the overall situation may be invoked.... Even the ideal use of precompiled responses is destined to fail when the problem is not caused by the suspected etiology or when it does not respond to the usual actions. Anesthesia cannot be administered purely by precompiled 'cookbook' procedures. Abstract reasoning about the problem utilizing fundamental medical knowledge still takes place in parallel with precompiled responses even when quick action must be taken. This seems to involve a search for high level analogies or true deductive reasoning using deep medical and technical knowledge and a thorough analysis of all possible solutions."

(Source: Gaba, "Human work environment and simulators", in R. Miller (ed.), p. 2654, *Anesthesia*, 4th edn. Churchill Livingstone, New York, 1994)

So here we see again the RPD model finding application in another world of emergency decision making, with the need to be able to apply a classical analytic approach under certain conditions (cf. Fredholm's unlimited situation). Extending Rasmussen's hierarchy (1983) of skill-based, rule-based and knowledge-based activities, Gaba, Fish and Howard (1994) postulate five levels of mental activity, the first three corresponding to Rasmussen's levels:

1. Sensorimotor: sensory perceptions and motor actions with minimal conscious control.
2. Procedural: familiar subroutines.
3. Abstract reasoning: for unfamiliar situations.
4. Supervisory control: allocation of attention.
5. Resource management: command and control of available resources.

Drawing on the work of cognitive psychologists (e.g. Klein 1989), as well as their own anaesthesiology experiences and research findings, they have integrated this taxonomy into a model of anaesthetists' decision making during operations (Figure 5.5).

While Figure 5.5 presents a specific description of decision making in a particular medical environment, the model appears to be transferable to other domains of emergency command. If we consider the five levels of thinking, then the processes at the sensorimotor level (1) may have most similarity to the basic level of pilots' decision making due to the hands-on, technical nature of the anaesthetist's task, which is not characteristic of

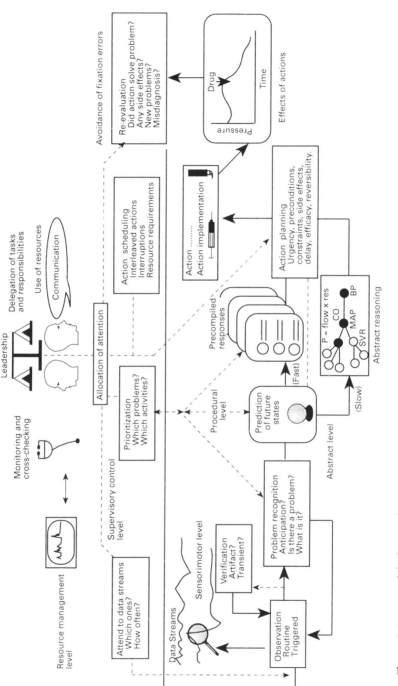

Figure 5.5 *A Model of Anaesthetists' Intraoperative Decision Making (Gaba, Fish and Howard 1994, figure 1.4). Reprinted with permission of Churchill Livingstone, New York.*

other commanders. However, the other four levels are relevant. The procedural level (2) operates on a recognition system activating precompiled responses. This is marked as a fast process and it is effectively an RPD method, with standard operating procedures and familiar routines being executed by an experienced anaesthesiologist. Where the decision maker does not know exactly what the problem is, but recognizes that there is serious risk to the patient and need for an immediate response, then a basic emergency protocol is used, which involves turning off all anaesthetics, maintaining 100% oxygenation and ensuring that pulse and blood pressure are acceptable:

"It should be implemented whenever a potentially catastrophic event is detected. Once underway, it can be modified or elements can be rescinded if necessary. Its use will allow you to retrieve more specific incident protocols, ... and to use your own knowledge and experience to produce an optimum plan for handling the underlying problem."

(Gaba, Fish and Howard 1994, p. 39)

This is typical of other domains such as aviation or high hazard industries, where there are non-specific emergency response procedures for non-diagnosed, high-risk situations.

The model also shows that abstract reasoning (3) may be employed, although Gaba, Fish and Howard (1994) say that they do not know how often this type of thinking is involved in anaesthesia crisis management. Their research from simulated crisis management indicates that most anaesthesiology decisions are of the procedural type, using the precompiled plans. As a consequence of this finding, they have developed a guidebook of optimum response procedures (hierarchical checklists) for 62 critical incidents. This is very like an aviation or industrial emergency procedures manual. The guide is not intended to be used as a "recipe book"; instead, it is designed to foster better decision making by "improving the recognition of and response to crises" (p. viii).

The fourth level is supervisory control, which concerns allocation of attention as well as prioritization, scheduling and coordination of actions. Similar mental processes will be required of an incident commander but he or she should not become involved in their execution, and this may be one reason why the incident commander has to mentally simulate what will happen if a certain instruction or plan is issued. In fact, Gaba, Fish and Howard (1994) note that while the mental simulation stage of the RPD model (Klein and Crandell 1995) would make sense to an anaesthetist, they have not observed this step in their research, and they suggest that this may be because the anaesthetist is able to execute actions in an incremental fashion, receiving immediate feedback, with the opportunity to alter the plan if necessary. Finally, the fifth level is resource management, which is basically teamwork or crew resource management (CRM) with particular focus on communication, delegation and coordination of activities (see Mackenzie et al. 1994). This would apply to any emergency response team.

Codified medical protocols for emergency decision making are increasingly being employed by the medical profession in the accident and emergency department for dealing with serious trauma cases. Again, anaesthetists are involved in this work but also general surgeons, orthopaedic surgeons, accident and emergency specialists, nursing and paramedical staff. One such system, which has been used in Britain since 1988, is Advanced Trauma Life Support (ATLS), which has been imported from the USA (Alexander and Proctor 1993). This technique is designed to improve the initial assessment and management of trauma patients in the first hour (the golden hour) of emergency care. It was instigated by an American orthopaedic surgeon, who crashed his private plane into a Nebraska cornfield, sustaining serious injuries to himself, killing his wife, and critically injuring three of his four children. The inadequacy of the emergency treatment they received shocked him (at one point he apparently had to get off his emergency trolley to assist in the resuscitation of one of his children) and as a result the ATLS programme of training was developed. ATLS is of interest because it is essentially a training mechanism for developing recognition-primed decision making.

ATLS is designed to assist medical decision makers working under conditions of high time pressure with a patient who has a serious chance of death. The situation is dynamic, the problem is likely to be ill-defined and not amenable to early diagnosis, and the patient may be able to provide little or no information. This is essentially a naturalistic decision making situation where conventional medical decision making based on a careful history and thoughtful review of alternative diagnoses is not possible. Treatment must be commenced without the doctors necessarily knowing the cause of the problem and continuing to diagnose as they go along. This is a somewhat alien concept in medicine, but is a common emergency response procedure in other domains, as discussed earlier. The system involves repeated cycles of situation assessment, stabilization, treatment and reassessment, concentrating on the primary causes of death to traumatized patients – airway, breathing and circulation, followed by disability or neurological status and environment or exposure considerations (ABCDE). What is of interest is how this system provides a valuable framework within which to undertake emergency response decisions. ATLS trainees are taught to prioritize by treating the greatest threat to life first, but always remembering that their actions must do no further harm to the patient. For doctors relatively inexperienced in dealing with serious trauma this is a highly stressful situation, and having a system to aid their decision making helps to prevent them "stalling" when faced with a sudden crisis. In their training they are told, "if things are not going well, stop, think, go back to ABC – airway, breathing, circulation – and you'll find a clue". They are taught to "retain a high index of suspicion" in their decision making approach and to remain vigilant in their repeated situation assessment, looking for signs and symptoms.

The aim, as in most NDM environments, is to reach a satisfactory solution. Therefore, when treating a patient with severe blood loss, the strategy is not to waste time seeking a perfect blood match but to use a blood type that is a satisfactory match and that will not cause further problems. There are both vertical and horizontal versions of ATLS, the former being employed by a single doctor, the latter being used by a team. Comments by doctors who have been trained in this technique demonstrate the importance of standard emergency protocols such as ATLS. One said, "I felt in control of the situation because I had a system I could use". I asked a class of ATLS students, "Which is the worst time period when you are dealing with these emergency admissions?". I assumed that they would reply, "the first five minutes", but in fact they said that the most stressful period is five to ten minutes into the situation, when they know that something is seriously wrong, but don't know what it is and have a sense that they are not controlling it. On reflection, this may also be the most difficult phase for other emergency commanders, although the time scale may be extended. The ATLS approach gives decision makers a degree of control and a sense of confidence in the knowledge that they are using a carefully developed system of emergency management.

The training is delivered in a three-day course consisting of lectures, demonstrations and practicals. These are designed to aid recognition-primed decision making so that the student can quickly deliver the correct response to a given pattern of symptoms (although, interestingly, no cognitive decision model is mentioned). At the end of the course students are formally assessed in a trauma centre simulator, where they are required to treat actors who have been trained to display certain symptoms and signs. Having watched a course undergoing their simulator assessments, there is no doubt that this is decision making under pressure, but it is also apparent that a codified procedure such as ATLS provides a valuable tool for the less experienced decision maker working under these highly stressful conditions.

Decision Making by Battle Commanders

This book is not about battle commanders; however, the military research agencies have been influential in the development of the naturalistic decision making theory. For instance, Klein's RPD work was partly funded by the US Army Research Institute. In this section a brief overview is presented showing how the NDM approach is being applied to decision making in the military domain, because this can help to expand our understanding of the strengths and weaknesses of the NDM approach and the RPD model in particular. In the United States, there is considerable military interest in naturalistic decision making, with the objectives of improving training methods and decision aids for warfare commanders. A US Marines Corps (1994) concept paper on command and control, written "to describe how we can reach and execute effective military decisions faster than an adversary, in any conflict setting on any scale", explicitly discusses Klein's RPD model, contrasting intuitive decision making (based on experience, judgement and focusing on situation assessment) with classical analytical decision making (based on reasoning and concentrating on comparison of multiple options), the latter being the method of decision making in which officers are trained. While the paper acknowledges that both styles have their merits, the view is taken that:

> "the intuitive approach clearly is more appropriate for the typically fluid, rapidly changing conditions of war, when time and uncertainty are critical factors. The analytical approach may be more useful in situations in which it is necessary to document or justify a decision (more likely to be the case in an environment of detailed control). Moreover, the analytical approach may have merit in situations in which commanders are inexperienced or in which they face never-before-experienced problems."
>
> (US Army Marine Corps 1994, p. 33)

This provides a further endorsement of the notion espoused earlier, that limited time and incident magnitude determine the necessity for an intuitive RPD style in experienced emergency commanders, especially at an operational or tactical level, whereas a strategic commander at a major incident or an inexperienced commander might be advised to use the more basic analytical approach.

There have been a number of empirical studies of military commanders' decision making using an NDM framework. Daniel Serfaty is particularly interested in capturing the nature of expertise in army commanders, saying, "Expertise has long been one of the most difficult concepts to capture and quantify in the field of decision making, planning, and problem solving" (Serfaty and Michel 1990, p. 257). They employ a four-level concept of expertise and decision-making, which could probably be usefully transferred to emergency commanders across professions:

1. Novice–novice: ruled-based decisions.
2. Expert–novice: has an enriched mental model but still rule-based.

3. Novice–expert: knowledge-based, recognizes when rules do not apply.
4. Expert–expert: knowledge-based, can develop new rules and solve complex problems.

In their first study, three retired US generals and three majors were interviewed and asked to discuss their decision making in relation to a fictional tactical scenario located in south-west Asia. In terms of decision making, Serfaty and Michel concluded that both classical and recognition-primed decision styles were being used by the commanders. The choice of style seemed to depend on the task, the available time, the stage of the operation (reactive or planning) and the experience of the decision maker. The process seems to be founded more on situation assessment and what they called "option evaluation", than on option generation and selection:

> "The process of initial generation of candidate options should not be an artificial process such as 'the best, the look-alike, and the throw-away', a habit often quoted by the interviewees as a way to satisfy the artificial doctrinal requirement to generate three options."
>
> (Serfaty and Michel 1990, p. 264)

They point out that often a single course of action will have many aspects and branches, which need to be fully considered using option evaluation – that is, a "what if?" strategy. The differences they found between novices and experts relate to the experts' sophisticated under-standing of uncertainty, their proactive information seeking driven by richer mental models of the tactical situation, and their tendency to seek disconfirming rather than confirming information. The expert commanders also store their memories and knowledge of tactical situations in the form of complex dynamic physical images or "war stories", which also appears to be a characteristic of expert emergency services commanders.

In a subsequent investigation, Serfaty et al. (in press) studied battle command decision making in 46 US Army officers ranging in rank from captain to general, all of whom had some tactical experience but whose expertise varied as a function of ability and/or experience. The officers were given a set of written materials and maps describing a battlefield scenario set in the Persian Gulf and were asked to develop tactical plans, written statements of intent and instructions for a number of tactical situations. The officers' level of expertise (from 1, novice to 7, expert) was judged independently by two or three "super experts" (i.e. retired three- and four-star generals recognized by the military community as experts in their field). There was general agreement as to the expertise ratings of the 46 officers, which ranged from novice to level 5; interestingly, years of military service did not predict the ratings of command decision expertise.

When the researchers examined the decision making behaviours of the officers, they found only partial support for Klein's theory, in that the lower expertise commanders were as likely to come up quickly with an initial course of action as the more expert commanders. (Serfaty et al. argue that the RPD model would predict that the experts would be more likely to do this than the novices, although they acknowledge that the design of their experiment may have produced this result.) However, they did find that the high-expertise commanders provided more detailed courses of action, with more contingencies, than the low expertise officers, which would be consistent with the RPD theory, and they suggest that perhaps the distinction is that experts can rapidly generate a better course of action than novices. They concluded that the expert decision makers build and use a more intricate mental model of the situation, and that they "see" more complexity in the situation and more things that could go wrong with their plan than do novices. (See Serfaty et al. (in press) for their model of command decision making.)

Military expertise was also investigated by Lipshitz and Ben Shaul (in press), who compared the decision making of expert and novice Israeli gunboat commanders using a computer-based sea-combat task. They found that experts undertook a more efficient information search, collected more information before making a decision, "read" the situation more accurately, and made fewer bad decisions. They believe that the RPD model provides a valuable framework for the description of expert decision processes, but they argue that the concepts of "schemata" and "mental models" need to be incorporated more explicitly into the situation awareness phase. The schemata are the stored templates of previous experiences which drive the search for information when the commander is faced with a new situation. The mental model is the picture in the head of the commander, which represents the available knowledge of the current state of events. The challenge for researchers is to discover how these schemata are developed as novices become experts, and what cues are used to create the mental model of the incident situation. (See also Lipshitz (1995) for an interesting analysis of decision making in the Desert Storm (Gulf War) operation.)

In a similar study of decision making in the British Army, Pascual et al. (1994) studied eight officers and seven NCOs who had varying degrees of experience in command and control operations headquarters tasks. Each subject took part in a training session followed by two scenarios (planning and dynamic) in a simulated HQ, which was equipped with maps, reference material, communications and support personnel. In the planning scenario the subject had to take decisions about resource planning and utilization under time pressure. In the dynamic scenario the subject was in command of a reserve demolition team in a screen force battle where friendly forces were under enemy harassment and the battle-field situation was changing rapidly. Analysis of video and audio record-ings, debriefs and observations indicated a predominance of a naturalistic decision strategy (87%), compared to classical (2%), hybrid (3%) and other strategies (8%). However, Pascual et al. pointed out that the scenario settings were familiar to the subjects and that if they had used a more novel setting (e.g. Bosnia or the Gulf) then they might have expected to see greater use of the classical analytic strategy. They endeavoured to match the decision making strategies with particular theoretical models, and found that Klein's RPD was the best match (60%), with another eight model types accounting for the remaining decisions. They concluded:

> "Although RPD-like decision making behaviour may indeed be easier to identify and/or code than other models, it is felt that the RPD model provides the most appropriate, accurate, and utilitarian concepts for describing a broad range of C^2 [command and control] decision making behaviour, particularly for those subjects with considerable military experi-ence."
>
> (Pascual and Henderson, in press)

They also discovered that the subjects rarely consulted the standard procedures manuals, such as the *Tactical Aide-Mémoire* or the *Staff Officers' Handbook*, because the inexperienced subjects did not know how to use them and the experienced subjects had developed their own personal *aides-mémoire*:

> "Although the SOPs [standard operating procedures] enable the principles underlying decision making to be proceduralized, they are perceived as too rigid and time consuming to be practically applied in time-pressured high workload operating environments. It is under these conditions that decision makers need to be trained to craft workable and effective solutions, often those previously learnt and applied by experienced colleagues."
>
> (Pascual and Henderson, in press)

In terms of expertise, they postulated a similar categorization to that of Serfaty and colleagues, which they called Complete Novice, Advanced Novice, Primitive Expert and Advanced Expert, and they argued that decision making support devices need to be designed to match the different decision strategies that are likely to be employed at these levels of expertise. Thus, novices tend to use methods of problem solving involving decomposition and analytical rule-based assessment, whereas the experts prefer a more holistic decision strategy based on situation assessment and the development of "satisfactory" decision solutions. Their work is now being used in the design of computer support tools for army commanders' decision making. One salient feature of this is derived from

Klein's RPD model – an emphasis on tools that will aid in the development and refinement of a single course of action, rather than forcing the commander to follow standard military doctrine, which advocates generating three alternatives and then choosing between them (i.e. the classical approach). Likewise, an RPD approach is being taken by American researchers who are designing tactical decision support systems for naval warfare commanders (Hutchins, in press, b).

Decision Making in an Offshore Platform Emergency

The research to date that has studied decision making in flight decks, firegrounds, medical emergencies and warfare zones has shown considerable support for the naturalistic decision approach, particularly Klein's RPD model. Very little research into naturalistic decision making appears to have been carried out with industrial managers who also may have to take decisions under pressure, with the exception of our own investigation of the offshore oil installation manager. This research programme was instigated in response to the public inquiry into the *Piper Alpha* disaster (Cullen 1990), which highlighted the emergency command responsibilities of offshore installation managers (OIMs) as an area of concern that the oil industry was directed to address. This section is a description of some preliminary work in this area to determine the decision making style used by these industrial managers (Flin, Slaven and Stewart, 1996) and it has particular relevance for managers of high hazard sites based onshore (e.g. nuclear or chemical) who will be required to manage an accident or crisis until the emergency services arrive.

The first step in investigating OIMs' decision making in an emergency was to review interview material collected in a study of the command and control of serious offshore incidents (Flin and Slaven 1994). The HSE Offshore Safety Division provided reports of 23 offshore incidents that were of a serious enough nature to be considered a potential crisis and that were not *sub judice*. With company approval, 16 of the OIMs involved agreed to be interviewed about seven incidents on production platforms and nine on drilling rigs. The main purpose of the interviews had been to discuss command experience and training, but as they had also covered the management of the incident, the material was re-examined to determine the characteristics of the OIMs' decision making. The following themes emerged:

- Experience
- Mental models
- Time pressure

- Preplanning
- Distributed decision making
- Organizational context.

Experience

One feature of NDM models is that decision makers have considerable experience of the domain in question. Does the OIM have sufficient expertise to engage in recognition-primed decision making? For the fireground commanders studied by Klein (1989), their decisions were based upon experience of many fires and rescues. Dealing with emergencies is a routine event for fire officers and police officers, and by the time they reach command positions they should have had considerable practice and feedback in high pressure decision situations. This is not the case for a manager, whose work, in the main, involves dealing with the day-to-day running of an industrial operation. Offshore emergencies are abnormal events for OIMs, but their lack of first-hand crisis management experience is to some extent compensated by their detailed knowledge of the risks they run (since these are calculated in their installation safety case), and by the fact that these hazards are far fewer than the range of risks that an emergency services commander will encounter. Moreover, the OIMs also have extensive knowledge of the installation itself (whereas fire and police commanders have limited information of the incident location), and in addition the OIMs are trained and well practised in the implementation of standard emergency procedures designed to deal with all anticipated threats to the installation. In terms of direct experience of emergency management, the OIMs may have more in common with commercial pilots or anaesthetists, rather than with the emergency services commanders. Thus, while the offshore managers do not have the depth or range of crisis decision making experience characteristic of an emergency services commander, they may have sufficient knowledge of their own domain and rehearsed procedures to enable them to use an NDM-type decision method rather than a classical analytic strategy.

Schemata and Mental Models

The idea of a "mental model" came from earlier research into thinking and reasoning, which postulated the necessity for internal mental representations of external objects, systems and concepts. See Johnson-Laird (1985) for a readable explanation. He highlighted the importance of Kenneth Craik's work on human ability to process information which was carried out in the early 1940s. Interestingly, one of Craik's examples has direct relevance to the present discussion:

"If the organism carries a 'small-scale model' of external reality and of its own possible actions within its head, it is able to try out various alternatives, conclude which is the best of them, react to future situations before they arise, utilize the knowledge of past events in dealing with the present and future, and in every way to react in a much fuller, safer, and more competent manner to the emergencies which face it."

(Craik 1943, p. 61)

Lipshitz and Ben Shaul (1996) argue that it is important to distinguish between the two kinds of mental representation used in recognition-primed decision making to process information: (i) stored knowledge or "schemata" and (ii) "mental models" of the current situation. There was some evidence that the OIMs were relying on both schemata (mental blueprints of what is already known – risk assessments, procedures, platform processes, previous incidents) and an evolving "mental model" of the state of the emergency. The schemata drive the search for information, which is then used to formulate the mental model. In other words, the OIMs use "old knowledge" about where the major hazards are, the stage of the drilling operation or where personnel will be located at a given time of day, to organize the search for the most important new information needed to assess the status and parameters of the emergency. One important schema (or set of schemata) is the site layout, in this case the platform or rig, its structure and functions. The fixed production platforms are particularly complex structures with drilling facilities, oil extraction and processing, subsea pipelines, power generation and utilities, hotel accommodation and a helicopter landing deck, all built on legs sitting on the seabed. The significant role of this prior knowledge was underlined by the OIMs, who emphasized the importance of knowing the installation geography, plant and processes. As one commented, "How can you expect to be able to commit emergency response teams in dangerous situations without a knowledge of the geography and technical hazards within an area?".

Ship knowledge is an important component of naval training, and more experienced damage control officers on the warships of the Royal Netherlands Navy have been shown to have better schemata (mental representations) of ship layout, which aided their decision making (Schraagen 1989, in press). Once an emergency occurs, the schemata are used to create an accurate mental model of the state of the incident area, to map the damage and to consider the implications of escalation for adjacent sectors. On an offshore platform this requires a mental image of subsea pipelines, connections to other installations and technical hazards, to know what pattern and severity of damage to predict, and what equipment and compartments would be affected, without having to search out technical drawings and diagrams. Those OIMs who had been involved in the construction, commissioning and hook-up of their installation said that they had the ability to form a three-dimensional mental picture of an incident site, even if this was physically impossible to see once the installation was operational. Two OIMs said that if they had had a better knowledge of their installation, the incident might not have happened or escalated to the level it did. Thus, it appeared that contextual knowledge stored as schemata (or blueprints) and a good mental model of the developing incident were integral parts of the OIMs' situation assessment during decision making.

Time Pressure

Several OIMs commented on the rapid pace of decision making required during the incident: "I probably made 100 decisions in a short space of time". The time pressure variable is elemental in the NDM situation and the decision maker's judgement of the time horizon is critical: "Situation assessment requires definition of the problem and assessment of risk level and time available to make the decision" (Orasanu and Fischer, in press). The OIMs felt that it was vitally important to be decisive in what might be a rapidly escalating situation. They also appreciated that in some instances, because of the time pressure, they would have to take a satisfactory rather than an optimal decision. In the words of one OIM, "minutely wrong decisions are better than no decisions at all". The decision maker's awareness that the aim is to reach a satisfactory rather than an optimal solution is characteristic of experts using recognition-primed decision making (Klein 1989).

Preplanning

Confidence in their own ability to manage an emergency appears to have been increased for those who had thought about possible eventualities during drills and exercises, and had previewed their options (cf. Craik 1943, quoted above). They said that they felt more comfortable with emergency procedures already worked out – whether formally or in their own minds – rather than having to think out possible courses of action and their implications during the event. This concept of preplanning to develop a workable knowledge base, and its resultant benefits on decision quality, appears throughout the NDM literature; the process is effectively the establishment of the necessary schemata for emergency response. Orasanu (1994a) found that one of the factors that distinguished between high and low performing airline cockpit crews was that the high performing crews spent the light workload phases of flight discussing what they would do in emergency situations. It seems reasonable to suggest that this type of thinking would involve a high degree of mental simulation of possible courses of action: the important point here is that through thinking about potential problems and eliminating inappropriate courses of action, the commander is preparing for similar problems in the future, with prethought solutions to call upon. However, the limitations of preplanning were also acknowledged; for one OIM, the existing emergency procedures did not cover the situation he faced and decisions had to be made on the spot. Another said, "The emergency you prepare for is never the one that happens". These comments illustrate the need for generalized emergency procedures and even creative decision making, as shown above in Orasanu's (1995b) model.

Distributed Decision Making: The Offshore/Onshore Interface

Like many other commanders, an OIM reports to more senior managers who are based onshore. In the event of a serious offshore incident, an onshore emergency response team is mustered in the company's shore base office, some of which have dedicated emergency control centres. This can create a distributed decision making situation, with onshore managers and specialists becoming involved. For some OIMs this had been helpful in preventing media interference, organizing evacuation helicopters, providing specialist knowledge and dealing with relatives' enquiries. Where the OIMs felt that the onshore/offshore interface caused problems was when the onshore managers failed to realize the severity of the situation, questioned the OIM's decisions, needlessly rearranged evacu-ation arrangements resulting in serious confusion, asked for information rather than giving it, or did not know enough about the installation. These behaviours were regarded by the OIMs as hindering their decision making, saying that at best they "ignored silly suggestions", but at worst "this uninformed interference could easily have resulted in the total loss of the platform". In one drilling incident, the OIM disregarded advice from his onshore management (not widely regarded as a career-enhancing strategy); his decision on the appropriate action to take was "too drastic for them but seemed to be the right thing to do and all on board relaxed when that decision was made". Two OIMs said that they had allowed themselves to be swayed by the opinions of others (onshore) and that they would rely on their own judgement in future. The interface of the decision approaches of commanders at different levels – operational, tactical and strategic – raises a number of interesting research issues. Moreover, when this is compounded by distributed decision making (where those involved in the decision making process are located apart, often by hundreds of miles) then the possibility of decision clashes begins to increase (see Chapter 6).

Organizational and Commercial Context

While it should be acknowledged that the UK operating and drilling companies have taken significant steps to emphasize safety before production, the organizational and commercial context for many decision makers in complex environments cannot be ignored. Three OIMs said that in the early stages of the incident, their decisions had been based on financial considerations (e.g. cost of downtime), but that their emphasis then switched to the safety of the personnel on board, whatever the cost. In the aviation industry there has been recent concern regarding pilots' perception of commercial pressures to make flight slots, labelled by safety experts as the "Hurry Up Syndrome" (McElhatton and Drew 1993), and Gaba (1994) talks openly of the "production" pressures that can influence the decision making of surgical teams. The possibility of decision makers being influenced by perceived (or misperceived) organizational priorities which conflict with safety needs to be openly addressed in both safety management and emergency response training (organizational factors are included as an NDM characteristic). It is also worth noting that nowadays emergency services commanders are not shielded from such pressures, and Murray's (1994b) fireground command model (Fig. 5.3) shows organizational considerations as an input in his model of decision making.

In essence, this examination of our interview material suggests that the offshore emergency is a typical NDM situation. The next question is: which decision making strategy or strategies are the OIMs using? There was some evidence that they might be using an RPD strategy, namely, their expertise, the reliance on schemata, mental models and prethought plans, with an emphasis on gathering information to make a situation assessment (achieving the big picture). However, our original interview protocol had not been designed to test this hypothesis and the elements of decision making revealed do not constitute a sufficient test of strategy use. A fundamental tenet of RPD is that on recognizing the problem from the situation assessment, a single course of action is recalled. From the interviews, we could tell that (i) the OIMs could be making decisions very quickly (hence limited time for option generation and evaluation) and (ii) their goal was a satisfactory rather than an optimal response, which weakens the case for a lengthy consideration of alternatives in order to find the most elegant, efficient and economic solution. As a precursor to a simulator-based research project, we have been examining the situation assessment and decision making skills of experienced OIMs.

In a pilot study (see Flin, Slaven and Stewart, 1996), a number of experienced OIMs were asked to describe the way in which they would deal with a hypothetical crisis scenario based on indications of a high-level gas leak. They were then asked to describe what actions they would take in order to manage the incident and what information they would require to formulate their plan. The OIMs were then interviewed about one or more of their decisions, using a version of the critical decision probes (Klein, Calderwood and McGregor 1989). After the interviews, the scenario transcripts were analysed using a coding scheme based upon the RPD model in order to identify statements that were indicative of situation assessment (goals, cues, expectancies, actions), mental simulation, story building or course of action generation. Of a total of 107 decision points 90% appeared to be of a single option type, possibly RPD or rule based. Preliminary analysis of the first six interviews presented little evidence of OIMs generating multiple options when faced with crisis decisions, and again they appeared to be seeking satisfactory rather than optimal solutions. When questioned about how he reached a particular decision, one OIM said, "in every real incident that I've been involved with it's been obvious what to do – to me at least.... I'm not seeking the perfect solution, I'm seeking something that works".

The majority of their decisions seem to be based upon recognition of a particular problem aspect, and the generation of a single course of action to deal with it drawn from their company's standard operating procedures. These seem to correspond to the pilots' condition–action rule decisions described by Orasanu and Fischer (in press). Observation of OIMs in exercises on their platforms and in simulators confirms their reliance on standard emergency response procedures, and we are now looking more carefully within one operating company at the percentage of decisions that are simply implementation of these "rules" as opposed to creative decisions (Skriver and Flin 1996). Orasanu and Fischer (in press) also identified another category of pilots' decisions, labelled "procedural management" decisions, in which standard operating procedures are applied in situations of recognized high risk but where the precise nature of the problem remains unclear. A very similar strategy is seen in the management of emergencies in other domains, such as medical trauma centres (as discussed above). This kind of decision making is also found in the early stages of an offshore emergency, where standard procedures such as stopping "hot-work" (e.g. welding), shutting down production or mustering personnel can be put into action before the problem has been fully identified. While it currently appears that experienced OIMs take crisis decisions without generating multiple options and assessing them in parallel, this does not necessarily mean that their decision making strate-gies are exactly in line with the RPD model. Nevertheless, we have used Klein's RPD model in training with OIMs and offshore control room operators and found that it appears to have good face validity (is regarded as a good description) for their own view of their decision making

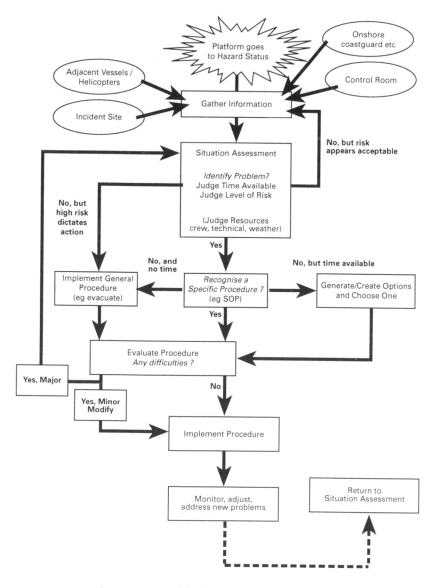

Figure 5.6 *Model of Emergency Decision Making.*

processes (Flin 1995b), although this does not prove its validity. Based on the interview material described above and our observations of OIMs handling simulated emergencies, a general model of emergency decision making, which includes an RPD-type component, is proposed (Figure 5.6).

As the figure shows, both recognition-primed type decisions (generally codified as standard operating procedures) and classical option comparison may be found. No distinction has been made between an SOP response and an RPD response that is not in the emergency manual, because we do not yet have the data to separate these modes. This diagram is in effect a simplified version of the Orasanu (1995b) taxonomy, with fewer decision modes evident. For example, the "go/no go" decision which would be taken in seconds by a pilot (e.g. aborting a take-off) is not shown (although this could be relevant for a control room operator in terms of shutting down production or a police commander in a firearms incident). Future research will enable us to test this model with the longer term objective of assisting the oil industry to tailor its OIM training and decision aids to fit naturalistic decision making styles.

As this section has illustrated, there is now considerable interest in the subject of incident commanders' decision making across a range of very different work environments. The naturalistic decision research has made some significant advances in this field, particularly Gary Klein's seminal work on recognition-primed decision making, which has achieved universal currency as the dominant model. There is general agreement among researchers and practitioners that the NDM approach is likely to be fruitful in the search for a better understanding of decision making in high-pressure domains. Nevertheless, there is still a need for fundamental cognitive research to unravel the mechanics of these fast decision processes. The implications of the naturalistic decision research for the selection and training of incident commanders is discussed in Chapter 7. The final section of this chapter returns to the question of stress, and assesses the effect of stress on classical and recognition-primed decision making.

STRESS AND DECISION MAKING

The causes and effects of stress for incident commanders were reviewed in Chapter 4. This final section considers the effects of stress on decision making in the light of the recent research into command decision making outlined above. Given the range of factors that are believed to be causes of stress (stressors) for incident commanders, e.g. dynamic events, time pressure, high risk, inadequate information (see Figure 4.3), it seems likely that any resulting physical or psychological effects will have some impact on their decision making ability. So how does stress affect decision making?

The prevailing view until very recently has been that stress can produce an impressive catalogue of debilitating effects on decision making performance. Typical reported problems are narrowing of attention ("tunnel vision"), lack of concentration, overreliance on heuristics and rules of thumb, and susceptibility to decision biases (see Svenson and Maule 1993). However, some of the research that has supported such conclusions may have limited application to emergency management. For example, a study entitled "The harassed decision maker" (Wright 1974), which initially looks promising, turns out to be based on students imagining they were choosing a car. Another, entitled "Decision making under stress" (Kienan 1987), is again students, this time doing a multiple-choice computer task, who think they might be given an electric shock. While laboratory experiments do have a significant role to play in the research process and simulating stress presents ethical problems for psychologists, generalizing from results such as these to an experienced incident commander facing a major incident presents something of a credibility gap.

The question of stress and decision making has not been investigated systematically for emergency services commanders, and little that is not anecdotal has been written on the topic. Weisaeth (1987), in his chapter on leader stress during accidents and crises, argues that beyond a moderate level of stress, the leader has a reduced ability to solve complex problems, due to a narrowing of attention, stereotyping of thought processes, and consideration of fewer alternative solutions to the problem than normal. However, Weisaeth (1994) suggests that leaders in emergencies use a classical analytic style of decision making, which he describes as: (i) recognizing and identifying the problem, (ii) collecting information, (iii) formulating alternative solutions and their consequences, (iv) choosing between alternatives and (v) implementing the solution. Klein agrees that this rigorous analytic style of decision making is likely to be affected by stress and that there is good evidence to support this claim. But, more controversially, he goes on to propose that the recognition-based style of decision making used by experienced commanders is far less susceptible to the damaging effects of incident stressors, such as time pressure, than the prescriptive analytic strategies:

> "If you are a Commanding Officer faced with a difficult situation, and you rapidly size up the situation and see what to do, the time pressure may not be a factor. On the other hand, if you try to go through a process of identifying all the possible courses of action, and the most important dimensions for evaluating these, and the appropriate weights, and if you then rate each option on each dimension, but are interrupted in the middle of all this by the need to decide NOW!, before you have finished your deliberations, you will be unable to respond. The prescriptive decision strategies are of limited relevance in most operational settings."
>
> (Klein, in press)

Klein (1996) proposes that the prescriptive strategies that are ideal for many other kinds of decisions (such as high-level policy planning) are particularly ill-suited to situations with very limited time available, missing and ambiguous information, frequent interruptions and changing goals. Thus, it is hardly surprising that experts use the RPD strategy. Having said that, he does accept that in more complex situations, requiring extensive situation assessment or option evaluation, stress can still affect these cognitive tasks (RPD, levels 2 and 3 in Figure 5.1). Dismissing the arguments for stress increasing experienced decision makers' susceptibility to decision biases (Tversky and Kahneman 1974) and hypervigilance (Janis and Mann 1977), he advocates that expert decision makers' reactions to stressors can in fact be regarded as adaptive rather than dysfunctional. For example, adaptive strategies that have been observed include more selective use of information, use of simpler strategies, increased conservatism, readiness to take action, and aiming for a satisfactory rather than an optimal solution. In a similar vein, Wickens et al. (1993) also suggested that pilots using RPD-type decision making might show a different pattern of reactions to stress:

> "The results highlight the emerging distinction between what Klein (1989) has referred to as recognition-primed decisions (direct long-term memory retrieval) and the more algorithmic form of decision making that is conventionally studied in the laboratory. To the extent that distinct and different stress effects are predicted by these two types, as suggested by the data reported here, then care must be taken in over-generalizing conclusions regarding the influence of stress on decision making."
>
> (p. 288)

More research needs to be carried out to check these propositions, but there are different training implications for the teaching of stress management depending on which decision method is being used. Our experience that OIMs and emergency services commanders report that they were not aware of stress while managing an incident provides some support for the notion that the intuitive recognitional, or rule-based, strategies they are using are fairly resistant to the prevailing stressors.

One of the cornerstones of stress management is good teamwork, and the following chapter looks at group behaviour in the incident command team.

6
Incident Command Teams

"Many of the senior group leaders had no idea which emergency plan group they belonged to, or what functions they were supposed to carry out."
(Norwegian Public Reports 1991)

Incident commanders may have ultimate responsibility for an operation but they rarely act alone; they take decisions in conjunction with a supporting command team, often based in some kind of emergency control centre. In the words of NASA Crew Factors psychologist Judith Orasanu (1994b), "Effective leaders do not function as 'lone rangers'" (p. 9). The job of an incident command group is to gather and process information in order to aid the commander's decisions to direct, coordinate and monitor the actions of the crews engaged in emergency response, damage control, rescue and recovery duties. Therefore, an important facet of the incident commander's remit is to effectively manage the command team, to ensure that they execute their duties, share an understanding of the evolving incident and are working on the same plan towards common goals. This chapter considers the relevant research into emergency command teams, with particular attention to the studies of real teams making decisions under the pressures of time and high risk, such as the TADMUS (tactical decision making under stress) project, which has focused on US naval teams. The concepts of shared mental models and distributed decision making are introduced. Finally, the aviation industry's commitment to team skills in the form of crew resource management (CRM) is described, because this can be adapted for emergency command team training beyond the flight deck.

FACTORS INFLUENCING TEAM PERFORMANCE

Teams of one kind or another are to be found throughout modern organizations, and there is an extensive literature on how teams should be managed to achieve maximum performance on the sports field, in the military, in industry, in operating theatres, in flight decks and in boardrooms (Hackman 1990; West 1995). While there has been a century of psychological experiments on group behaviour, it should be noted that not all groups are teams, thus limiting the application of much of the laboratory-based research. A team can be defined as:

> "a distinguishable set of two or more people who interact, dynamically, interdependently, and adaptively toward a common and valued goal/ objective/mission, who have each been assigned specific roles or functions to perform, and who have a limited life-span of membership."
>
> (Salas et al. 1992, p. 4)

Using this definition to search the literature, it appears that there has been significantly less research into team performance, and few studies of teams working in situations of time pressure and high risk. Perhaps surprisingly, given the reliance of the emergency services on teamwork, there has been hardly any research into how their incident command teams function. David Wynne (1995), an assistant chief officer at Hereford and Worcester Fire Brigade, who has studied the potential application of airline CRM training for the fire service, comments:

> "The Fire Service is highly dependent upon teams to fulfil its statutory duties. To be effective the Service needs to know how well teams perform. ... There has, however, been very little research carried out upon fire command teams operating in natural settings."
>
> (p. 2)

The importance of teamwork in both industrial and military settings has been illustrated by a number of high profile accidents in complex systems where poor teamwork was implicated as a contributing factor. Rouse, Cannon-Bowers and Salas (1992) examined the accident reports for five such incidents: the USS *Vincennes* shooting down of a commercial airliner, the Three Mile Island nuclear plant accident, the collision between the Pan Am and KLM planes at Tenerife, the Flixborough chemical plant explosion and the Pan Am 401 crash in Miami. They identified three main teamwork problems:

1. Roles not clearly defined, resulting in tasks falling through the cracks.
2. A lack of explicit coordination, therefore goals not balanced appropriately.
3. Miscommunication problems.

Similar analyses of aircraft accidents had already revealed that poor crew judgement and decision making were contributory causes to 47% of accidents between 1983 and 1987 (NTSB 1991). A subsequent safety study (NTSB 1994) of crew errors in 37 accidents between 1978 and 1990 found that the most common problem was crews making procedural errors or tactical decision errors. Interestingly, they also found that in 31 out of 37 cases, there were secondary errors in which one crew member (usually the co-pilot) failed to detect and challenge another's error (usually the captain's). Orasanu (1994b) says, "The influence of role, status, and ambiguity of a dynamically deteriorating situation are relevant here. Our analyses of crew performance in simulators support these findings" (p. 7). Such investigations encouraged the development of psychological research programmes into teams working in naturalistic decision making environments characterized by high stakes, time pressure and dynamic problems (e.g. Foushee and Helmreich 1988; Guzzo and Salas 1995; Orasanu 1990; Swezey and Salas 1992; Zsambok, in press).

This chapter deals with one such natural work environment, namely, incident command teams who are at or near the scene of the event and who have responsibility for managing the operational response. For the emergency services, this would be commanders at an operational or tactical level and their support staff who establish an on-scene command centre or incident control point (see Figure 1.2). These teams usually have five or more participants, depending on the services involved and the incident in question. Similar management teams are used in ship control centres, public venues, entertainment complexes and in industry to coordinate on-site and off-site emergency response. For example, in the nuclear industry, "The operator's emergency response organisation would be directed by the Site Emergency Controller who would be located in the emergency control centre on the site and would be supported by a team of engineers, scientists and administrative staff" (HSE 1994b, p. 15). A typical emergency command centre team for an offshore oil platform is displayed in Figure 6.1, with the external communication links shown in Figure 6.2. The on-board emergency response organization consists not only of the incident commander and his or her team in the emergency command centre (ECC), but also an on-scene commander at the site of the damage, as well as fire teams, rescue teams and first aid teams. The on-site teams report via phone and personal radio into the ECC, where information exchange and a record of the situation assessment are facilitated by personnel updating whiteboards and time/action logs, regular team time-out briefings and updates, plus open communication between ECC team members. All of this information is used by the OIM for assessment and ongoing monitoring of the situation as part of his or her decision making process.

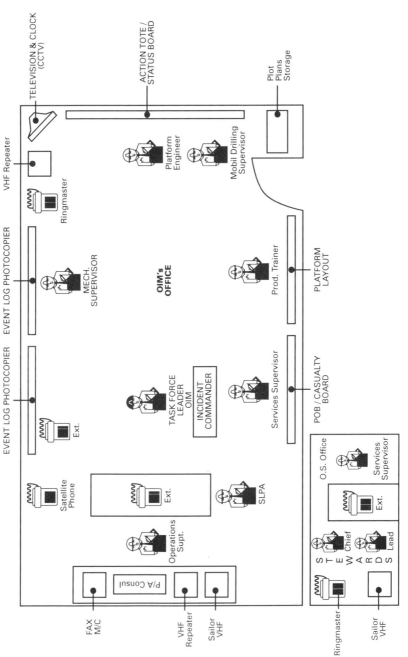

Figure 6.1 *Offshore Oil Platform Emergency Command Centre Team. Reprinted with permission of Mobil North Sea Ltd.*

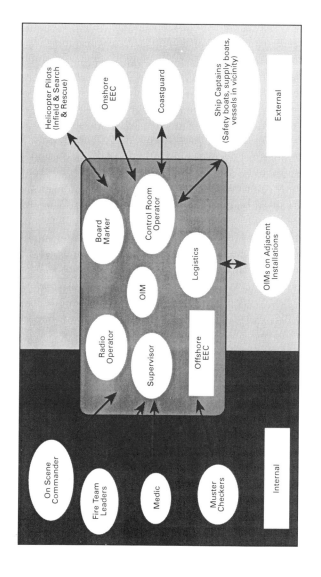

Figure 6.2 *Offshore Emergency Command Centre: Communication Flow.*

If we consider an emergency command team of this type, which could also be found in an onshore industrial organization, such as a chemical or nuclear plant site, or an emergency services incident command post, then we can examine the factors that influence the performance of such teams. There are innumerable lists of the variables that determine effective teamwork across a range of operational environments, and these can be used to create a model of command team performance in emergencies. This framework has not been empirically evaluated and it is only intended as an illustration of the complexity encountered when analysing team performance. For an incident command team, the critical performance measure would be the quality (e.g. speed, accuracy) of their decision making *en route* to a successful resolution of the situation.

The model of command team performance shown in Figure 6.3 is based on general models of group behaviour (e.g. McGrath 1984), as well as more precise analyses of team decision making (Klein 1995; Orasanu 1994a; Salas, Cannon-Bowers and Blickensderfer 1995; Zsambok, in press), which will be discussed below. There are four principal elements:

1. The input factors. These include: the leader's characteristics, the individual team members' characteristics and the structure and experience of the team as a whole. In many organizational settings, the group leader or commander does not have the luxury of hand picking the team members and therefore has to work with the team provided, making individual members' team skills a critical variable.
2. The context in which the team is operating must also be considered, for example, the organizational culture ("the way we do things around here") and the particular task demands and circumstances of the emergency.
3. The group processes or dynamics (throughput); that is, the manner and style of team working, such as how they communicate, the coordination of activities, their method of decision making, how they achieve a shared picture of events, the support and cooperation among team members.
4. The output variables, including the team's performance (e.g. effectiveness, speed, number of errors), individual members' performance, the incident commander's performance and the degree of job satisfaction and stress experienced during the operation.

Studies of team performance attempt to measure all four sets of variables, although rarely all at once, given the complexity of their interaction. Leadership characteristics and commanders' decision making skills have been discussed in earlier chapters, and the following section concentrates on the latest research into team decision making, because this is the

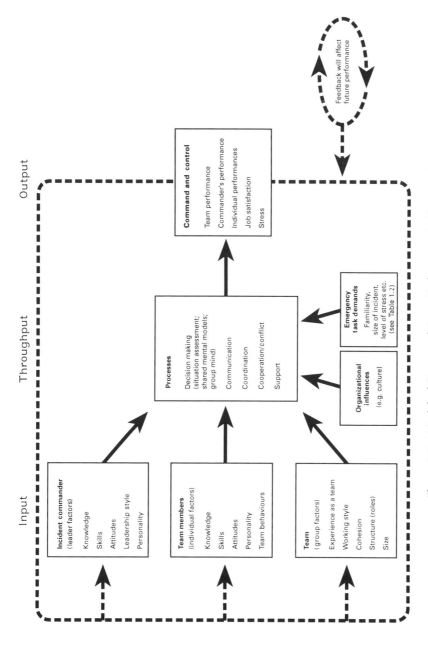

Figure 6.3 *Model of Command Team Performance in Emergencies.*

central function of an emergency command centre team. The material has been drawn from studies of teams functioning in high pressure environments, such as military command centres, nuclear plant control rooms, operating theatres and flight decks. As in the previous chapter, the emphasis is on research that has been carried out in naturalistic environments, typically in simulators, because emergencies in the real world are often life threatening, and for obvious reasons do not lend themselves to re-enactment or participant observation.

RESEARCH INTO TEAM PERFORMANCE

To my knowledge, there have been no major empirical research studies of team performance by incident command teams in industry or the emergency services. Nevertheless, there are data available from scientific investigations into teams making decisions under pressure that have direct relevance to the incident command situation. This section briefly outlines the work from three research programmes based in the United States, all of which are concerned with team performance, especially decision making in demanding environments:

1. "Dream teams"
2. Advanced team decision making
3. Crew factors.

While most of the work reviewed is from the military or aviation arena, it has general applicability to emergency commanders across occupations. This claim has been reinforced by the feedback we received from industrial managers, police officers, fire service officers, anaesthetists, and helicopter pilots, when this research was presented at a series of conferences and seminars we held in Aberdeen with leading American researchers presenting their findings (Kaempf 1992; Klein 1995; Orasanu 1994b; Salas and Cannon-Bowers 1995).

"Dream teams"

One of the most influential research groups in this area is based at the Training Systems Division of the US Naval Air Warfare Center in Orlando, Florida. Senior research psychologists Dr Eduardo Salas and Dr Jan Cannon-Bowers (1993) have conducted investigations with more than 300 navy teams, using both laboratory experiments and detailed observations and performance ratings of real teams in command and control centres and cockpits. They concluded that high performance teams – dream teams – are made, not born, and have the following characteristics:

Basics:

- Individual task proficiency
- Clear concise communication
- Task motivation
- Collective orientation
- Shared goal and mission.

In order to have a team of basic effectiveness, team members must be individually competent not only at their own tasks but must also have the necessary teamworking skills, such as being able to communicate clearly. The group need to feel like a team, to be motivated to perform well and to have a clear idea of the team's objectives. These are the minimum requirements for an effective team, but for enhanced performance the following are also required:

Advanced:

- Shared understanding of the task
- Shared understanding of other team members' responsibilities
- Team leadership
- Collective efficacy (sense of "teamness")
- Anticipation: "getting ahead of the power curve"
- Flexibility: (i) adjust allocation of resources to fit task; (ii) alter strategies to suit task (recognize cues)
- Efficient implicit communication (aware of each other's needs)
- Monitor own performance (self-correcting).

The analysis of team functioning by Salas and Cannon-Bowers (1995) shows that to achieve superior performance, teams also need to have a very clear understanding not only of the overall task, but also of each other's roles and responsibilities; they can anticipate each other's needs. The psychologists use the example of the "blind pass" in basketball to illustrate this, where players exhibit supreme team coordination without explicit communication. Leadership is important, and the leader must enable the team to think ahead (rather than be chasing the situation). In the words of a jet pilot, "If you know where you are now, it's too late because you were there five miles ago". The high performance teams monitor their own performance and remain self-critical, correcting and adjusting their methods of working as necessary. These findings have implications for staffing, job design and team training in the form of cross-job training, teamwork skills, team leadership, guided practice, stress exposure training and mental model training (i.e. helping teams to build and share a common picture of the situation). (See Swezey and Salas 1992; Cannon-Bowers et al. 1995, for techniques used to train team competencies.)

More recent work has emphasized an important distinction between "taskwork" behaviours (specific duties or tasks) and a set of independent "teamwork" behaviours, which are the skills of being an effective team member (Salas et al. 1995). These teamwork skills have become the focus of interest, with various attempts being made to define and categorize them with a view to developing better measures of team performance. Cannon-Bowers et al. (1995) have recently reviewed these studies and produced a useful synthesis, which identifies the following eight key dimensions of teamwork skills found in a number of operational settings:

- adaptability
- shared situational awareness
- performance monitoring and feedback
- leadership/team management
- interpersonal relations
- coordination
- communication
- decision making.

Appropriate subskills are also shown for each dimension (see Cannon-Bowers et al. 1995, table 10.1). Most of these team skills are contingent on team members having a good mental model of each other's roles and responsibilities, operating procedures and common goals. This concept of a shared team mind will be returned to below.

One of the strengths of this research programme is the concentration on training evaluation and performance measurement. The investigators emphasize that processes need to be assessed as well as outcomes:

> "This is an important, but often overlooked distinction. While it is important to measure the outcomes of team effort, it is equally important to understand the specific behaviour that led to those outcomes."
>
> (Salas et al. 1995, p. 94)

This notion has led to the development of behavioural observation scales to rate the frequency of the critical teamwork behaviours outlined above, as well as assessing overall outcomes. For fuller descriptions of how to train, manage and measure team performance, see McIntyre and Salas (1995), Cannon-Bowers and Salas (in press) and Salas, Cannon-Bowers and Johnston (in press).

Advanced Team Decision Making

Dr Caroline Zsambok and her colleagues at Klein Associates were sponsored by the US Army Research Institute to develop a model of Advanced Team Decision Making (ATDM). The aim of their project was to develop a theory-based training programme for senior officers, which would enable them to achieve more effective strategic team decision making (Klein, Zsambok and Thordsen 1993; Zsambok et al. 1992). Their observations of strategic decision making teams (military, aviation, fire command) led to the identification of 13 key behaviours, which they believe are essential to high-level team performance, in terms of both teamwork and taskwork demands, with an outcome of better, faster, more effective plans, decisions and reactions (Klein 1995). These are organized into a framework of four main components, as shown in Table 6.1.

This ATDM taxonomy has been developed into a training technique and an assessment scheme. Preliminary studies with students engaged in strategic decision making exercises at the US Air Force Institute of Technology and the Industrial College of the Armed Forces have shown significant improvements in team performance in groups using the model compared to control groups (Klein 1995). There is considerable overlap between the team skills behaviours identified in this model and those in the work of Salas and colleagues described above, and this emerging consensus should enable future research to adopt a common foundation, which will allow a more rigorous comparison of the essential team skills in different settings (Zsambok, in press). While observations of emergency services and industrial command teams lead me to believe that these models are adaptable, I have no evidence to prove this and the next stage

Table 6.1 *Advanced Team Decision Making (Klein 1995)*

Team resources:	How good are team members?
	Are they still struggling with basic procedures?
Team identity:	Does everyone know who does what?
	Is anyone "out of it"?
	Do people help each other out?
	Is anyone "micromanaging"?
Team self-management:	Is the leader competent?
	Do they spot and correct problems?
Team thinking:	Are they headed for the same goals?
	Does everyone have the same picture?
	Are they behind the power curve?
	Do they get paralysed by uncertainty?

of our research is to test this, using the assessment protocols derived from these models. A recent study by Bonney (1995) with London Fire Brigade teams using the ATDM model does suggest that there may indeed be useful applications within the emergency services.

Crew Factors Research

An internationally acclaimed programme of team research has been undertaken by NASA to examine crew performance on the flight deck. Since the late 1970s, investigations into commercial aircraft accidents have highlighted the crucial role of teamwork in the cockpit. Helmreich and Foushee (1993), in a review of this research, explained that there are a number of central issues regarding flight crew group processes:

1. The formation of a cohesive team from a group of strangers (in the large airlines pilots rarely fly with the same crews).
2. Workload management and delegation.
3. Methods of integrating ambiguous and incomplete data to reach optimum decisions.
4. The effects of stress induced by fatigue, emergencies or personal experiences on team communications and operations.
5. The nature of ineffective and effective leadership in flight crews.

As these issues are applicable to many incident command teams, the most relevant findings from the flight crew simulator studies are described below.

In one of the earliest experiments (Ruffell Smith 1979), 18 crews "flew" in a Boeing 747 simulator from Washington to New York, then on to London. They were presented with an oil pressure problem and later a hydraulic failure, complicated instructions from air traffic control, bad weather and a cabin crew member who repeatedly asked for information and assistance when they had a high workload. The findings showed marked differences in crews' ability to deal with this scenario, some performing well and others committing serious errors:

> "The primary conclusion drawn from the study was that most problems and errors were induced by breakdowns in crew coordination rather than by deficits in technical knowledge and skills. For example, many errors occurred when individuals performing a task were interrupted by demands from other crew members or were overloaded with a variety of tasks requiring immediate action. In other cases poor leadership was evident and resulted in a failure to exchange critical information in a timely manner."
>
> (Helmreich and Foushee 1993, p. 17)

These are not problems unique to teams on flight decks. Harrington and Gaddy (1993), discussing nuclear power plant control room crews responding to emergencies, say "Numerous simulated scenarios have been observed in which one crew member had valuable information that was not communicated for one reason or another" (p. 3).

Subsequent NASA studies (e.g. Orasanu 1990) that analysed voice records from simulator studies confirmed the importance of team communication; gave flight crews who communicated more, and with more command and acknowledgement statements, performed better (as judged by expert pilots). Communication in the cockpit is used to share information, direct actions, reflect thoughts and provide emotional support. Captains of high performing crews were found to be more explicit in stating their goals, plans and strategies, making predictions or warnings, and providing explanations. These captains were also more likely to accept suggestions by first officers than the captains of low performance crews, who were more likely to ignore them. In another study, it was found that more effective first officers demonstrated higher levels of inquiry and assertion. Under conditions of high workload, the better crews' communications became more selective; they talked less to each other, thus reducing unnecessary load on attention and mental resources (see Orasanu 1994a for an overview).

The better flight crews spent time during normal conditions on long flights working on contingency planning and thinking ahead. Consequently, in an emergency they were able to quickly reassess their allocation of resources, recognizing critical cues in their environment and adjusting their strategies accordingly. They also monitored their own performance, engaged in self-correcting behaviours and were supportive to other team members. Good crews engage in a thorough situation assessment, paying particular attention to the dimensions of time and risk, and they can match their decision making strategies to the demands of the situation. Orasanu and Fischer (in press) summarized the generalized strategies that characterized higher performing crews as follows:

"1. They monitored the environment closely and appreciated the significance of cues that signalled a problem;
2. They used more information in making decisions and if necessary they manipulated the situation to obtain additional information in order to make a decision;
3. They adapted their strategies to the requirements of the situation, demonstrating a flexible repertoire;
4. They planned for contingencies and kept their options open when possible;
5. They did not overestimate their own capabilities or the resources available to them;

6. They appreciated the complexity of decision situations and managed their workload to cope with it."

(p. 6)

The crew factors research from the aviation psychologists on effective crew performance has implications for crews working in many other domains: the six characteristics quoted above could apply to teams in an incident command post, a ship control centre, an operating theatre or an industrial control room. The programme of aviation psychology research from NASA and other laboratories has contributed to the current programmes of human factors training for pilots, in the form of crew resource management (see below).

SHARED MENTAL MODELS: TEAM MIND

One of the most influential concepts to emerge from flight crew and military team research has been that of the "group mind" – team members holding a shared mental model of their functioning or of the presenting problem. Mental models have been defined as "the mechanisms whereby humans generate descriptions of system purpose and form, explanations of system functioning and observed system states, and predictions of future system states" (Rouse and Morris 1986, p. 351). These models are regarded as a mechanism by which teams develop the explanations and expectations that underpin the coordination required for superior performance (Rouse, Cannon-Bowers and Salas 1992). The term "shared mental model" has been used interchangeably in the literature to refer to different kinds of team knowledge, often unsupported by any empirical evidence (for a recent review and attempted synthesis, see Klimoski and Mohammed 1994). For example, Cannon-Bowers and Salas (1990) proposed that effective teams had a "shared mental model" of the task in hand, and of team members' knowledge, skill, attitudes and roles. They later espoused the view that several different mental models are likely to be required, such as of equipment, of the team and of the task (Cannon-Bowers, Salas and Converse 1993). Orasanu (1990, 1994a) found that flight deck crews operating on the same shared mental model of a developing incident and of the current response plan (goals, cues, strategies and roles) performed better in emergencies. She stated that this mental model "is not to be confused with shared background knowledge about the crew's work domain, which is simply a common baseline" (p. 4). In a subsequent article, Orasanu and Salas (1993) refer to "shared mental models" of the team members' knowledge, skill, anticipated behaviours and needs, and "shared problem models" of the specific situation or emergency.

Thus (and as discussed earlier in the context of individual decision making), it is helpful to distinguish between (i) the mental representation of the team's personnel, duties and standard operating procedures, and (ii) the mental model of a given incident or emergency scenario. The former stored models can be thought of as schemata, and the new internal conceptions of the situation or problem as the mental models (Lipshitz and Ben Shaul in press). There is no doubt that both mental representations are critical to effective team functioning. The development and maintenance of the shared schema (blueprint) of team roles and tasks is achieved through training and job experience, and this enables the team to coordinate their activities implicitly (i.e. without explicit communication), particularly when working under pressure. In an emergency, the mental model of the current situation is created and shared within the team by timely and explicit communications, especially the use of feedback to ensure closed-loop communication. A shared mental model of the problem would be needed if teams operating in high pressure environments were using a recognition-primed decision strategy (see Chapter 5), and there is some evidence for this. Klein and Thordsen (1989), examining decision making in military command and control, crisis management, firefighting and cockpit crews, found that the team strategy was to assess and classify the situation they faced in order to recall the appropriate course of action, rather than using an option generation and comparison decision strategy. The notion of team situation awareness (Salas et al. 1995) would have to be incorporated into a recognition-primed decision strategy, and this would be an important element of the shared mental model of the problem.

Both Cannon-Bowers, Salas and Converse (1993) and Orasanu (1994a) voice a note of caution in relation to the team holding a shared mental model or having "one mind": namely, the risk of the group maintaining the wrong picture of the situation. They advise critical review and the encouragement of "devil's advocates" within the group. For example, Janis (1972) identified a pattern of group behaviour, which he called "groupthink", that can occur when consensus and group harmony begin to override the group's ability to appraise its actions critically and to consider alternative courses of action. Another problem (discussed above) is when the group members uncritically accede to the leader's commands and lack the assertiveness to challenge the leader's stated view of events. In such circumstances the drive to share a single mental model, if this is done uncritically, would be more of a liability than an asset.

If we apply this concept of shared mental model of the emergency to the incident command team, then the basic premise appears to be intuitively appealing. However, Orasanu's work at NASA is based on small crews of two or three pilots on a flight deck with a single external communication channel to air traffic control. Our observations and debriefing of offshore oil industry emergency control centre (ECC) teams indicated that the shared mental model concept (in terms of all team members having isomorphic models) was unworkable due to the size of the ECC team (5–9), the multidimensionality of the problem and the multiplicity of communication channels (see Figure 6.2).

Instead, it appeared that what is necessary in this type of command situation is to identify which players need "the big picture". Not all members of the ECC team need to have this overview because they need to concentrate on maintaining a current and accurate mental representation of the present and future states of their own area of responsibility (e.g. status of casualties, fire teams, incoming helicopters, adjacent shipping). Certainly, the incident commander (OIM), the deputy OIM (who will have to take command if the OIM is incapacitated, but who may be acting as on-scene commander and remote from the ECC), and the board marker who is logging the incident all need a high degree of overlap of their mental models. This would be in terms of what has happened (initiating incident, damage status, injuries/fatalities), the current position (deployment of fire and rescue teams; the status of damage control operations; evacuation options relating to lifeboat availability, helicopter and ship positions; the muster count; the integrity status of plant and structure; the weather and sea conditions) and the plan of action. A hydrocarbon production installation is a very large, complex structure – there could be 300 people on board – and a marine rescue operation is a multifaceted operation. Hence, no single individual can hold all the information necessary for effective emergency response; rather, the ECC team need to know who is holding which details and who needs what information. This requirement appears to reflect Wegner's (1987) concept of transactive memory systems and group mind. According to Orasanu and Salas (1993), who apply this to the notion of shared team models:

> "The critical components include labels that signify particular information and knowledge about which group member has what information. Transactive memory results in expansion of personal memory through interdependence on other members of the group. The concept does not mean that everyone shares all the stored knowledge, but that they share knowledge of the labels (which may be idiosyncratic to the group) and knowledge of who possesses specialized information."
>
> (p. 333)

This demands a considerable degree of shared role understanding, as well as partially shared (or overlapping) mental models (Cannon-Bowers et al. 1995). Our experience working with ECC teams (see below) is that valuable exercises and group discussions can be built round the questions,

"Who needs the big picture?" and "Who holds what information?". If questionnaires can be introduced during training scenarios during "time-outs" or "situation reports", then one has the possibility of assessing the various mental models being held by team members and the extent to which they overlap or otherwise. Analysis of team communications during real and simulated incidents can also enable researchers to estimate the decision making process and the use of shared models (see Rogalski and Samurcay 1993).

The shared mental model concept is being used widely by researchers and trainers working with military teams and aviation crews in North America. We have used the idea with emergency command teams from the offshore oil industry, and it is likely to have similar application for incident command teams in the emergency services, where it may be a valuable means of examining shared situational understanding between agencies. However, while the concept has general appeal, we actually know very little about what form these "models" take, what information they contain, how they are developed and why they may provide a mechanism for enhancing team decision making. A full examination of such issues is beyond the scope of this volume; for further discussion see Cannon-Bowers, Salas and Converse (1993), Klimoski and Mohammed (1994) and Orasanu (1994a).

DISTRIBUTED DECISION MAKING

Incident command teams typically form part of a larger network of decision makers; for example, at a major incident, the emergency services will have operational, tactical and even strategic groups involved. For offshore oil installations, there are both onshore and offshore emergency control centres, and industrial sites such as nuclear plants have on-site as well as off-site emergency control centres. Pilots take decisions in conjunction with air traffic controllers, who have a critical role to play in many types of aviation emergency (see, for example, Haynes 1992). Brunacini (1985) says of the fireground:

> "Complex scenarios present widespread and dynamic (always changing) settings which absolutely defy the capacity for on-site appraisal by one person. Decentralized units and sectors must be used as information centres. No amount of road work will enable you to run fast enough or far enough to keep yourself informed."
>
> (p. 49)

In all these cases, those involved in the decision making process are not located together as a group; they may be miles (even hundreds of miles) apart. What do we know of this aspect of team working known as distributed decision making?

Brehmer (1991a) distinguishes group decision making from distributed decision making by indicating that in the latter the problem is to achieve coordination among participants who have to work together towards a common goal in a dynamic environment, where each has a limited picture of the problem as a whole. In his words, "each decision maker is looking at the problem through his or her own limited window" (Brehmer 1996, p. 30), and no one has a "window" that allows him or her to see the whole problem. This can apply in the workplace or on a battlefield, as well as in emergency command (see Rasmussen, Brehmer and Leplat 1991). Our theoretical understanding of distributed decision making systems is actually quite limited, but what is clear is that communication is the foundation of effective decision making in this deployment. The requirement for passed information to be accurate, relevant, timely and complete is paramount when the decision makers are not working in a face-to-face setting. Moreover, each agent needs a level of awareness of how their decision making role interfaces with that of others in the system – what Brehmer (1991a) calls a "more reflective kind of decision making" (p. 13).

How can command and control be achieved across these distributed decision making systems? Brehmer (1991b) argues that coordination in such distributed decision making systems is achieved by the use of a hierarchical management structure, and he contrasts two complex systems of this kind, namely military command and emergency management. In a military system, the problem of information delays between levels in the command hierarchy is dealt with by focusing on goals in the transmission of orders rather than precise details of how a given order should be executed. The more senior commander will never have a completely accurate or current picture of the battle situation, therefore the decision as to how goals should be achieved has to be left to a more junior commander at the scene of events. Those at the top of the hierarchy, in the senior command positions, work on a different and slower time frame than those at the "front" or the "sharp end" of the system. The front-line troops and their leaders not only respond to commands, but they must also take minute to minute decisions as the conditions around them change:

> "in so far as what happens in this environment has not been foreseen by the higher levels, control is transferred to the soldiers, and the system takes on a self-organizing character. This is why commanders at the higher levels in the hierarchy await news from the lower levels with such anxiety, for in the actual battle, control has often slipped from their hands."
>
> (Brehmer 1991b, p. 344)

Distributed decision making is a common feature of emergency management, and in an escalating incident, decisions sometimes have to be made at the lowest levels in the hierarchy, as Duckworth's (1986) interviews with police officers who were on duty at the Bradford fire illustrated:

> "As the fire developed with a speed and intensity that none had envisaged possible, each officer had to make a whole series of rapid decisions about where to station himself, what to tell people, where to direct them, who to help, and so forth."
>
> (p. 318)

To maintain control in the command system in such situations, where feedback is likely to be slow, each team member should be working to a similar idea or plan of how the emergency should be managed, and should know what the appropriate actions are for a given condition (feedforward control). This is precisely the reason why standard operating/response procedures are employed and why all team members need to have a very clear idea of each other's roles and responsibilities.

Brehmer (1996) has been using a version of his computer simulation of a forest fire (FIRE; discussed in Chapter 5) to study distributed decision making in teams of four. The players' communications are all recorded and analysed to examine differences in team decision making and performance. While acknowledging the limited realism of such laboratory research, Brehmer reported two interesting findings:

1. The critical information required for effective coordination is information about intentions rather than past actions.
2. The best communication system was found to be the use of one central decision maker rather than an open system. However, it is emphasized that the optimum communication network may be a function of time pressure.

A similar computer programme (CITIES) has been developed to study distributed decision making in relation to an emergency control centre that dispatches police-tow and fire-rescue units across a city-based scenario (Wellens 1993). By working with these very simplified simulations in the controlled conditions of a laboratory, we can further our understanding of the structures and processes that underpin successful performance in the real world of team decision making in emergencies.

TEAM DECISION MAKING UNDER STRESS

The question of whether the incident commander's decision making ability is likely to be affected by stress was considered in the previous chapter. What do we know of teams involved in decision making under pressure?

How are they likely to respond to stress? There are reports indicating that under conditions of stress, team performance and communication can break down and the role of the leader may alter. As mentioned earlier "all eyes swivel to the captain when the crew perceive themselves to be under threat". Research has shown that leaders are regarded as more competent and more responsible when the team is under stress, consequently group members may be willing to shift more of the decision making load on to them. This can hinder as well as help team performance. Foushee and Helmreich (1988) reported that on the flight deck, subordinate crew members are more reluctant to question the captain under emergency conditions, and there have certainly been aircraft crashes where this has been a contributory factor. They illustrated this by referring to an alarming set of results from a simulator study in which aircraft captains feigned incapacity during a final landing approach and 25% of the planes "crashed" because the co-pilots failed to take over control. The introduction of assertiveness training as part of CRM courses is a direct result of research findings of this kind. Driskell and Salas (1991b) tested the stress-rigidity theory, which predicts that under conditions of stress or threat, higher status group members are accorded more power. Their study of status effects in teams of two, working together under conditions of stress (the threat of an unpleasant tear gas drill), showed that low status subjects were even more willing to defer to others when under stress. However, the higher status members actually became more receptive to the contributions of the other team members, which may be due to a search for more information under stress or the desire to share responsibility. However, they note that this finding would not necessarily apply when larger teams are involved.

According to Burgess et al. (1992), in the presence of stressors, team performance can be degraded by a drop in morale, less cooperation, inferior coordination, a higher error rate and poorer communication. They looked at how leaders' behaviours with the team could change under stress, and concluded that team leaders initiated more communication under stress, with more commands, suggestions, observations and statements. Drawing on an earlier literature review, they developed guidelines for training team leaders, which included leaders providing performance feedback to team members, clarifying team roles, aiding coordination, using strategic and concise communications, remaining responsive to others' needs, and being unintimidating and approachable. In a more recent discussion of the literature, Morgan and Bowers (1995) begin by pointing out that:

"as with other types of stress, it is recognized that under certain conditions teamwork stress can serve to stimulate or energize relevant behaviors, whereas under other conditions (unspecifiable at this time) the stressors will

certainly inhibit or reduce the occurrence of adaptive teamwork behaviors.
... in addition to its impact on individuals, teamwork stress also has an
impact on the processes required for effective team coordination and
cooperation."

(p. 268)

They identify the following seven potential stressors (causes of team
stress) which appear to have an impact on the performance of decision
making teams in naturalistic environments (characterized by high
workload, ambiguous information, time pressure and risk):

1. Team training load (presence of new team members).
2. Team workload (increase in load will enhance level of demand).
3. Team size (increasing size makes coordination and communication
   more difficult).
4. Team composition (heterogeneity of team members may increase
   conflict but may also improve problem solving).
5. Team structure (a less hierarchical structure may reduce status
   problems but could be less well coordinated).
6. Team cohesion (increased mutual attraction usually improves performance).
7. Goal structure (individual or group goals).

Unfortunately, few clear predictions regarding the effects of stress on
teamwork can be made at this stage; studies do not always yield compat-
ible results, and much of the work has been laboratory based using small
teams of two or three rather than the larger teams one would encounter in
an emergency control centre. There is, however, a new project on military
tactical teams making decisions under pressure, which may provide some
valuable data pertinent to the emergency command team.

TADMUS

A major research project into command decision making has been carried
out under the auspices of the TADMUS (Tactical Decision Making Under
Stress) programme. This multi-million dollar research programme ($12.8
million by 1993) was instigated following a series of US Navy casualties in
the Persian Gulf, which resulted in Congress hearings concerning the
impact of stress on combat decision making. In May 1987 the aircraft
carrier USS *Stark* lost 37 of her crew following a direct hit from an Iraqi
warplane, and the commanding officer and tactical action officer were
criticized for their inadequate defence of the ship. The watershed incident
was in 1988, when the USS *Vincennes* accidentally shot down an Iran Air

commercial plane, killing all 290 passengers. The crew of the *Vincennes* mistook the track of the airliner for a fighter plane on their computer screens. (See Rogers and Rogers (1992) for the commander's personal account of events; see Klein (1996) for an analysis based on transcripts from the ship's command centre; see also Woodward (1992, p. 102) for a graphic description of a very similar decision problem, in which he narrowly avoided shooting down a commercial airliner during the Falklands War.) After the *Vincennes* disaster, post-incident investigations focused on commanders' and their teams' decision making under stress and identified a need for a dedicated programme of research into this problem.

Consequently, the US Office of Naval Research launched a six-year (1990–1996) interdisciplinary programme of research into tactical decision making under stress in warfare command teams. The work has been principally concerned with US naval teams' decision making, in the combat information centre of a battle cruiser, where the computer operators are constantly watching their screens for signs of aircraft in their vicinity. When the ship is under threat and they decide that an incoming plane is potentially hostile, then they have less than a minute to make the decision to shoot it down before it attacks them, even though it may be several miles away. There is no doubt that this is a prime example of decision making under pressure for the commanders on these ships, as their decision tasks involve rapidly unfolding events, multiple plausible hypotheses, highly ambiguous information, extreme time pressure and severe (often catastrophic) consequences of errors.

Psychologists and computer scientists at a number of research centres across the USA have been working on a series of TADMUS projects, typically using simulations of command team anti-air warfare scenarios (Cannon-Bowers, Salas and Grossman 1991). The principal stressors being studied are:

- workload/time pressure
- uncertainty
- auditory overload/interference
- fatigue/sustained operations.

Two main Navy laboratories were involved in the work, the Naval Training Systems Centre in Orlando and the Naval Command, Control and Ocean Surveillance Centre in San Diego (Hutchins in press, a). The aims of the programme were to define and measure critical decision tasks, to examine the effects of stress on decision making, and to develop principles of training, simulation, decision support and computer displays. In Orlando, the group have been working on the effects of stress on decision making, and the development of team training and simulation principles. At the San Diego base, their objective is to apply new decision making models to the design of a computer-based support system for enhancing decision making under very complex conditions. Special laboratories have been set up, called "Decision-Making Evaluation Facility for Tactical Teams" (DEFTT). These are simulators that recreate six computer workstations of a US Navy Aegis cruiser's combat information centre, manned by the commanding officer, tactical action officer, anti-air warfare coordinator, identification supervisor, tactical information coordinator and electronic warfare supervisor (see Hutchins and Kowalski (1993) for technical details). The actions taken by each team member are recorded as they respond to anti-air warfare scenarios while the experimenters manipulate workload and ambiguity conditions to measure changes in performance. Performance is measured by error counts, expert reports, observations of critical behaviours (e.g. issuing warnings to aircraft) and communication analyses. Certain types of error have been identified that a decision support system or specific team training can improve, such as losing the tactical picture, failing to take appropriate response, communications within the team not being acted upon and failures to inform higher authority. Following the finding of Kaempf et al. (1992) that anti-air warfare officers relied on a recognition-primed strategy (see Chapter 5) for most of their decisions, the prototype software tools for the DEFTT simulator are based on Klein's (1993) RPD model, and situation assessment by explanation-based reasoning (Pennington and Hastie 1993).

In one of the studies of decision making in the DEFTT simulator (Hutchins in press, a), twelve naval officers performed four test scenarios of naval anti-air warfare in a littoral (near land) situation. All team and off-ship communications were recorded, then used to identify errors. A large number of decision errors (on average, 16 per scenario) was found. These errors were categorized into the three stages of recognition-primed decision making: recognizing a problem (15%), situation assessment (46%) and course of action selection (40%). At one point during each scenario, the officers' situation awareness (a "snapshot" of the tactical situation in terms of contacts of interest, probable intent, etc.) was assessed. The responses of the commanding officer were then compared with those of the tactical action officer and with the "ground truth" (known identification and intent for each contact). The results showed a low percentage of matches between the situation awareness of the commanding officer and that of the tactical action officer. Hutchins (in press, a) explains:

> "The implication is that when these two command-level decision makers do not share the same view of the situation, it could result in a delay in taking action or, if the person with the less accurate view makes the final decision

regarding course of action, and it turns out to be the wrong decision, the effects could be grievous."

The research groups are now working on the design of several decision support devices which will aid decision makers and help to reduce these problems (e.g. Klein et al., in press). For emergency command teams, the idea of taking a "snapshot" of each team member's assessment of the situation during exercises might also provide some illuminating results and help to identify gaps in coordination or communication within the team.

The effects of stress on team decision making are not well understood, and are only now receiving serious attention, given the critical tasks undertaken by military and industrial teams in hazardous environments. It cannot necessarily be assumed that the presence of an accepted stressor will degrade team performance, because well-managed teams have far more resources than an individual to cope with an increase in demand. Another of the TADMUS studies, by Serfaty, Entin and Volpe (1993), studied four-person teams in naval combat information centres. They found that an increase in time pressure initially resulted in more errors, but, surprisingly, as the time pressure continued to increase, the teams' error rates decreased. Serfaty, Entin and Volpe realized that the teams were in fact changing their decision making strategies – when the time pressure first increased, team members still waited for information requests from the commander (their normal mode) but responded faster with less success. With the higher time pressure, they became more proactive and gave the commander information they anticipated he would need. This is a good illustration of the dangers of making assumptions that teams' decision making abilities will be affected in the same fashion as those of individuals working alone. Opportunities for conducting research in this area have recently improved, with the wider implementation of simulator-based training for emergency decision making teams (see Chapter 3).

CREW RESOURCE MANAGEMENT

The final section of this chapter describes a particular type of team training, CRM, initially developed by the aviation industry and now adopted by a number of other professions, such as medicine and the merchant navy. It has also been used in the nuclear industry, and an outline is provided of our recent work developing CRM packages for emergency response training in the offshore oil industry. To my knowledge, it has not yet been used with emergency services teams in

Britain, although a senior fire service officer has recently suggested that it could and should be adapted for fire and rescue services team training (Wynne 1995).

The term "cockpit resource management" (now crew resource management) was first used in 1977 by the American aviation psychologist John Lauber, who defined it as "using all the available resources – information, equipment, and people – to achieve safe and efficient flight operations" (1984, p. 20). By 1980 many of the international airlines had become interested in human factors aspects of their flight operations and had introduced training in flight crew coordination. There were several reasons for example statistics on aircraft accidents showed that a significant percentage of losses were due to flight crew failures rather than technical problems (NTSB 1991, 1994). Moreover, research carried out at NASA Ames in the 1970s using accident analyses, pilot interviews and simulator observations had confirmed the need for non-technical training, which would focus on pilots' leadership, command, decision making, communication and team work (Orasanu 1994b).

CRM is now used almost universally by the major international airlines, typically taking the form of initial three-day training courses, continuation training and subsequent monitoring of CRM skills during simulator flights (line-orientated flight training; LOFT):

> "LOFT provides the organisation with a means of creating conditions requiring the practice of effective crew coordination to resolve complex emergency situations. It is also the instrument for reinforcing and evaluating the concepts learned in the CRM classroom."
>
> (Wiener, Kanki and Helmreich 1993, p. xxi)

In the UK, human factors training and examination are required for a Flight Crew Licence, and CRM training is an annual Civil Aviation Authority (CAA) requirement for commercial pilots.

What do CRM courses include? There is no standard CRM course; however, the CAA issued an information circular (AIC 143/1993) that suggested a syllabus for a three-day course. This syllabus was neither exhaustive nor compulsory, and individual operators designed their own courses, with the CAA issuing approval on inspection. For example, the British Airways CRM training programme covers six main topic areas: (i) choosing behaviour, (ii) communications, (iii) decision taking, (iv) feedback, (v) medical and (vi) self-awareness. During the course a variety of delivery techniques are used, including lectures, discussion, video film and exercises, as well as a peer assessment questionnaire called "Cockpit 2000". Their programme of regular simulator flights allows crews to develop and practise their team skills, having trained their flight crew trainers to observe and evaluate a crew's performance as a team (Thomas

1994). For a full account of the development of CRM and current research, see Jensen (1995) and Wiener, Kanki and Helmreich (1993); details of CRM programmes in companies such as KLM, Lufthansa, and Qantas can be found in Johnston, Fuller and McDonald (1995) and McDonald, Johnston and Fuller (1995) and a description of CRM for helicopter pilots is given in David (1996). There are dual benefits in CRM training: one is to improve human performance and teamwork in order to minimize the risk of emergencies or accidents occurring; the other is that CRM should help teams to perform more efficiently once an emergency has occurred. Captain Al Haynes, who, with the help of his crew and an air traffic controller, landed a desperately stricken DC-10 aircraft, thus saving many lives, acknowledged the role of CRM in this extraordinary accomplishment:

> "I am firmly convinced that CRM played a very important part in our being able to land at Sioux City with any chance of survival. I also believe that its principles apply no matter how many crew members are in the cockpit."
>
> (Haynes 1992, p. 13)

CRM courses are now used beyond the flight deck. In recent years there has been a similar interest in human factors and teamwork in the prevention and management of merchant shipping emergencies (Esbensen, Johnson and Kayten 1985). This has resulted in the parallel development of CRM courses for the merchant navy, in the form of bridge resource management (BRM) programmes. The two-day BRM course run at the US Merchant Marine Academy in New York for harbour and river pilots covers situational awareness, error chains, communications, dynamics of group performance, decision making, human factors and problems in pilot–bridge crew integration. The bridge team management course held at the Southampton Institute, Maritime Operations Centre uses a full mission bridge simulator for a five-day course that deals with teamwork, communication, confidence building for junior team members, risk awareness and resource management. The Danish Maritime Institute offers a four-day CRM course that includes human factors, decision making, stress, communication and crew synergy. Some transport companies, such as Braathens SAFE in Norway, have developed CRM courses for their marine officers and marine pilots as well as aircraft pilots. Their two-day marine course includes leadership, crew coordination, maritime culture, social atmosphere, communication, workload, decision making and situational awareness. It is taught by a maritime instructor, a CRM instructor airline pilot and a psychologist. This CRM course is now mandatory for Norwegian high-speed vessel navigators (Solberg 1995, personal communication).

In the USA (e.g. Stanford University) and Canada (e.g. Toronto University) CRM training is also used in medicine. Dr David Gaba of Stanford University has developed anaesthesia crisis resource management training, which is derived from the aviation CRM programmes. Candidates use operating theatre simulators to practise teamwork when dealing with critical situations, and examine issues of leadership, communication, assertiveness and decision making in much the same fashion as pilots rehearsing problems that can occur on the flight deck (Gaba, Fish and Howard 1994; Howard et al. 1992). Gaba (1992) explains that the major part of the course involves simulation exercises followed by debriefings, where each participant takes a turn at acting as the " 'primary anesthesiologist' ('in the hot seat') for one block (30 minutes), and is a 'silent partner' anesthesiologist for another block" (p. 141). There is rather less evidence of CRM courses being used in industry, although similar team training courses using simulators have been used in nuclear power companies in the USA (Gaddy and Wachtel 1992; Harrington and Kello 1993). The next subsection describes their use in the North Sea oil industry (Flin 1995b).

CRM for Offshore Control Room Operators' Emergency Response Training

Our first awareness that CRM could be adapted for industrial emergency response training was in 1992 when we became involved in human factors training, which was part of a four-day programme of offshore control room operator (CRO) competence assessments and emergency response training, being staged by a major North Sea oil company. The assessments were being carried out in an onshore simulator facility, and the company had decided to intersperse these scenarios and feedback sessions with four specially designed training modules. The trainers had already looked at one of the CRM courses being used by a commercial airline, and, with regard to their standard of competence for CROs, had decided that the most relevant elements to incorporate into their training programme would be modules on communication, decision making, stress and assertiveness.

In the airlines, the content of the CRM courses has been based on research findings from aviation psychologists (such as NASA) and the expertise of experienced pilots. In this case a similar approach was adopted; we drew on relevant psychological research (although little had been carried out offshore, see Flin and Slaven, 1996b) and the expertise of the trainers, who had considerable experience in control room operations. Our remit was to design the training packages for the trainers to deliver. The development phase therefore consisted of the initial design of the materials followed by an extensive redesign in order to tailor the presentations and exercises to meet the trainers' exacting standards of validity and applicability to the offshore control room. The module content as prepared is described briefly in the following subsections.

Decision Making

The objectives of this module were that participants would be able to recognize the essential differences between decision making under normal operating conditions and in an emergency, and in addition that they would be able to identify the factors that hinder or help decision making under stress in the control room and would know how to apply the latter if required. A model of the human memory system was used, which illustrated both long-term memory and working memory (Baddeley 1992), with specific exercises to demonstrate information processing limitations under normal conditions. The RPD model of decision making (Kaempf 1992; Klein 1993) was used as a framework for understanding decision making in high-pressure situations (see Figure 5.1).

Communication

This module covered the basic communication process, barriers to effective communication and awareness of strengths and weaknesses in personal communication skills. Exercises highlighted the importance of feedback and listening skills, the role of non-verbal communication and effective communication techniques. An actual offshore incident involving a communication problem was also presented and discussed.

Assertiveness

This module began by defining what was meant by assertiveness, why it was relevant to CROs, how it differed from passive and aggressive styles of behaviour and the signs that indicate each mode. The impacts of different behaviour styles on oneself and on others were discussed. (This covers similar ground to the British Airways "choosing behaviour" module; Thomas 1994.)

Exercises were used to allow role playing of different styles of behaviour in control room situations which would merit an assertive response from the CRO, such as:

> "You have a major process upset and you receive the second phone call from the Toolpusher to say that he wants fresh water immediately. What do you say to the Toolpusher?"

Participants were encouraged to discuss situations they had experienced in relation to different styles of behaviour and their outcome.

Stress

The stress module was designed to improve understanding of the causes and effects of stress, recognition of the signs of stress, and ability to cope with the effects of stress. A widely accept model (Cox, 1993) was used to explain the psychological and physiological processes of stress, and particular emphasis was placed on sources of stress in an offshore emergency, and in particular in the control room. Personal experiences of stress and resulting effects were discussed, then available coping strategies were considered.

This was not a full CRM course, but the underlying philosophy was very similar, with human factors modules being designed by psychologists and subject experts together but being delivered by the latter in conjunction with a programme of simulator assessments. The course content covered standard CRM topics, although the materials were adapted for the environment and operations of the offshore production platform control room. Teaching methods included lectures as well as exercises and discussion of personal experiences relating to the topic areas. In the longer term, such courses can be developed and refined by incorporating operational experience, incident analyses and research findings from control room studies.

CRM for OIMs and their Emergency Response Teams

A CRM training approach has also been used with offshore managers (OIMs) and their teams, who were undergoing emergency response team training in a high-fidelity offshore control room simulator facility. We were again asked by the same operating company to design training modules that would be used in between scenarios and debrief sessions. By this time, we were drawing on a much richer vein of research material and expertise, having completed our study of OIMs' crisis management (Flin and Slaven 1994), examined command training in other organizations (Flin and Slaven 1995) and visited British Airways and NASA Ames to learn more of CRM research and practice. We had reviewed our current research on emergency response team performance with Dr Orasanu from NASA, who had visited one of the company's control room simulators during her visit to Aberdeen. In addition, we were able to discuss CRM developments with other psychologists at the 1994 European Aviation

Psychology conference (Johnston, Fuller and McDonald 1995) and with the other researchers working on emergency decision making at the Naturalistic Decision Making conference in June 1994 (Zsambok and Klein, in press). Two of our psychologists had joined the British CRM group (affiliated to the Royal Aeronautical Society), which meets several times a year to discuss current CRM philosophy and practice. Finally, we had been invited to attend a special meeting, which took place in January 1993, when the oil company invited several members of the British Airways CRM flight crew training team to brief one of their operational training groups on the CRM approach.

On this basis, we were aware of a number of elements that appeared to be particularly critical for effective team performance in emergency command centres and which were applicable to an offshore platform. These elements included understanding of team roles, communications, group decision making/problem solving, assertiveness, team attitudes, stress management and shared mental models. Working closely with the trainers, we were able to design materials to introduce these topics, suggest scenario modifications that would allow these facets of team performance to be tested, and discuss these issues with the team in the feedback sessions. Our aim was not only to help the team under training to improve its performance, but also to teach individual crew members portable team skills, because the composition of an emergency response team will change over time as personnel move or rotas are altered. Details of some of these elements are given below.

Team Attitudes

Behaviour is governed to a significant degree by the attitudes we hold, and any attempt to change behaviour should begin with an attempt to identify underlying attitudes and beliefs relevant to the behaviours in question. Research carried out by aviation psychologists showed clearly that pilots' attitudes were a predictor of their behaviour on the flight deck, and one of the objectives of CRM is to produce attitude change where required. In fact, measuring attitudes before and after CRM training is one of the techniques used for evaluating its effectiveness (Gregorich and Wilhelm 1993). The scale most commonly used with pilots is the Cockpit Management Attitudes Questionnaire (CMAQ) (Gregorich, Helmreich and Wilhelm 1990). The CMAQ, containing 25 attitude items covering a range of issues regarding crew coordination, communication, role definitions and personal capabilities under stress, revealed substantial variability in attitudes among pilots. This scale is composed of three factor-analytically derived dimensions: (i) communication and coordination, (ii) command responsibility and (iii) recognition of stressor effects. It has been used in a number of research studies as well as in CRM evaluation. The CMAQ has been adapted for use in other domains where crew coordination is important, such as in the nuclear industry, where control room operators may have to take critical command decisions in the opening stage of an emergency (Harrington and Kello 1993), and with dispatchers in an emergency communications centre (Rhodenizer, Peppler-Swope and Bowers, in press). The scale has also been modified for use with police officers (Flin and Stewart, in preparation) and fire service officers (Murray 1995). As no research of this kind had been carried out with offshore crews, we adapted the CMAQ with reference to Harrington's nuclear industry version, substituting offshore terms where appropriate. This scale, called the Offshore ER Team Attitudes Questionnaire, contains 25 attitude items in a Likert format dealing with command responsibility, team coordination and personal performance (Table 6.2).

Respondents are asked to indicate whether they agree or disagree with each item on a five-point scale, and the questionnaire takes about ten minutes to complete. This scale is still under development and, to date, it has only been used as an attitude sensor, with summary data fed back to emergency response teams, where it has generated lively discussion and facilitated the introduction of the human factors training packages during the course. Our intention is to develop this instrument to be used for both training and course evaluation with offshore and emergency services incident command teams.

Table 6.2   *Sample Items from Offshore ER Team Attitudes Questionnaire*

Number	Item
1	Team members should avoid disagreeing with each other because conflicts create tension and reduce team effectiveness
2	Some people in this team find it difficult to be assertive
4	OIMs should leave technical matters to other members of the team
11	Team members should not question the decisions or actions of the OIM except where they threaten the safety of the platform
13	Even when fatigued, I perform effectively during critical platform operations
16	We have a procedure for anything that could go wrong on this platform
18	It is easier to make decisions when under pressure
21	Team leaders should use the same management style in an emergency as they use every day
24	During an emergency communications within our team will improve
25	My decision making ability is as good in emergencies as in routine operations

Roles and Responsibilities

Models of team performance generally emphasize that members of high performing crews have a clear understanding not only of their own roles and responsibilities but also of the role demands of other team members. For an offshore emergency response organization, this is particularly critical because team members will be assigned roles that probably will not correspond with their everyday duties (e.g. muster checker, board writer, on-scene commander). Where platforms have small crews, it is possible for an individual's role to change if the incident escalates. One exercise was developed which involved groups of three outlining their own roles in the ECC team and the roles of the other members. This allows an assessment of role clarity and reveals any unwarranted assumptions that are being held about the roles and duties of other team members.

Assertiveness

The need for assertive behaviour in more junior team members has been sharply highlighted in aviation accident analysis and simulator observations, which revealed the reluctance of co-pilots to challenge captains' authority even when they had made a poor decision or an actual error. This was compounded by an attitude held by some captains that it was not the co-pilot's place to question their decisions. The need for assertive behaviour is greatest where team members are not of equivalent status and the more junior or lower status members do not feel comfortable questioning the instructions of the leader. Research shows clearly that high performing (low error) crews have a climate of openness and trust, where team leaders are receptive to alternative views and team members are not afraid to express them. Our experience of watching many offshore ECC teams is that this is as relevant on an oil platform as it is on a flight deck. The training package used for this module involves a video, which gives an excellent demonstration of the need for assertiveness in operational conditions, a scenario in the simulator where skill balance can be demonstrated and a review of assertiveness skills and their role in team effectiveness.

Team Decision Making

One of our main research interests is the area of OIM and team decision making (Flin, Slaven and Stewart, 1996; Stewart and Skriver 1996), and in this module we use a group decision making exercise that highlights the need for team members to share and review incoming information in order to build a picture of the problem at hand. We review the types of decision making that may be appropriate with particular reference to the RPD model. An outline process of decision making is discussed and, if necessary, refined as the result of group discussion. We have begun to chart communication networks and the concept of the shared mental model with the help of course participants.

Our experience suggests that CRM training can be successfully tailored for offshore teams who have responsibilities for managing emergency response procedures. While CRM training was initially designed to reduce operational errors and improve emergency response performance in aircraft crews, there is increasing evidence that it can be adapted for other teams who have to produce consistently high performance under difficult conditions. The great strength of CRM is that it is founded on an ongoing investigation of the human factors element in accident causation and in successful emergency management. If it is to be implemented in other domains, then it will require to be underpinned by post-incident analysis and psychological research into leader and team performance when managing real or simulated incidents. Incidentally, aviation companies using CRM have reported significant spin-off benefits for normal operational performance. As Wynne (1995), who visited NASA and United Airlines to assess the value of simulator research and CRM training for the Fire Service, concluded:

> "The Fire Service does not as yet have the technology or the funding to create high fidelity simulator scenario training. One of the main contributions that the CRM programmes could bring to the Fire Service is in the design, implementation and debriefing of fire ground exercises.... The first important stage in the process will require the Fire Service to determine the key elements that constitute effective team performance on the fire ground."
>
> (p. 51)

The research now being carried out by the Fire Service College (Gunter 1996) and London Fire Brigade (Bonney 1995) represents a significant contribution to the achievement of this first stage.

CONCLUSION

As Salas and Cannon-Bowers (1993) point out, while we have a good idea of what constitutes the essential ingredients for the "dream team", failing to achieve this may leave an incident commander in charge of the "nightmare team" – a horror that some incident commanders may have experienced already. This chapter has examined the available psychological research into team performance in demanding conditions for decision making, where the risks and costs of errors are high. There are practical lessons for incident commanders to be learned from the team studies carried out in other domains, especially in military, medical and aviation environments. While there has been no major research of this kind into the performance of incident command teams in the UK, it is encouraging to note that British fire service officers are beginning to see direct applications for practices and procedures in their own brigades (Bonney 1995; Wynne 1995).

7
Conclusions and Future Developments

"Having read the report I believe that he, and now the HSE are looking for the perfect being, somebody like Clark Kent, who will sit in his office chair carrying out mind numbing admin for 364 days with a wry grin on his granite hewn features, only to disappear into the closet on hearing the general alarm and to appear in a trice with flowing cape, a pair of tights, complete with modesty knickers over them and a huge OIM emblazoned on the chest. Ready to take on the world. Where they are going to find him, God only knows and when they do I want to be there to read the job description and see the salary grade."

(Ullman 1994, p. 5)

LEGAL RESPONSIBILITIES OF THE INCIDENT COMMANDER

Clark Kent or Superman?

The quotation comes from an experienced offshore manager, who was asked in a survey about his views on the criticisms of the offshore managers in the public inquiry report into the *Piper Alpha* disaster. I suspect that incident commanders from other disciplines would have some sympathy with Ullman's comment. Is the incident commander Clark Kent or Superman? Increasing management accountability, public expectations, prosecution by media, changing legislation and a trend towards litigation (Young 1993) mean that this is not a trivial question. Command and control in emergency management, and especially the performance of the incident commander, is coming under increasing public and media attention.

In several public inquiry recommendations and conditions imposed by HSE improvement notices or reviews, there has been a focus on the organizational procedures for selection and training of incident commanders (outlined in Chapter 1). Accountability for command can be raised in criminal charges of negligence, in civil actions and even in insurance claims, although to date, on-scene command decisions appear to have escaped the brunt of such litigation. Gibson (1995), discussing lawsuits against Canadian fire departments, comments:

> "It seems to us that command decisions made at the fire ground during the course of battle will receive considerable sympathy from our courts. Everyone realises that firefighters put their lives on the line every time they leave the fire hall."
>
> (p. 30)

Are British judges likely to be equally sympathetic? There have been several legal cases from the English courts that have examined the decisions taken by incident commanders. In a Court of Appeal judgment (*Knightley* v. *Johns and Others* [1982] 1 WLR 349), Police Constable Knightley claimed against four defendants, including the Chief Constable of West Midlands and Police Inspector Sommerville. The latter had been called by radio to the scene of an accident involving a car overturning in the Queensway Tunnel, Birmingham, and had forgotten to close the tunnel to traffic immediately, as required by police standing order. He ordered Knightley and another constable to ride their motorcycles into the tunnel against the flow of traffic in order to close the tunnel. A car struck and injured Knightley, who sued the Inspector for negligence for instructing him, or at least permitting him, to drive the wrong way. The Appeal Court reversed the original judgment and found that the Inspector "was negligent in failing to close the tunnel and in ordering or allowing his subordinates to do a very dangerous thing contrary to the standing order" (p. 357).

In another appeal case involving the police (*Hughes* v. *National Union of Mineworkers and Others* [1991] ICR 669), the plaintiff, Police Constable Hughes, had brought an action against a number of people, including the Chief Constable of North Yorkshire, for an injury he received when on duty during a miners' strike riot. The claim was for negligence in causing, permitting or requiring the plaintiff to take up an unsupported and unprotected position; and failing to implement proper riot control and exercise proper coordination, namely failing to implement a safe system of work. The Chief Constable's initial application to have the proceedings struck out as disclosing no reasonable cause of action had been refused. However, the appeal was allowed. Two earlier cases of police commanders' negligence in operational decision making were cited in the judgment. Firstly, the Knightley case received the following comment:

"This case shows that a police officer may owe a duty of care to an officer under his command in what may broadly be called 'operational circumstances' where his decisions were no doubt taken in the heat of the moment."

(p. 679)

The second case of negligence which was cited, concerned an erroneous operational command decision where a chief inspector had a CS gas canister fired into a gun shop in an effort to flush out a dangerous psychopath, resulting in a fire when there was no firefighting cover present (*Rigby* v. *Chief Constable of Northamptonshire* [1985] 1 WLR 1242).

In contrast to these earlier decisions, the judgment in Hughes relating to the public order incident stated:

"It will no doubt often happen that in such circumstances critical decisions have to be made with little or no time for considered thought and where many individual officers may be in some kind of physical danger or another. It is not in the public interest that those decisions should generally be the potential target of a negligence claim if rioters do injure an individual officer, since the fear of such a claim would be likely to affect the decisions to the prejudice of the task which the decisions are intended to advance."

(p. 680)

Thus, in situations where police commanders have taken decisions "in the heat of the moment" we have two cases (*Knightley*, *Rigby*) where the officers were found to have been negligent and one (*Hughes*) where the circumstances of the critical decision were such that negligence was not accepted. There is clearly no general ruling and such claims will be dealt with on a case by case basis. Fire service commanders have similar legal responsibilities as a recent civil case has shown.

"Hampshire County Council faces a compensation bill of up to £6m after a judge held the County fire brigade liable for the partial destruction in a fire of a prestige company headquarters.... Judge Richmond Harvey QC, ... held there was no justification for the fire officer in charge to depart from the principle that sprinklers should be kept operating until fire was completely under control. He said the decision was a 'bad blunder'."

(*Fire Prevention*, 289, May 1996, p. 3)

Furthermore, questions of liability and duty of care are not only of concern to emergency services commanders: other incident commanders, such as industrial managers (Flin and Slaven 1994), business managers (Mahoney 1994), ships' officers (Hesler 1995) and hospitality managers (Wembley Stadium Health and Safety Department 1995) may also find themselves in an equivalent position of accountability regarding decisions taken during an emergency. Today, there is a new emphasis on the commander's responsibilities for the health and safety of subordinates deployed at an incident. The need for commanders to take a serious approach to risk assessment and risk management is becoming very clear. In the early 1990s, Phoenix Fire Chief, Alan Brunacini (1991) was alerting fireground incident commanders:

> "A whole new group of personnel has entered the fire fighter safety process. Surviving fire fighters and their relatives, smart lawyers, insurance representatives, public administrators, and fire service safety advocates all represent a very special set of agendas before and after a firefighter is injured or killed.... This group typically has radar that can detect goofy explanations and lame excuses for unsafe practices. ... Anyone who has not started to understand and respond to the current shift in the safety responsibility of the command system needs a wake-up call."
>
> (p. 76)

Against this increasing scrutiny of command and control procedures, the first objective of this volume was to collate and analyse what was known about the skill of incident command. While the organizations studied demonstrate considerable expertise, incident command seems to be regarded as a black art rather than a science. Little of the expert knowledge of command is written down and stored. The organizations in question have a great fondness for documenting technical advances, but managerial skill developments seem to be transferred by folklore, anecdotes, oral history and war stories, at the risk of significant memory fade and distortion through the mists of time. Therefore, it has been difficult to obtain from secondary sources detailed accounts or analyses of incident command from the perspective of the commander. These do not generally exist in any accessible form in the UK, and those that were discovered from further afield are included in Chapter 5. However, it was possible to gather material from a variety of sources on the operational principles of command and control, and to collect details of the selection, training and competence assessment of on-scene commanders. There is significant commonality across organizations but a limited transfer of knowledge and expertise between them.

SELECTION, TRAINING AND COMPETENCE ASSESSMENT

By studying famous warfare commanders, authors such as van Creveld (1985) and Keegan (1987) have attempted to extract the essence of command and to define the "right stuff" for military leadership. Serfaty and Michel (1990) studied these texts and concluded, "They both agree that although individual innate qualities are essential, inherent factors in the experience and training of military commanders determine the success or failure of their mission." (p. 262).

In Chapter 2 an attempt was made to define the characteristics of the ideal incident commander. The resulting list of personality attributes was fairly obvious (namely, an individual who likes to take a leadership role, has a stable temperament, and is a calm decision maker under pressure) and added little to our existing understanding of the basic profile required. The conclusion at this juncture has to be that beyond these fundamental qualities, there is no one precise "right stuff" profile. (There are certainly characteristics that predict the "wrong stuff", including arrogant, untrustworthy, excitable, shy, loner and over-confident individuals, as well as any psychiatric symptomatology.) The research to date indicates that, excluding deviant or difficult personality types, a range of personality profiles will be found within a group of successful incident commanders, albeit that, as a group of people who have chosen professions that require incident command, they may show some distinct characteristics (such as those listed above) when compared to managers from other occupations. For the present population of incumbent and prospective incident commanders, what is most important is that they have awareness of the strengths and weaknesses of their personality profile in relation to incident command, and secondly that they have the skills to cope with decision making and teamwork under pressure.

Moore (1986), discussing police commanders in public order incidents, gives us an insight into those skills:

> "All police commanders, in their several grades, must have a good knowledge of staging the many and varied operations that their group or unit may be called upon to undertake in the event of public disorder, whether it be offensive or defensive action. They must be able to understand and be able to stage manage the situation; they must have the ability to concentrate on the tasks in hand without worrying over other things; they must be capable of thinking quickly in order to make rapid decisions (there is often no time for consultation when the disorder is ongoing); and finally they must have a flair for improvisation and the ability to see things with clarity."
>
> (p. 98)

These skills are now enshrined in the new standards of competence for incident command in a number of professions – including fire service officers, oil industry managers and commercial pilots – which provide a definition of the key behaviours required for effective performance. In all cases the commander is required to assess the situation, evaluate risk, judge and deploy the required resources, formulate a plan of action and communicate this to the response teams. The standards of competence enable a clearer focus for career development and training and allow a fair assessment of performance against an agreed national behavioural specification.

The training methods used in different organizations for incident commanders were reviewed in Chapter 3, and great similarity of content and technique was found across organizations. Incident command is not an innate skill, and for hazardous site managers, ships' captains and airline pilots, incident command, although included in their job description, is an abnormal element of their duties. Emergency services commanders do have extensive experience of routine incidents, but they too can encounter the larger or more complex situations, which are much rarer and therefore present difficulties for the acquisition of command skills. In both cases the problem of providing commanders with sufficient experience is addressed by the widespread use of simulators, both high and low fidelity. The simulators present first class training and research opportunities, providing that those involved do not become so seduced by the technology that they miss the fundamental learning objectives. The crucial role of structured, critical and constructive feedback sessions when conducting command training for both individuals and teams was widely emphasized.

For the majority of the organizations contacted, managing emergencies was either their *raison d'être* or was a fundamental aspect of their work, and accordingly they had each developed their own traditions and methods for emergency management. As a result, incident commanders from different agencies have their own preferred command procedures and *modus operandi*. For example, the site manager of a petrochemical plant that has just suffered an explosion and fire will have to work with on-scene commanders from the police service, the fire brigade and the ambulance service, as well as with local authority emergency response coordinators. There have been examples where inter-agency cooperation and communication have not functioned as smoothly as would be desired. Managing this interaction is a critical facet of modern incident command, and in practice is typically improved by joint training exercises or the participation of visiting lecturers from sister organizations on emergency management courses. An open and critical examination of past successes and failures needs to be encouraged, particularly for major incidents. Thornley, a chief ambulance officer, says:

> "We never know when or where a major incident will occur next. Our level of preparedness will always depend on how much we learn from the tragedies of others. In the UK we are, in my view, still complacent about disaster planning."
>
> (Thornley 1990, p. 36)

Another interface that is very important is that between commanders of different status within a given organization. The skills of operational, tactical and strategic command are quite distinct, and it remains to be seen whether the "right stuff" for operational command is also the "best stuff" for strategic command. For the management of very large-scale incidents and disasters, a command and control model may in fact be inappropriate (Jackson 1994; Turner 1994). A foray into this particular debate is beyond the scope of this book, but it raises a number of significant issues for those responsible for disaster planning.

STRESS, DECISION MAKING AND TEAMWORK

The psychological foundations for effective incident command relate principally to stress management, decision making and team working, and these were examined in Chapters 4–6. Leadership may be a surprising omission from this list, but, as discussed below, the bulk of conventional research on leadership is not well focused and has limited relevance for the incident commander. In general, little research into these topics has been undertaken in relation to emergency services commanders, although there is a valuable body of data from the military and aviation psychologists. My second goal was to raid the psychological research literature for all that could be found of relevance to the role of the incident commander.

Incident commanders, almost by definition, will be operating in demanding and potentially stressful situations. They need to be able to manage their own stress reactions as well as those of their teams. While there is a well-developed literature on stress in rescue and emergency services personnel, almost none of this relates to incident commanders: either they are deemed to be immune to stress or they are so successful at managing it that no one ever asks them how they cope. In Chapter 4 a model of stress for incident commanders was developed and this was used as a framework against which to discuss the causes, buffers and effects of stress in incident command. The model is a mixture of guesswork, extrapolation, anecdote and creativity, but it has been examined by a number of commanders, and the version presented does incorporate their suggestions. On reflection, slightly different models may have to be developed for operational, tactical and strategic commanders as incident command research progresses.

The linchpin of incident command is decision making – in fact, the word "crisis" comes from the Greek *krisis*, to decide. This is the essential skill, particularly in the critical "golden hour" at the start of an incident, and it transpires that we actually know very little about the psychological mechanisms underpinning this ability. What we do now know is that incident commanders at an operational level are likely to be using a naturalistic decision method rather than a traditional analytic strategy. To them, it seems more like "gut feel" or intuition. Yet where decision making is taught in command training, an analytic approach is typically recommended. Chapter 5 reviewed the latest psychological research into decision making from military, fire service, aviation, medical and industrial scientists. A number of very promising lines of investigation have emerged, particularly from the field of naturalistic decision making. The NDM researchers study individuals taking decisions in dynamic situations under conditions of high risk, time pressure, responsibility for lives, and ambiguous and incomplete information (Zsambok and Klein, in press). The dominant model is that of Klein (1993), whose ideas on recognition-primed decision making have begun to attract serious interest:

> "The US Marine Corps has recognized intuitive decision making doctrinally as a viable decision-making method and has implemented measures to introduce training in intuitive decision making into the curricula of its professional schools."
> (Major John Schmitt, US Marine Corps, personal communication, May 1996)

In the UK, the NDM models are now being considered by the Defence Research Agency, the fire service, the oil industry and the police.

A common theme that emerged when organizations were asked about training was the emphasis on developing not only leadership skills but also team working abilities. It was repeatedly emphasized that incident commanders do not, and should not, work alone: they function in a team setting, from very small flight deck teams to the enormously complex inter-agency teams one would find at a major incident. Although there have been many studies of group behaviour, few of these have dealt seriously with the demands facing a command team working under real risk and high time pressure. In Chapter 6 the latest studies of team decision making under stress were considered, as well as the aviation industry's Crew Resource Management programmes, which transfer the psychologists' findings directly into the workplace. Very little of this research seems to be used in the training of British incident commanders, and any teaching on the psychology of group behaviour is more likely to be covered in general management courses. This is not to say that the importance of team functioning is not emphasized or tested in simulations. An elemental principle conveyed is that leaders should be as familiar as possible with the strengths and weaknesses of the teams they would have to rely on in an emergency. Deficiencies in team performance frequently relate to communication and coordination problems (both within and between agencies), and these can be minimized by training teams together in emergency response procedures. One aspect of team management that was not accorded a separate chapter is leadership, a nebulous subject at best, as the following section illustrates.

LEADERSHIP THEORY

Fundamentally, incident management training focuses on developing the knowledge and skills that are required for effective command and control in an emergency, and the content of training programmes appears to be broadly similar, irrespective of agency or organization (Flin and Slaven 1995). When the syllabus content of courses for incident commanders is examined, it appears that the weight of emphasis is placed on the standard operational procedures rather than on the management or cognitive skills that are required to achieve the desired result. However, one underlying theme is the development of leadership skills, a topic that has a long military pedigree. This section looks at the theoretical basis of leadership training for commanders and compares this with the prevailing views on leadership from the field of management development.

Leadership ability is generally deemed to be a key attribute of an incident commander, and to some extent may be regarded as an umbrella term for the required competencies that have to be trained. However, finding a precise specification of the required behaviours or the style of leadership is rather less frequently articulated. Leadership within a military context embodies the concepts of command, control, organization and duty, and there has been extensive military research into leadership training (e.g. Bartone and Kirkland 1991; Popper, Landau and Gluskinos 1992; Schmitt 1994), much of which, unfortunately, never sees the light of day outside the defence research community.

If one looks at the training of incident commanders from the emergency services, this is derived from military doctrine but there appears to have been little experimental research into the optimal leadership styles of civil emergency commanders (Flin 1995a). In contrast, there are Norwegian studies of leaders under stress (Weisaeth 1987), the Swedish Fire Research Board has commissioned research into the development and training of rescue tactics for fire commanders (Fredholm 1991, 1995) and the French Public Safety Ministry has funded research into decision making in high ranking fire officers (Samurcay and Rogalski 1993).

The dominant model of leadership for training in the British armed services, the emergency services and lower level management is Adair's (1983) Action Centred Leadership, with its simple three-circle model. Adair developed his ideas from his experience as a British Army officer, and he maintained that the effective leader must focus on the needs of the individual, the task and the team. This functional model has not changed significantly since its initial exposition in the 1960s, and it continues to be taught in a wide range of management courses. While the three-circle diagram and the associated advice to leaders is intuitively appealing, there has been little empirical work to test whether it can actually function as an explanatory theory of leadership in routine managerial duties or emergency command situations. However, what else is on offer to provide an explanatory and (predictive) theory of leadership in emergency command situations that can be used for training?

Leadership is one of the most researched topics by industrial psychologists, and military and political scientists, but few – if any – theories, or their underpinning research, focus on situations that equate to dangerous, ambiguous, dynamic conditions facing the on-scene commander at a major incident. References to studies of "leadership in crisis" usually concern political or policy strategists (e.g. Janis 1989, 1992), or chief executives whose companies are the subject of hostile takeovers, industrial and environmental accidents, contaminated products (e.g. the Perrier or Tylenol cases), fraud or other business disasters (see Barton 1993; Booth 1993; Darling 1994; Mitroff and Pearson 1993; Syrett and Hogg 1992; Rosenthal and Hart 1991). More generally, there is a wide range of alternative theoretical approaches to leadership and the extent of the published literature is overwhelming (for recent reviews, see Hogan, Curphy and Hogan 1994; Shackleton 1995; Syrett and Hogg 1992; Yukl 1994).

What can be distilled from this managerial research literature on leadership is a progression from a centuries-old focus on leadership characteristics, to research in the 1960s on leader behaviours (e.g. autocratic versus democratic; team versus task), to an awareness that "one size fits all" recommendations of the best leadership style are unlikely to work. The contingency theories of the 1970s emphasized that leadership style cannot be considered in isolation (see Bass 1990). Effective leadership behaviour is likely to be dependent on the leader's personality and skills, the situation, and the competence and motivation of the group being led. Thus, the most effective leader needs to be able to (i) diagnose the situation (the task/ problem, the mood, the competence and motivation of the team), (ii) have a range of styles available (e.g. delegative, consultative, coaching, facilitating, directive) and (iii) match his or her style to the situation (e.g. Hersey and Blanchard's (1993) model of situational leadership). In an emergency, which has by definition high time pressure and risk, it is unlikely that a consultative leadership style would be appropriate, and while the incident commander needs to solicit advice from available experts and to listen to more junior commanders (or operational team leaders), the appropriate style is likely to be closer to directive than democratic. Weisaeth (1987), who has studied leaders of emergency response teams, states:

> "Management and leadership must be situation-determined. In industrial crises and during accidents/catastrophes the situation changes suddenly and radically. Such situations require a leader style in its more authoritarian and commando-like form."
>
> (p. 3)

The need for a perceptible change in leadership style is very obvious in simulated emergency exercises when the time pressure and task demands are increased. Moreover, this sends a very important message to the rest of the team that the situation is serious and that they will also have to "change gear" and sharpen their performance. For those individuals who will only on the rarest of occasions have to act as incident commanders (e.g. industrial managers), a necessary part of their training is the opportunity to practise the directive style that they will require in a fast moving emergency. However, the precise tailoring of this style will depend on the commander's personality, the organizational culture, the team's expertise and expectations, and the operational management structure.

Within the business world, there is fairly general agreement that key leadership traits include drive, desire to lead, honesty and integrity, self-confidence (emotional stability), cognitive ability and knowledge of the business (Kirkpatrick and Locke 1991). These show considerable overlap with the fundamental characteristics sought in incident commanders. The current fashions in leadership style are the delegative, consultative styles, couched in notions of empowerment (Byham and Cox 1988), and trans-formational leadership (Bass and Avolio 1994), which are widely taught in multinational corporations but are also permeating military thinking (Popper, Landau and Gluskinos 1992). These approaches have not been developed with the incident commander in mind, and although it was argued above that a consultative style may be inappropriate, particularly in the opening stages of an incident, this does not mean that there should be no delegation to more junior commanders. In a major incident consider-able authority has to be devolved to sector commanders or fire and rescue team leaders, who will be required to take critical decisions and who will not have the time or the opportunity to seek the opinion of the senior commander. These individuals need to have the expertise and the confidence to make decisions as the need arises, and the senior commander is often more in the role of overseer, commanding (as in many military settings) by negation. That is, he or she will be informed of the decisions being taken but will only intervene if it is felt necessary to countermand a decision. The essential points are that the commander should be comfort-able with the style required and that the front-line commanders should have a clear understanding of their delegated authority and the incident commander's plan of action.

FUTURE DIRECTIONS

Where do we go from here? In a sense, the formal, scientific study of incident command is only just beginning, and it would be unusual if a book written by a researcher did not make the perennial plea for further research. What are the longer term practical objectives of such research? I would argue that selection, training and competence assessment of on-scene commanders need to be grounded in a proper understanding of their decision making and team management behaviours. An examination of novice/expert differences can help to reveal the essential skills that characterize the proficient commander. If, indeed, a recognitional decision strategy is employed by experts, then the implications for incident command training relate firstly to developing stored mental models by experience, simulation and accident reviews – the expert's mental models being rich in cues and expectations with related courses of action. Secondly, an emphasis should be placed on the use of mental simulation using the mental model to preplay the retrieved course of action to check for contraindications before implementation. Thirdly, it would discourage training based on classical decision making, which advises option generation and concurrent evaluation to achieve an optimal solution. Under the time pressure and high risk typical of emergencies in oil installations, aircraft, battle zones, firegrounds, rioting crowds and hospital trauma centres, the aim is to rapidly achieve a satisfactory solution that will ensure the safety of the individuals in danger. The complexity of the decision making and teamwork in these environments presents a significant challenge, not only to the on-scene commanders, but also to the research psychologists who work with them.

A number of developments are taking place involving psychologists and incident commanders. The first international scientific group on naturalistic decision research was established in October 1995 as a specialist section of the Human Factors and Ergonomics Society (USA). Our research group at Robert Gordon University is one of the few non-military centres studying incident command across professions. We are currently working with Grampian Fire Brigade, Fife Fire and Rescue service, Bond Helicopters, Grampian Police, the Fire Service College and the offshore oil industry on incident command research projects. The US Army Research Institute sponsored the first European NDM meeting in September 1996 (Flin, Strub and Salas, in preparation). The Fire Service College has established a research group of senior officers studying various facets of incident command (several as doctoral candidates), and London Fire Brigade now has a number of projects running on incident command involving its own occupational psychologist. The Home Office, Police Research Group have awarded a personal research grant to an Inspector at Grampian Police to study decision-making. An annual workshop on Critical Incident Management is held by Portsmouth University, attended by British and American police and fire service officers. Plans are now under way to form a British network of scientists and practitioners who can work together to develop a better understanding of incident command with regard to selection, training and operational procedures. (The first UK conference on Critical Incident Management will be held in March 1997). In essence, our joint efforts will be geared to supporting those who find themselves "sitting in the hot seat".

Appendix 1

For this project, a number of organizations involved in incident command were contacted (see Flin and Slaven, 1994 for further details) and those who provided most information are listed below. Organizations that were visited are marked *

Aberdeen College (Marine and
Offshore Technology Unit)
Aberdeen Royal Infirmary,
Anaesthetics Dept (ATLS training*)
Air Accidents Investigation Branch*
Australian Department of Defence
Bond Helicopters*
Bristows Helicopters*
British Airways*
British Army (Gordon
Highlanders*)
British International Helicopters*
British Nuclear Fuels Ltd
British Petroleum Exploration*
Defence Research Agency
Disaster Research Center, Delaware
Emergency Planning Unit,
Aberdeen*
Fire Service
Cote san Luc Fire Department,
Quebec
Ecole Nationale des Officiers
Sapeurs-Pompiers, Paris
The Fire Service College*,
Moreton-in-Marsh
Grampian Fire Brigade*

London Fire and Civil Defence
Authority*
New York Fire Department,
Manhattan
Glasgow Nautical College
HM Coastguard, Aberdeen*
Home Office
Home Office Emergency Planning
College, Easingwold
Klein Associates (Ohio*)
Marine Accident Investigation
Branch
Merchant Navy (Dept of Transport)
Ministry of Defence
Mobil North Sea Ltd*
Montrose Fire and Emergency
Training Centre*
NASA
Crew Factors Group, NASA
Ames, California*
Space Human Factors Life
Sciences Division, Washington
DC
Nautical Institute, London
Offshore Command Training
Organization (OCTO)*

Police
  FBI Academy, Quantico, Virginia
  Metro Dade SWAT Team,
    Miami*
  Metropolitan Police, Negotiator
    Training, Hendon*
  Miami City Police Department*
  Police Staff College, Bramshill*
  Queensland Police
  Scottish Police College, Tulliallan*
Royal Air Force (Officers and
  Aircrew Selection Centre, Biggin
  Hill)*
Royal Navy
  Flag Officer Sea Training,
    Portland*
  HMS *Excellent* (NBCD School),
    Portsmouth*
  Leadership School, HMS *Royal
    Arthur*

Submarine Command Course,
  Faslane*
Scottish Ambulance Service,
  Aberdeen*
Scottish Nuclear, Hunterston*
Scottish Prison Service
Shell Expro*
Southampton Institute (Centre for
  Maritime Operations)
Swedish Defence Research
  Establishment (Department of
  Human Studies)
Swedish Fire Research Board
US Marine Corps
US Navy
  Naval Airwarfare Center,
    Orlando (Human Factors
    Division)
  TADMUS project, Ocean
    Surveillance Center, San Diego*

References

AAIB (1990) *Report on the Accident to Boeing 737-400 G-OBME near Kegworth, Leicestershire on 8 January 1989*, Aircraft Accident Report 4/90. London: HMSO.

AAIB (1992) *Memorandum on the Investigation of Air Accidents*. Farnborough: Department of Transport, Air Accidents Investigation Branch.

ACPO (1991) *Major Incident Emergency Procedures Manual*. London: HMSO (restricted).

Adair, J. (1983) *Effective Leadership*. London: Pan.

AFAC (1995) *Australian Fire Agencies Competency Standards*. Australian Fire Agencies Council, PO Box 713, Mount Waverley, Victoria, Australia.

Akesson, T. (1995) Rescue simulator with virtual reality, Emergency Services Institute report, Kuopio, Finland.

Alexander, D. and Wells, A. (1991) Reactions of police officers to body-handling after a major disaster: a before and after comparison. *British Journal of Psychiatry*, **159**, 547–555.

Alexander, R. and Proctor, H. (1993) *Advanced Trauma Life Support*. Chicago, IL: American College of Surgeons.

Algar, P. (1992) *Managing Industrial Emergencies. A Planning and Communications Guide*. London: Financial Times Management Reports.

American Psychiatric Association (1994) *Diagnostic and Statistical Manual of Mental Disorders*, 4th edn. Washington, DC: American Psychiatric Association.

Anderson, N. and Herriot, P. (eds) (1989) *Assessment and Selection in Organizations* (with 1994 and 1995 supplements). Chichester: John Wiley.

Armstrong, K., Lund, P., McWright, L. and Tichenor, V. (1995) Multiple stressor debriefing and the American Red Cross: the East Bay Hills fire experience. *Social Work*, **40**(1), 83–90.

Atterbury, D. (1992) Training and assessing warships in damage control and firefighting. In Collected Papers of the First Offshore Installation Management Conference: Emergency Command Responsibilities, Robert Gordon University, Aberdeen, April.

Auf der Heide, E. (ed.) (1989) *Disaster Response. Principles of Preparation and Coordination*. St Louis, MI: C.V. Mosby.

Backer, P. and Orasanu, J. (1992) Stress, stressors, and performance in military operations: a review. Report for the US Army Institute, contract DAAL03-86-D-001.

Baddeley, A. (1992) Working memory. *Science*, **255**, 556–559.

Barnett, M. (1991) LICOS – A liquid cargo operations simulator and its use in training for the handling of potential emergencies. Paper presented at the Human Factors in Offshore Safety Conference, Aberdeen, April.

Barton, L. (1993) *Crisis in Organizations: Managing and Communicating in the Heat of Chaos*. Cincinnati, OH: South-Western.

Bartone, P. and Kirkland, F. (1991) Optimal leadership in small army units. In R. Gal and D. Mangelsdorf (eds) *Handbook of Military Psychology*. Chichester: John Wiley.

Bartram, D. (ed.) (1995) *Review of Personality Assessment Instruments (Level B) for Use in Occupational Settings*. Leicester: British Psychological Society.

Bartram, D. and Baxter, P. (1995) Cathay Pacific Airways pilot selection validation. In N. Johnston, R. Fuller and N. McDonald (eds) *Aviation Psychology: Training and Selection*. Aldershot: Avebury Aviation.

Bartram, D. and Dale, H. (1982) The Eysenck Personality Inventory as a selection test for military pilots. *Journal of Occupational Psychology*, **55**, 287–296.

Bass, B. (1990) *Bass and Stogdill's Handbook of Leadership*, 3rd edn. New York: Free Press.

Bass, B. (1992) Stress and leadership. In F. Heller (ed.) *Decision-making and Leadership*. Cambridge: Cambridge University Press.

Bass, B. and Avolio, B. (1994) *Improving Organizational Effectiveness through Transformational Leadership*. New York: Sage.

Bawtree, D. (1995a) Safety culture and our response to its failure. Paper presented at the Third Emergency Planning and Disaster Management Conference, Lancaster University, July.

Bawtree, D. (1995b) Learning from the *Estonia* disaster. *Civil Protection*, **35**, 6–7.

Beaton, R., Murphy, S., Pike, K. and Jarrett, M. (1995) Stress symptom factors in firefighters and paramedics. In S. Santer and L. Murphy (eds) *Organizational Risk Factors for Job Stress*. Washington, DC: American Psychological Association.

Belardo, S., Karwan, K. and Wallace, W. (1984) An investigation of system design considerations for emergency management decision support. *IEEE Transactions on Systems, Man and Cybernetics*, **14**(6), 795–804.

Berge, D. (1990) *The First 24 Hours. A Comprehensive Guide to Successful Crisis Communications*. Oxford: Basil Blackwell.

Bohl, N. (1995) Professionally administered critical incident debriefing for police officers. In M. Kurke and E. Scrivner (eds) *Police Psychology into the 21st Century*. Hillsdale, NJ: Lawrence Erlbaum.

Bonney, J. (1995) Fire command teams. What makes for effective performance? International project report, Brigade Command Course, Fire Service College, Moreton-in-Marsh.

Booth, S. (1990) Interactive simulation and crisis management training. *Contemporary Crises*, **14**, 381–394.

Booth, S. (1993) *Crisis Management Strategy. Competition and Change in Modern Enterprises*. London: Routledge.

Boyle, S., Fullerton, J. and Yapp, M. (1993) The rise of the assessment centre: a survey of AC usage in the UK. *Selection and Development Review*, **9**(3), 1–4.

Brehmer, B. (1991a) Distributed decision making: some notes on the literature. In J. Rasmussen, B. Brehmer and J. Leplat (eds) *Distributed Decision Making: Cognitive Models of Cooperative Work*. Chichester: John Wiley.

Brehmer, B. (1991b) Organization for decision making in complex systems. In J. Rasmussen, B. Brehmer and J. Leplat (eds) *Distributed Decision Making: Cognitive Models of Cooperative Work*. Chichester: John Wiley.

Brehmer, B. (1992) Dynamic decision making: human control of complex systems. *Acta Psychologica*, **81**, 211–241.

Brehmer, B. (1996) Dynamic and distributed decision making. *Journal of the Fire Service College*, **1**(2), 17–36.

Brown, J. and Campbell, E. (1994) *Stress and Policing*. Chichester: John Wiley.

Bruder, C. (1995) The psychological lifeguard: a new model for catastrophic disaster mental health. Paper presented at the American Psychological Association Conference, New York, August.

Brunacini, A. (1985) *Fire Command*. Quincy, MA: National Fire Protection Association.

Brunacini, A. (1991) Command safety: a wake-up call. *National Fire Protection Association Journal*, January, 74–76.

Burgess, K., Salas, E., Cannon-Bowers, J. and Hall, J. (1992) Training guidelines for team leaders under stress. Paper presented at the 36th Annual Meeting of the Human Factors Society, Atlanta, Georgia, October.

Burke, E. and Hendry, C. (1995) Decision making on the London incident ground. Paper presented at the Fourth European Congress of Psychology, Athens, July.

Burke, E., Hendry, C., Bonney, J. and Collins, N. (1996) Understanding and developing fireground decision making competence. Paper presented at the British Psychological Society Annual Conference, Brighton, April.

Byham, B. and Cox, J. (1988) *ZAP. The Lightning of Empowerment*. New York: Harmony.

CACFOA (1991) *Major Incidents Emergency Procedures Manual*. London: HMSO.

Cameron, K. (1994) An international company's approach to managing major incidents. *Disaster Prevention and Management*, **3**, 61–67.

Cammish, J. and Richardson, M. (1989) Emergency arrangements within BNFL with specific reference to Sellafield. *Disaster Management*, **2**(1), 3–7.

Canadian Royal Commission (1984) *The Loss of the Semisubmersible Drill Rig* Ocean Ranger *and its Crew*. Ottowa: Canadian Government Publishing Service.

Cannon-Bowers, J. and Salas, E. (1990) Cognitive models and team training: shared mental models in complex systems. Paper presented at the Society for Industrial and Organizational Psychology, Miami, Florida, April.

Cannon-Bowers, J. and Salas, E. (in press) A framework for developing team performance measures in training. In M. Brannick, E. Salas and C. Prince (eds) *Team Performance Assessment and Measurement: Theory, Methods and Applications*. Hillsdale, NJ: Lawrence Erlbaum.

Cannon-Bowers, J., Salas, E. and Converse, S. (1993) Shared mental models in expert team decision making. In J. Castellan (ed.) *Individual and Group Decision Making*. Hillsdale, NJ: Lawrence Erlbaum.

Cannon-Bowers, J., Salas, E. and Grossman, J. (1991) Improving tactical decision making under stress. Research directions and applied implications. Paper presented at the International Applied Military Psychology Symposium, Stockholm, Sweden, June.

Cannon-Bowers, J., Salas, E. and Pruitt, J. (1996) Establishing the boundaries of a paradigm for decision-making research. *Human Factors*, 38, 2, 193–205. (Special issue: Decision Making in Complex Environments).

Cannon-Bowers, J., Tannenbaum, S., Salas, E. and Volpe, C. (1995) Defining competencies and establishing team training requirements. In R. Guzzo and E. Salas (eds) *Team Effectiveness and Decision Making in Organizations*. San Francisco, CA: Jossey Bass.

Canter, D. (1990) *Fires and Human Behaviour*, 2nd edn. London: David Fulton.

Canter, D., Comber, M. and Uzzell, D. (1989) *Football in its Place*. London: Routledge.

Cardwell, M. (1994) Survival among the ruins. *Security Management*, **38**(4), 64–68.

Chappell, S. (1994) Using voluntary incident reports for human factors evaluations. In N. Johnston, N. McDonald and R. Fuller (eds) *Aviation Psychology in Practice*. Aldershot: Avebury Technical.

Charlton, D. (1991) Stress and the submarine command course. The manipulation of stress as an aid to training. *Review of Naval Engineering*, **45**, 25–31, Classified.

Charlton, D. (1992) Training and assessing submarine commanders on the Perishers' course. In Collected Papers of the First Offshore Installation Management Conference: Emergency Command Responsibilities, Robert Gordon University, Aberdeen, April.

Cook, M. (1993) *Personnel Selection and Productivity*, 2nd edn. Chichester: John Wiley.

Cooper, C. (1982) Personality characteristics of successful bomb disposal experts. *Journal of Occupational Medicine*, **24**(9), 653–655.

Corneil, W. (1995) Traumatic stess and organizational strain in the Fire Service. In L. Murphy, J. Hurrell, S. Santer and G. Keita (eds) *Job Stress Interventions*. Washington, DC: American Psychological Association.

Cox, T. (1993) *Stress Research and Stress Management: Putting Theory to Work*. Contract report 61/1993. Sudbury: HSE Books.

Craik, K. (1943) *The Nature of Explanation*. Cambridge: Cambridge University Press.

Crainer, S. (1993) *Zeebruge. Learning from Disaster*. London: Herald Charitable Trust.

Crego, J. (1995) Wisdom's way. *Police Review*, 28 July, 24–25.

Crego, J. and Powell, J. (1994) The exercising of critical decision makers and their teams: a simulation approach using digital video and a multi-station computer network. Paper presented at the Society for Applied Learning Technologies Conference, Washington, DC, August.

Cullen, The Hon. Lord (1990) *The Public Inquiry into the Piper Alpha Disaster*, vols I and II (Cm 1310). London: HMSO.

Dale, M. and Iles, P. (1992) *Assessing Management Skills*. London: Kogan Page.

Darling, J. (1994) Crisis management in international business: keys to effective decision making. *Leadership and Organization Development Journal*, **15**(8), 3–8.

David, G. (1996) Human factors in helicopter operations. In R. Flin and G. Slaven (eds) *Managing the Offshore Installation Workforce*. Tulsa, OK: Penn Well Books.

De Cort, R. (1994) The development of UK and European major hazards legislation and the review of the Seveso Directive: the implications for industry. *Disaster Prevention and Management*, **3**(2), 8–14.

Department of Health (1991) *Disasters: Planning for a Caring Response*. London: HMSO.

Department of Transport (1988) *Certificates of Competency in the Merchant Navy*. London: HMSO.

Dickson, J. (1992) Contingency planning for emergencies. *Long Range Planning*, **25**(4), 82–89.

Dobson, P. and Williams, A. (1989) The validation of the selection of male British army officers. *Journal of Occupational Psychology*, **62**, 313–325.

Dobson, R. (1995) Starting as you mean to go on. A study of compliance with operational procedures during the first 10–15 minutes of incidents. International project report, Brigade Command Course, Fire Service College, Moreton-in-Marsh.

Donald, I. and Canter, D. (1992) Intentionality and fatality during the King's Cross underground fire. *European Journal of Social Psychology*, **22**, 203–218.

Donovan, S. (1992) Chemical companies formulate proactive emergency plans. *Safety and Health*, **145**(4), 34–38.

Dorner, D. and Pfeifer, E. (1993) Strategic thinking and stress. *Ergonomics*, **36**(11), 1345–1360.

Dowell, J. (1995) Coordination in emergency operations and the tabletop training exercise. *Le Travail Humain*, **58**, 85–102.

Downes, C. (1991). *Special Trust and Confidence: The Making of an Officer*. London: Frank Cass.

Drabek, T. (1986) *Human System Responses to Disaster*. New York: Springer-Verlag.

Drager, H. and Furnes, O. (1994) MEMbrain, a decision support system for emergency management. Paper presented at EUREKA conference, Lillehammer, Norway, June (available from A/S Quasar Consultants, Postboks 388 Skoyen, 0212 Oslo, Norway).

Driskell, J. and Salas, E. (1991a) Overcoming the effects of stress on military performance: human factors, training and selection strategies. In R. Gal and A. Mangelsdorf (eds) *Handbook of Military Psychology*. Chichester: John Wiley.

Driskell, J. and Salas, E. (1991b) Group decision making under stress. *Journal of Applied Psycholology*, **76**(3), 473–478.

Driskell, J. and Salas, E. (eds) (1996) *Stress and Human Performance*. Hillsdale, NJ: Lawrence Erlbaum.

Dror, Y. (1988) Decision making under disaster conditions. In L. Comfort (ed.) *Managing Disaster: Strategies and Policy Perspectives*. Durham, NC: Duke University Press.

Duckworth, D. (1986) Psychological problems arising from disaster work. *Stress Medicine*, **2**, 315–323.

Dudgeon, P. (1991) After the fire: "the old Kwasi is there, somewhere, at the core". *The Observer*, 17 November, 56–58.

Dunbar, E. (1993) The relationship of subjective distress and emergency response experience to the effective use of protective equipment. *Work and Stress*, **7**(4), 365–373.

Dunn, V. (1994) Command procedures at high rise fires. *WNYE* (New York Fire Department magazine).

Durham, T., McCammon, S. and Allison, E. (1985) The psychological impact of disaster on rescue personnel. *Annals of Emergency Medicine*, **14**(7), 73–77.

Dynes, R. (1993) Guidelines for emergency management at fixed site installations. *Disaster Prevention and Management*, **2**(4), 6–16.

Dynes, R. (1994) Community emergency planning: False assumptions and inappropriate analogies. *International Journal of Mass Emergencies and Disasters*, **12**, 141–158.

Dyregrov, A. (1989) Caring for the helpers in disaster stuations: psychological debriefing. *Disaster Management*, **2**, 25–30.

Elliott, D. and Smith, D. (1993) Coping with the sharp end: recruitment and selection in the fire service. *Disaster Management*, **5**(1), 35–41.

Elsensohn, R. (1991) Training seastaff for emergencies and safe ship operation through simulation – deck and engine. In *The Management of Safety in Shipping*. London: The Nautical Institute.

EMA (1995) *National Emergency Management Competency Standards*. Dickson, ACT: Emergency Management Australia.

Emery, M. and Grimsted, B. (1994) "Both starboard engines have gone!" *Pilot*, October, 34–38.

Endsley, M. (1995) Toward a theory of situation awareness in dynamic systems. *Human Factors*, **37**(1), 32–64.

Endsley, M. (in press) The role of situation awareness in naturalistic decision making. In C. Zsambok and G. Klein (eds) *Naturalistic Decision Making*. Hillsdale, NJ: Lawrence Erlbaum.

Ersland, S., Weisaeth, L. and Sund, A. (1989) The stress upon rescuers involved in an oil rig disaster. "Alexander L. Kielland" 1980. *Acta Psychiatrica Scandinavica*, suppl. 355, **80**, 38–49.

Esbensen, P., Johnson, R. and Kayten, P. (1985) The importance of crew training and standard operating procedures in commercial vessel accident prevention. Paper presented to the Society of Naval Architects and Marine Engineers, Norfolk, VA, May.

Everly, G. and Mitchell, J. (1995) Prevention of work-related posttraumatic stress: the critical incident debriefing process. In L. Murphy, J. Hurrell, S. Santer and G. Keita (eds) *Job Stress Interventions*. Washington, DC: American Psychological Association.

Feltham, R. (1989) Assessment centres. In N. Anderson and P. Herriot (eds) *Assessment and Selection in Organizations*. Chichester: John Wiley.

Fennell, D. (1988) *Investigation into the King's Cross Underground Fire*. Department of Transport, London: HMSO.

Fiedler, F., Potter, E. and McGuire, M. (1992) Stress and effective leadership decisions. In F. Heller (ed.) *Decision-Making and Leadership*. Cambridge: Cambridge University Press.

Fink, S. (1986) *Crisis Management: Planning for the Inevitable*. New York: American Management Association.

Fischer, H. (1994) *Response to Disaster. Fact versus Fiction and Its Perpetuation*. Maryland: University Press of America.

Fischer, U., Orasanu, J. and Wich, M. (1995) Expert pilots' perceptions of problem situations. In R. Jensen (ed.) *Proceedings of the Eighth International Symposium on Aviation Psychology*. Columbus, OH: Ohio State University Press.

Fisher, B. (1978) Disasters and major incidents. *Police Journal*, **60**(2), 196–200.

Fletcher, S. (1991) *NVQs. Standards and Competence*. London: Kogan Page.

Flin, R. (1995a) Incident command: decision making and team work. *Journal of the Fire Service College*, **1**(1), 7–15.

Flin, R. (1995b) Crew resource management: training teams in the offshore oil industry. *Journal of European Industrial Training*, **19**(9), 33–37.

Flin, R. and Slaven, G. (1993) Managing offshore installations: a survey of UKCS offshore installation managers. *Petroleum Review*, **47**, 68–71.

Flin, R. and Slaven, G. (1994) *The Selection and Training of Offshore Installation Managers for Crisis Management*. London: HSE Books.

Flin, R. and Slaven, G. (1995) Identifying the right stuff. Selecting and training on-scene commanders. *Journal of Contingencies and Crisis Management*, **3**, 113–123.

Flin, R. and Slaven, G. (1996a) Personality and emergency command ability. *Disaster Prevention and Management*, **5**, 40–46.

Flin, R. and Slaven, G. (eds) (1996b) *Managing the Offshore Installation Workforce*. Tulsa, OK: Penn Well Books.

Flin, R., Slaven, G. and Stewart, K. (1996) Emergency decision making in the offshore oil and gas industry. *Human Factors*, **38**, 2, 262–277.

Flin, R. and Stewart, E. (in preparation) Police incident command – a case of naturalistic decision making?

Flin, R., Strub, M., Salas, E. and Martin, L. (eds) (in preparation) *Decision Making under Stress: Emerging Themes and Applications*.

Foster, D. (1992) HM Coastguard. A twofold "service" to the offshore oil industry. Paper presented at the Theory and Practice of Offshore Safety Cases. London, November.

Foster, D. (1995) Communication is the key. *Coastguard*, July, 34–36.

Foushee, C. and Helmreich, R. (1988) Group interaction and flightcrew performance. In E. Wiener and D. Nagel (eds) *Human Factors in Aviation*. San Diego, CA: Academic Press.

Franklin, L. and Hunt, E. (1993) An emergency situation simulator for examining time-pressured decision making. *Behavior Research Methods, Instruments and Computers*, 25(2), 143–147.

Frederico, P. (1995) Expert and novice recognition of similar situations. *Human Factors*, 37(1), 105–122.

Fredholm, L. (1991). *The Development of Rescue Tactics*. Sundbyberg: Swedish National Defense Establishment.

Fredholm, L. (1995) Decision making in fire fighting and rescue operations. Paper presented at the Third Emergency Planning and Disaster Management Conference, Lancaster University, July, pp. 22–30.

FSAB (1995) *Emergency Fire Services. Supervision and Command N/SVQ Level 3*. Fire Service Awarding Body, Arndale Centre, Luton LU1 2TS.

Furnham, A. (1992) *Personality at Work*. London: Routledge.

Fuselier, D. (1991) Hostage negotiation: issues and applications. In R. Gal and A. Mangelsdorf (eds) *Handbook of Military Psychology*. Chichester: John Wiley.

Gaba, D. (1992) Dynamic decision-making in anesthesiology: cognitive models and training approaches. In D. Evans and V. Patel (eds) *Advanced Models of Cognition for Medical Training and Practice*. Berlin: Springer-Verlag.

Gaba, D. (1994) Human work environment and simulators. In R. Miller (ed.) *Anesthesia*, 4th edn. New York: Churchill Livingstone.

Gaba, D., Fish, K. and Howard, S. (1994) *Crisis Management in Anesthesiology*. New York: Churchill Livingstone.

Gaddy, C. and Wachtel, J. (1992) Team skills training in nuclear power plant operations. In R. Swezey and E. Salas (eds) *Teams. Their Training and Performance*. New York: Ablex.

Gibson, G. (1995) Fire departments' legal liability in Canada. *Canadian Firefighter*, 19, 27–31.

Gibson, M. (1991) *Order From Chaos. Responding to Traumatic Events*. Birmingham: Venture Press.

Ginnett, R. (1993) Crews as groups: Their formation and their leadership. In E. Wiener, B. Kanki and R. Helmreich (eds) *Cockpit Resource Management*. New York: Academic Press.

Glendon, A. and Glendon, S. (1992). Stress in ambulance staff. In E. Lovesey (ed.) *Contemporary Ergonomics*. London: Taylor & Francis.

Goodwin, P. and Wright, G. (1991) *Decision Analysis for Management Judgement*. Chichester: John Wiley.

Greatrex, J. and Phillips, P. (1989) Oiling the wheels of competence. *Personnel Management*, August, 36–39.

Green, R. (1990) Human error on the flight deck. In D. Broadbent, J. Reason and A. Baddeley (eds) *Human Factors in Hazardous Situations*. Oxford: Clarendon Press.

Greenstone, J. (1995) Hostage negotiations team training for small police departments. In M. Kurke and E. Scrivner (eds) *Police Psychology into the 21st Century.* Hillsdale, NJ: Lawrence Erlbaum.

Gregorich, S. and Wilhelm, J. (1993) Crew Resource Management training assessment. In E. Wiener, B. Kanki and R. Helmreich (eds) *Cockpit Resource Management.* New York: Academic Press.

Gregorich, S., Helmreich, R. and Wilhelm, J. (1990) The structure of cockpit management attitudes. *Journal of Applied Psychology,* **75,** 682–690.

Grimwood, P. (1992) *Fog Attack. Firefighting Strategy and Tactics – An International View.* Redhill, Surrey: FMJ Publications.

Gunter, D. (1996) Effective crew command. Research report, Fire Service College, Moreton-in-Marsh.

Guzzo, R. and Salas, E. (1995) (eds) *Team Effectiveness and Decision Making in Organizations.* San Francisco, CA: Jossey Bass.

Hackman, R. (ed.) (1990) *Groups that Work (and those that Don't): Creating Conditions for Effective Teamwork.* San Francisco, CA: Jossey Bass.

Haines, J. (1995) Emergency management and incident control on offshore installations. MSc thesis, Cranfield University.

Hansen, J. (1995) *Oklahoma Rescue.* New York: Ballantine.

Hardinge, N.M. (1989) Personnel selection in the military. In N. Anderson and P. Herriot (eds) *Assessment and Selection in Organizations.* Chichester: John Wiley.

Harrington, D. and Gaddy, C. (1993) Overcoming the effects of acute stress through good teamwork practices (Report). Winston-Salem, NC: Team Formation.

Harrington, D. and Kello, J. (1993) Systematic evaluation of nuclear operator team skills training: a progress report. In *Proceedings of the IEEE 5th Conference on Human Factors in Power Plants,* Monterey, CA, June 1992.

Harvie, C. (1994) *Fool's Gold. The Story of North Sea Oil.* Harmondsworth: Penguin.

Haynes, A. (1992) United 232: Coping with the "one chance-in-a-billion" loss of all flight controls. *Flight Deck,* **3,** Spring, 5–21.

Helmreich, R. (1984) Cockpit management attitudes. *Human Factors,* **26,** 583–589.

Helmreich, R. (1987) Theory underlying CRM training: psychological issues in flight crew performance and crew co-ordination. In H. Orlady and H. Foushee (eds) *Cockpit Resource Management Training,* NASA conference publication 2455. Moffett Field, CA: NASA Ames Research Centre, pp. 15–23.

Helmreich, R. and Foushee, C. (1993) Why Crew Resource Management? Empirical and theoretical bases of human factors training in aviation. In E. Wiener, B. Kanki and R. Helmreich (eds) *Cockpit Resource Management.* New York: Academic Press.

Helmreich, R., Holland, A., McFadden, T., Rose, R. and Santy, P. (1990) Strategies for crew selection for long duration missions. Paper presented at the American Institute of Aeronautics and Astronautics, Space Programs and Technologies Conference, Alabama, September (paper no. AIAA-903762).

Hendry, C. (1994) Looking for clues. International project report, Brigade Command Course, Fire Service College, Moreton-in-Marsh.

Hersey, P. and Blanchard, K. (1993) *Management of Organizational Behavior,* 6th edn. Englewood Cliffs, NJ: Prentice Hall.

Hesler, B. (1995) Training ships' crew for effective firefighting and emergency incident command. Paper presented to the Institute of Marine Engineers. London, May.

Hidden, A. (1989) *Investigation into the Clapham Junction Railway Accident.* Department of Transport, London: HMSO.

Hilton, P. (1992) A match for the crowd. *Personnel Management*, June, 57–58.
Hilton, T. and Dolgin, D. (1991) Pilot selection in the military of the free world. In R. Gal and A. Mangelsdorf (eds) *Handbook of Military Psychology*. Chichester: John Wiley.
Hirsh, W. and Bevan, S. (1991) Managerial competences and skill languages. In M. Silver (ed.) *Competent to Manage*. London: Routledge.
Hodgkinson, P. and Stewart, M. (1991) *Coping with Catastrophe*. London: Routledge.
Hogan, R., Curphy, G. and Hogan, J. (1994) What we know about leadership. *American Psychologist*, **49**, 493–504.
Home Office (1978) *Principles of Operational Command and Control at Incidents* (Joint Committee on Fire Brigade Operations). London: Home Office Fire Department.
Home Office (Fire Department) (1981) *Manual of Firemanship*, Practical Firemanship 1, Book 11. London: HMSO.
Home Office (1992) *The Human Elements of Disaster Management*. London: Home Office Central Advisory Facility on Organisational Health and Welfare.
Home Office (1994) *Dealing with Disaster*, 2nd edn. London: HMSO.
Horlick-Jones, T. (1994) Planning and coordinating urban emergency management. *Disaster Management*, **6**(3), 141–146.
Horlick-Jones, T., Amendola, A. and Casale, R. (eds) (1995) *Natural Risk and Civil Protection*. London: E & FN Spon.
Howard, S., Gaba, D., Fish, K., Yang, G. and Sarnquist, F. (1992) Anesthesia crisis resource management training: teaching anesthesiologists to handle critical incidents. *Aviation, Space and Environmental Medicine*, **63**, 763–770.
HSE (1984) *Training for Hazardous Occupations: A Case Study of the Fire Service*. London: HMSO.
HSE (1985a) *The Brightside Lane Warehouse Fire*. London: HMSO.
HSE (1985b) *The Control of Industrial Major Accident Hazards Regulations 1984 (CIMAH): Further Guidance on Emergency Plans*, HS(G) 25. Sudbury: HSE Books.
HSE (1992) *A Guide to the Offshore Installations (Safety Case) Regulations 1992*. Sudbury: HSE Books.
HSE (1994a) *The Management of Health and Safety at Atomic Weapons Establishments Premises*, Parts 1 and 2. Sudbury: HSE Books.
HSE (1994b) *Arrangements for Responding to Nuclear Emergencies*. Sudbury: HSE Books.
HSE (1995) *Stress at Work: A Guide for Employers*. Sudbury: HSE Books.
Hunter, D. and Burke, E. (in press) *Handbook of Pilot Selection*. Aldershot: Avebury.
Hutchins, S. (1996) Decision making errors demonstrated by experienced naval officers in a littoral environment. In C. Zsambok and G. Klein (eds) *Naturalistic Decision Making*. Hillsdale, NJ: Lawrence Erlbaum.
Hutchins, S. (in press) Principles for intelligent decision aiding. In E. Park (ed.) *Human Interaction with Complex Systems*. Norwell, MA: Kluwer.
Hutchins, S. and Kowalski, J. (1993) Tactical decision making under stress: preliminary results and lessons learned. Paper presented at the Symposium on Command and Control Research, Washington, DC, June, pp. 85–96.
Hytten, K. and Hasle, A. (1989) Fire fighters: a study of stress and coping. *Acta Psychiatrica Scandinavica*, suppl. 355, **80**, 50–55.
Hytten, K., Jensen, A. and Skauli, G. (1990) Stress inoculation training for smoke divers and free fall lifeboat passengers. *Aviation, Space and Environmental Medicine*, **61**, 983–988.
Idzikowski, C. and Baddeley, A. (1983) Fear and dangerous environments. In G. Hockey (ed.) *Stress and Fatigue in Human Performance*. Chichester: John Wiley.

Inzana, C., Driskell, J., Salas, E. and Johnston, J. (1996) The effects of preparatory information on enhancing performance under stress. *Journal of Applied Psychology*, **81**(4), 1–7.

Ireland, R. (1991) Fatal accident inquiry into the death of Timothy John Williams on board the *Ocean Odyssey*, Aberdeen Sheriff Court.

Irwin, R. (1989) The incident command system (ICS). In E. Auf der Heide (ed.) *Disaster Response. Principles of Preparation and Coordination*. St Louis, MI: C.V. Mosby.

Jackson, A. (1994) Recent developments in civil protection and the implications for disaster management in the United Kingdom. *International Journal of Mass Emergencies and Disasters*, **12**(3), 345–355.

Jackson, G. (1995) "It's not over yet": Mitigating the effects of disasters and traumatic incidents. In N. McDonald, N. Johnston and R. Fuller (eds) *Applications of Psychology to the Aviation System*. Aldershot: Avebury Aviation.

Jacobs, B. and t'Hart, P. (1992) Disaster at Hillsborough stadium: a comparative analysis. In D. Parker and J. Handmer (eds) *Hazard Management and Emergency Planning*. London: James and James.

James, A. (1988) Perceptions of stress in British ambulance personnel. *Work and Stress*, **2**, 319–326.

James, A. (1992) The psychological impact of disaster and the nature of critical incident stress for emergency personnel. *Disaster Prevention and Management*, **1**(2), 63–69.

Janis, I. (1972) *Victims of Groupthink*. Boston, MA: Houghton Mifflin.

Janis, I. (1989) *Crucial Decisions: Leadership in Policymaking and Crisis Management*. New York: Free Press.

Janis, I. (1992) Causes and consequences of defective policy making. In F. Heller (ed.) *Decision-making and Leadership*. Cambridge: Cambridge University Press.

Janis, I. and Mann, L. (1977) *Decision Making: A Psychological Analysis of Conflict, Choice, and Commitment*. New York: Free Press.

Jensen, R. (1995) *Pilot Judgement and Crew Resource Management*. Aldershot: Avebury Aviation.

Johnson, R. and Hansen, H. (1994) Caring for the human side. Developing a critical incident debriefing (CID) response plan in a midsize international oil and gas company. In Proceedings of the Society of Petroleum Engineers 3rd Safety, Health and Environment Conference, Jakarta, January, pp. 427–439 (SPE 27257).

Johnson-Laird, P. (1985) Mental models. In A. Aikenhead and J. Slack (eds) *Issues in Cognitive Modelling*. Sussex: Lawrence Erlbaum.

Johnston, N., Fuller, R. and McDonald, N. (eds) (1995) *Aviation Psychology: Training and Selection*. Aldershot: Avebury Aviation.

Jolly, R. (1982) Personality, individual differences, and experience of command in war. Defence Fellowship thesis, University College, London.

Jones, A. (1991). The contribution of psychologists to military officer selection. In R. Gal and A. Mangelsdorf (eds) *Handbook of Military Psychology*. Chichester: John Wiley.

Jones, A., Herriot, P., Long, B. and Drakeley, R. (1991) Attempting to improve the validity of a well-established assessment centre. *Journal of Occupational Psychology*, **64**, 1–21.

Joseph, S., Yule, W., Williams, R. and Hodgkinson, P. (1994) Correlates of post-traumatic stress at 30 months: the *Herald of Free Enterprise* disaster. *Behaviour Research and Therapy*, **32**(5), 521–524.

Joyce, D. (1989) Why do police officers laugh at death? *The Psychologist*, September, 380–381.

Kaempf, G. (1992) Emergency decision making. In Collected Papers of the First Offshore Installation Management Conference: Emergency Command Responsibilities, Robert Gordon University, Aberdeen, April.

Kaempf, G. and Militello, L. (1992) The problem of decision making in emergencies. *Fire International*, **135**, 38–39.

Kaempf, G., Wolf, S., Thordsen, M. and Klein, G. (1992) Decision making in the AEGIS combat information centre. Report for Naval Command, Control and Ocean Surveillance Centre, San Diego (contract N66001-90C6023). Ohio: Klein Associates.

Keegan, J. (1987) *The Mask of Command*. London: Jonathan Cape.

Keller, A. (1990) The Bradford disaster scale. In A. Keller and H. Wilson (eds) *Disaster Prevention, Planning and Limitation*. London: The British Library.

Keller, K. and Koenig, W. (1989) Management of stress and prevention of burnout in emergency physicians. *Annals of Emergency Medicine*, **18**, 42–47.

Kienan, G. (1987) Decision making under stress: scanning of alternatives under controllable and uncontrollable threats. *Journal of Personality and Social Psychology*, **52**(3), 639–644.

Kirkpatrick, S. and Locke, E. (1991) Leadership: do traits matter? *Academy of Management Executive*, **5**(2), 48–60.

Klein, G. (1989) Recognition-primed decisions. *Advances in Man–Machine Systems Research*, **5**, 47–92.

Klein, G. (1991) Naturalistic decision making. Paper presented at the American Psychological Association Conference, San Francisco, CA, August.

Klein, G. (1993) A recognition-primed decision (RPD) model of rapid decision making. In G. Klein, J. Orasanu, R. Calderwood and C. Zsambok (eds) *Decision Making in Action*. New York: Ablex.

Klein, G. (1995) Naturalistic decision making: Individual and team training. Seminar presented at the Offshore Management Centre, Robert Gordon University, Aberdeen, March.

Klein, G. (1996) The effect of acute stressors on decision making. In J. Driskell and E. Salas (eds) *Stress and Performance*. Hillsdale, NJ: Lawence Erlbaum.

Klein, G. (in press) The recognition-primed decision (RPD) model: looking back, looking forward. In C. Zsambok and G. Klein (eds) *Naturalistic Decision Making*. Hillsdale, NJ: Lawrence Erlbaum.

Klein, G. and Crandell, B. (1995) The role of mental simulation in problem solving and decision making. In P. Hancock, J. Flach, J. Caird and K. Vicente (eds) *Local Applications of the Ecological Approach to Human–Machine Systems*. Hillsdale, NJ: Lawrence Erlbaum.

Klein, G. and Thordsen, M. (1989) Recognitional decision making in C^2 organizations. In *Proceedings of 1989 Symposium on Command-and-Control Research*. McLean, VA: Science Applications International Corporation, pp. 239–244.

Klein, G., Calderwood, R. and Clinton-Cirocco, A. (1985) Rapid decision making on the fireground (KATR 84417). Contract report (MDA 90385G0099) for the US Army Research Institute, Alexandria, VA.

Klein, G., Calderwood, R. and McGregor, D. (1989) Critical decision method for eliciting knowledge. *IEEE Transactions on Systems, Man and Cybernetics*, **19**(3), 462–472.

Klein, G., Zsambok, C. and Thordsen, M. (1993) Team decision training. Five myths and a model. *Military Review*, April, 36–42.

Klein, G., Orasanu, J., Calderwood, R. and Zsambok, C. (eds) (1993) *Decision Making in Action*. New York: Ablex.

Klein, G., Kaempf, G., Wolf, S., Thordsen, M. and Miller, T. (in press) The uses of decision requirements. *International Journal of Human Computer Studies*.

Klimoski, R. and Mohammed, S. (1994) Team mental model: construct or metaphor? *Journal of Management*, 20(2), 403–437.

Kline, P. (1993) *The Handbook of Psychological Testing*. London: Routledge.

Kobasa, S. (1982) The hardy personality: toward a social psychology of stress and health. In G. Sanders and J. Suls (eds) *Social Psychology of Health and Illness*. Hillsdale, NJ: Lawrence Erlbaum.

Kornicki, R. (1990) The Home Secretary's announcement on civil emergencies and the future role of the civil emergencies adviser. In A. Keller and H. Wilson (eds) *Disaster Prevention and Limitation*. London: The British Library.

Kroon, M. and Overdijk, W. (1993) Psychosocial care and shelter following the Bijlmermeer air disaster. *Crisis: The Journal of Psychosocial Care and Suicide Prevention*, 14, 117–125.

Lagadec, P. (1990) *States of Emergency*. London: Butterworth-Heinemann.

Lagadec, P. (1991) *Preventing Chaos in a Crisis*. Maidenhead: McGraw-Hill.

Lang, J. (1986) Training for command. In *The Nautical Institute on Command*. London: Nautical Institute.

Larken, J. (1992) The command requirement and OIM qualification. In Collected Papers of the First Offshore Installation Management Conference: Emergency Command Responsibilities, Robert Gordon University, Aberdeen, April.

Lauber, J. (1984) Resource management in the cockpit. *Air Line Pilot*, 53, 20–23.

Le Marquand, P. (1991) Preparing for emergencies at sea. In *The Management of Safety in Shipping*. London: The Nautical Institute.

Lewis, G. (1994) *Critical Incident Stress and Trauma in the Workplace*. Indiana: Accelerated Development Inc.

LFCDA (1994) *London Fire Brigade: Standards Framework*. London: London Fire and Civil Defence Authority.

Lindstrom, B. and Lundin, T. (1982) Yrkesmassig exponering for katastrof [Stress reactions in rescue personnel]. *Nordisk Psykiatrisk Tidsskrift*, 36, 1–41.

Lindy, J. (1985) The trauma membrane and other clinical concepts derived from psychotherapeutic work with survivors of natural disasters. *Psychiatric Annals*, 15, 153–160.

Lipshitz, R. (1994) Decision making in three modes. *Journal for the Theory of Social Behaviour*, 24(1), 47–65.

Lipshitz, R. (1995) The road to Desert Storm. *Organization Studies*, 16(2), 243–263.

Lipshitz, R. and Ben Shaul, O. (in press) Schemata and mental models in recognition-primed decision making. In C. Zsambok and G. Klein (eds) *Naturalistic Decision Making*. Hillsdale, NJ: Lawrence Erlbaum

Lovas, E. and Leitao, J. (1991) Organisation of psychosocial disaster management in an exploration and production company. In Proceedings of the Society of Petroleum Engineers 3rd Health, Safety and Environment Conference, the Hague, November, pp. 743–750 (SPE 23503).

Mackenzie, C., Craig, G., Parr, M. and Horst, R. (1994) Video analysis of two emergency tracheal intubations identifies flawed decision-making. *Anesthesiology*, 81(3), 763–771.

Mahoney, P. (1994) Business and bombs. Preplanning and response. *Facilities*, 12(10), 14–21.

MAIB (1991) *Report of the Chief Inspector of Marine Accidents into the collision between* the Passenger Launch MARCHIONESS and MV BOWBELLE with loss of life on the River Thames on 20 August 1989, Department of Transport, Marine Accident Investigation Branch. London: HMSO.

MAIB (1992) *Report of the Chief Inspector of Marine Accidents into the collision between the Fishing Vessel ANTARES and HMS TRENCHANT with the loss of four lives on 22 November 1990*, Department of Transport, Marine Accident Investigation Branch. London: HMSO.

MAIB (1995) *Summary of Investigations*, no. 1/95. London: Department of Transport, Marine Accident Investigation Branch.

Mashburn, M. (1993) Critical incident counselling. *FBI Law Enforcement Bulletin*, **62**, 5–8.

Mathis, R., McKiddy, R. and Way, B. (1982) Police emergency operations. The management of crisis. *The Police Chief*, November, 48–52.

McDonald, N., Johnston, N. and Fuller, R. (eds) (1995) *Applications of Psychology to the Aviation System*. Aldershot: Avebury Aviation.

McElhatton, J. and Drew, C. (1993) Time pressure as a causal factor in aviation safety incidents. In R. Jensen (ed.) *Proceedings of the Seventh International Symposium on Aviation Psychology*. Columbus, OH: Ohio State University Press.

McFarlane, A. (1988) The phenomenology of posttraumatic stress disorders following a natural disaster. *Journal of Nervous and Mental Disease*, **176**(1), 22–29.

McGrath, J. (1984) *Groups: Interaction and Performance*. Englewood Cliffs, NJ: Prentice Hall.

McIntyyre, R. and Salas, E. (1995) Measuring and managing for team performance: lessons from complex environments. In R. Guzzo and E. Salas (eds) *Team Effectiveness and Decision Making in Organizations*. San Francisco, CA: Jossey Bass.

Meichenbaum, D. (1985) *Stress Inoculation Training*. New York: Pergamon Press.

Milgram, N. (1991) Personality factors in military psychology. In R. Gal and A. Mangelsdorf (eds) *Handbook of Military Psychology*. Chichester: John Wiley.

Mitchell, J. (1988) The effects of stress on emergency service personnel. In L. Comfort (ed.) *Managing Disaster*. Durham, NC: Duke University Press.

Mitchell, J. and Bray, G. (1990) *Emergency Services Stress*. Englewood Cliffs, NJ: Prentice Hall.

Mitroff, I. and Pearson, C. (1993) *Crisis Management. A Diagnostic Guide to Improving Your Organization's Crisis Preparedness*. New York: Jossey Bass.

MoD (1994a) *Ship NBCD Manual*. London: MoD (restricted).

MoD (1994b) *Guide to Ship Firefighting*. London: HMSO.

Montgomery, B. (1958) *The Memoirs of Field Marshall Montgomery of Alamein*. London: Collins.

Montgomery, B. (1961) *The Path to Leadership*. London: Collins.

Moore, T. (1985) Simulation and its use at the Police Staff College. *Training and Development*, August, 13–16.

Moore, T. (1986) Public order; the police commander's role. *Policing*, **2**(2), 85–100.

Moore, T. (1988) Police training for crisis: the use of simulation. *Police Journal*, **61**(2), 119–136.

Moore, T. and von Gierke, H. (1991) Military performance in acoustic noise environments. In R. Gal and A. Mangelsdorf (eds) *Handbook of Military Psychology*. Chichester: John Wiley.

Moran, C. and Colless, E. (1995) Positive reactions following emergency and disaster response. *Disaster Prevention and Management*, **4**(1), 55–60.

Morgan, B. and Bowers, C. (1995) Teamwork stress: implications for team decision making. In R. Guzzo and E. Salas (eds) *Team Effectiveness and Decision Making in Organizations.* San Francisco, CA: Jossey Bass.

Morrell, B. (1994) Keeping the Queen's peace. *Metropolitan Police Journal*, **10**, July, 6–9.

Muir, H. (1994) Passenger safety. In N. Johnston, N. McDonald, and R. Fuller (eds) *Aviation Psychology in Practice.* Aldershot: Avebury Technical.

Murphy, J. (1993) Fireground command: The "STICK" method. *Fire Engineering*, **146**, August, 113–124.

Murray, B. (1993) Operational command. Progress report on the development of a command doctrine, CPT review, paper 3/93, Fire Service College, Moreton-in-Marsh.

Murray, B. (1994a) More guidance needed for senior commanders on the fireground. *Fire*, **87**, June, 21–22.

Murray, B. (1994b) Training for operational command. *Fire Professional*, Autumn, 67–71.

Murray, B. (1995) Incident command expertise. International project report, Brigade Command Course, Fire Service College, Moreton-in-Marsh.

Murray, D. and Harrison, V. (1994) Validity and utility of police extended interviews, report 9, Home Office Assessment Consultancy Unit, London, February.

Nautical Institute (1986) *The Nautical Institute on Command.* London: Nautical Institute.

NFPA (1990) *Fire Department Incident Management System.* Quincy, MA: National Fire Protection Association.

Noorderhaven, N. (1995) *Strategic Decision Making.* Wokingham: Addison-Wesley.

Norwegian Public Reports (1981) *The* Alexander L. Kielland *Accident.* Oslo: Ministry of Justice and Police (English translation).

Norwegian Public Reports (1991) *The* Scandinavian Star *Disaster of 7 April 1990.* Oslo: Ministry of Justice and Police (English translation).

Noy, S. (1991) Combat stress reactions. In R. Gal and A. Mangelsdorf (eds) *Handbook of Military Psychology.* Chichester: John Wiley.

NTSB (1990) *Aircraft Accident Report: United Airlines Flight 232, McDonnell Douglas DC-10-10, Sioux City Gateway Airport, Iowa, July 19th 1989*, NTSB/AAR/90/06. Washington, DC: NTSB.

NTSB (1991) *Annual Review of Aircraft Accident Data: US Air Carrier Operations Calendar Year 1988*, NTSB/ARC-91/01. Washington, DC: NTSB.

NTSB (1994) *Safety Study. A Review of Flight Crew-Involved Major Accidents of US Air Carriers 1978–1990*, NTSB/SS94/01. Washington, DC: NTSB.

O'Brien, K. (1995) Occupational stressors and command decision making in fire officers. Paper presented to the Institution of Fire Engineers, Salford, September 13th.

OPITO (1992) *OPITO Units of Competence Governing the Management of Offshore Installations.* Montrose: Offshore Petroleum Industry Training Organisation.

Orasanu, J. (1990) Shared mental models and crew decision making, technical report 46, Cognitive Science Laboratory, Princeton University, NJ.

Orasanu, J. (1994a) Shared problem models and flight crew performance. In N. Johnston, N. McDonald and R. Fuller (eds) *Aviation Psychology in Practice.* Aldershot: Avebury Technical.

Orasanu, J. (1994b) Decision making in action: meeting the challenge of emergency events. In Collected Papers of the Third Offshore Installation Management Conference, Robert Gordon University, Aberdeen, April.

Orasanu, J. (1995a) Situation awareness: its role in flight crew decision making. In

R. Jensen (ed.) *Proceedings of the Eighth International Symposium on Aviation Psychology*. Columbus, OH: Ohio State University Press.

Orasanu, J. (1995b) Training for aviation decision making: the naturalistic decision making perspective. In Proceedings of the Human Factors and Ergonomics Society 39th Annual Meeting, San Diego. Santa Monica, CA: The Human Factors and Ergonomics Society.

Orasanu, J. and Backer, P. (1996) Stress and military performance. In J. Driskell and E. Salas (eds) *Stress and Performance*. Hillsdale, NJ: Lawrence Erlbaum.

Orasanu, J. and Connolly, T. (1993) The reinvention of decision making. In G. Klein, J. Orasanu, R. Calderwood and C. Zsambok (eds) *Decision Making in Action*. New Jersey: Ablex.

Orasanu, J. and Fischer, U. (in press) Finding decisions in natural environments: the view from the cockpit. In C. Zsambok and G. Klein (eds) *Naturalistic Decision Making*. Hillsdale, NJ: Lawrence Erlbaum.

Orasanu, J. and Salas, E. (1993) Team decision making in complex environments. In G. Klein, J. Orasanu, R. Calderwood and C. Zsambok (eds) *Decision Making in Action*. Norwood, NJ: Ablex.

Orasanu, J., Dismukes, K. and Fischer, U. (1993) Decison errors in the cockpit. In Proceedings of the Human Factors and Ergonomics Society 37th Annual Meeting, Seattle, WA, October.

Orasanu, J., Fischer, U. and Tarrel, R. (1993) A taxonomy of decision problems on the flight deck. In R. Jensen (ed.) *Proceedings of the 7th International Symposium on Aviation Psychology*. Columbus, OH: Ohio State University Press.

O'Sullivan, D. (1992) Management training software system simulates disaster situations. *Chemical Engineering News*, 70(38), 21–23.

Pandele, P. (1994a) *Methode de Raisonnement Tactique [Method of Tactical Reasoning]*, Ecole Nationale des Officiers Sapeurs-Pompiers. Paris: Ministere de l'Interieur.

Pandele, P. (1994b) *Le Chef de Site [The Incident Commander]*, Ecole Nationale des Officiers Sapeurs-Pompiers. Paris: Ministere de l'Interieur.

Parker, D. and Handmer, J. (1992) (eds) *Hazard Management and Emergency Planning*. London: James and James.

Pascual, R. and Henderson, S. (in press) Evidence of naturalistic decision making in command and control. In C. Zsambok and G. Klein (eds) *Naturalistic Decision Making*. Hillsdale, NJ: Lawrence Erlbaum.

Pascual, R., Henderson, S., Fernall, R., Ahmed, Q. and McGahan, C. (1994) *Fundamental C2I Research*, strategic research package AS01BW05, vols 1–3. Fort Halstead, Kent: Defence Research Agency.

Paton, D. (1991) Major incident and disaster stress in firefighters. *Disaster Management*, 3, 216–223.

Paton, D. (1992) International disasters: issues in the management and preparation of relief workers. *Disaster Management*, 4, 183–190.

Paul, J. (1995) Do we need emergency management competencies? In *Proceedings of the Third Emergency Planning and Disaster Management Conference*, Lancaster University, July, pp. 96–104.

Pearson, R. (1995) JAA psychometric testing: the reason. In N. Johnston, R. Fuller, and N. McDonald (eds) *Aviation Psychology: Training and Selection*. Aldershot: Avebury Aviation.

Pennington, N. and Hastie, R. (1993) A theory of explanation-based decision making. In G. Klein, J. Orasanu, R. Calderwood and C. Zsambok (eds) *Decision Making in Action*. New York: Ablex.

Penwell, L. (1990). Leadership and group behaviour in human space flight operations. Paper presented at the American Institute of Aeronautics and Astronautics Conference, Alabama, September.

Perrow, C. (1984) *Normal Accidents. Living with High Risk Technologies.* New York: Basic Books.

Phillips, M. (1993) Design of an emergency response center. *Journal of Petroleum Technology*, January, 63–65.

Police Review (1989) Wright reveals full scale of Hillsborough police trauma. 17 November, p. 2312.

Popper, M., Landau, O. and Gluskinos, U. (1992) The Israeli defence forces: an example of transformational leadership. *Leadership and Organization Development Journal*, **13**(1), 3–8.

Popplewell, O. (1985) *Committee of Inquiry into Crowd Safety and Control at Sports Grounds. Interim Report.* Home Office. London: HMSO.

Popplewell, O. (1986) *Committee of Inquiry into Crowd Safety and Control at Sports Grounds. Final Report.* Home Office. London: HMSO.

Powell, J., Wright, T., Newland, P., Creed, C. and Logan, B. (1992) Fire play: ICCARUS. *Interactive Learning International*, **8**, 109–126.

Proulx, G. (1993) A stress model for people facing a fire. *Environmental Psychology*, **13**, 137–147.

QPS (1994) *Competency Acquisition Program.* Queensland Police Service, Brisbane, Australia.

Quarantelli, E. (1988) Disaster crisis management: a summary of research findings. *Journal of Management Studies*, **25**, 373–385.

Quarantelli, E. (1995) Disasters are different, therefore planning for and managing them requires innovative as well as traditional behaviors. In *Proceedings of the Third Emergency Planning and Disaster Management Conference*, Lancaster University, July.

Raphael, B. (1986) *When Disaster Strikes.* London: Unwin Hyman.

Raphael, B., Singh, B., Bradbury, L. and Lambert, F. (1983) Who helps the helpers? The effects of a disaster on the rescue workers. *Omega*, **14**(1), 9–20.

Rasmussen, J. (1983) Skills, rules and knowledge: signals, signs and symbols, and other distinctions in human performance models. *IEEE Transactions on Systems, Man and Cybernetics*, **13**(3), 257–267.

Rasmussen, J. (1986) A framework for cognitive task analysis in system design. In E. Hollnagel, G. Mancini and D. Woods (eds) *Intelligent Decision Support in Process Environments.* Berlin: Springer-Verlag.

Rasmussen, J. (1993) Deciding and doing: decision making in natural contexts. In G. Klein, J. Orasanu, R. Calderwood and C. Zsambok (eds) *Decision Making in Action.* New York: Ablex.

Rasmussen, J., Brehmer, B. and Leplat, J. (eds) (1991) *Distributed Decision Making: Cognitive Models of Cooperative Work.* Chichester: John Wiley.

Regester, M. (1987) *Crisis Management. How to Turn a Crisis into an Opportunity.* London: Hutchinson.

Regester, M. (1989) *Crisis Mangement. What To Do When the Unthinkable Happens.* London: Hutchinson.

Rhodenizer, L., Peppler-Swope, M. and Bowers, C. (1996) Toward enhanced training in the communication center. *Emergency Medical Services*, **25**, 66–69.

Rogalski, J. and Samurcay, R. (1993) Analysing communication in complex distributed decision-making. *Ergonomics*, **36**, 1329–1343.

Rogers, W. and Rogers, S. (1992) *Storm Center. The USS Vincennes and Iran Air Flight 655.* Annapolis, MD: US Naval Institute.

Rolfe, J. and Taylor, A. (1989) The training and management of personnel who will respond to aircraft disasters. *Disaster Management*, **1**(3), 36–41.

Rosenberg, L. (1991) A qualitative investigation of the use of humor by emergency personnel as a strategy for coping with stress. *Journal of Emergency Nursing*, **17**(4), 197–203.

Rosenthal, U. and Hart, P. (1991) Experts and decision makers in crisis situations. *Knowledge, Diffusion, Utilization*, **12**, 350–372.

Rosenthal, U., Charles, M. and Hart, P. (eds) (1989) *Coping with Crises. The Management of Disasters, Riots and Terrorism*. Chicago, IL: C.C. Thomas.

Roth, E. (in press) Analysis of decision making in nuclear power plant emergencies: an investigation of aided decision making. In C. Zsambok and G. Klein (eds) *Naturalistic Decision Making*. Hillsdale, NJ: Lawrence Erlbaum.

Roth, E., Mumaw, R. and Lewis, P. (1994) *An Empirical Investigation of Operator Performance in Cognitively Demanding Simulated Emergencies*, prepared for the US Nuclear Regulatory Commission. Pittsburgh, PA: Westinghouse Science and Technology Center.

Rouse, W. and Morris, N. (1986) On looking into the blackbox: prospects and limits in the search for mental models. *Psychological Bulletin*, **100**, 349–363.

Rouse, W., Cannon-Bowers, J. and Salas, E. (1992) The role of mental models in team performance in complex systems. *IEEE Transactions on Systems, Man and Cybernetics*, **22**(6), 1296–1308.

Ruffell Smith, H. (1979) A simulator study of the interaction of pilot workload with errors, vigilance, and decisions, NASA Technical Memorandum 78482. Moffett Field, CA: NASA Ames Research Center.

Salas, E. and Cannon-Bowers, J. (1993) Making of a dream team. Paper presented at the American Psychological Association conference, Toronto, August.

Salas, E. and Cannon-Bowers, J. (1995) Team performance and training in complex systems. In Collected Papers of the Fourth Offshore Installation Management Conference, Robert Gordon University, Aberdeen, April.

Salas, E., Cannon-Bowers, J. and Blickensderfer, E. (1995) Team performance and training research: emerging principles. *Journal of the Washington Academy of Science*, **83**(2), 81–106.

Salas, E., Cannon-Bowers, J. and Johnston, J. (in press) How can you turn a team of experts into an expert team? In C. Zsambok and G. Klein (eds) *Naturalistic Decision Making*. Hillsdale, NJ: Lawrence Erlbaum.

Salas, E., Dickinson, T., Converse, S. and Tannenbaum, S. (1992) Toward an understanding of team performance and training. In R. Swezey and E. Salas (eds) *Teams. Their Training and Performance*. New York: Ablex.

Salas, E., Prince, C., Baker, D. and Sherestha, L. (1995) Situation awareness and team performance: implications for measurement and training. *Human Factors*, **37**, 123–136.

Sale, R. (1992) Towards a psychometric profile of the successful army officer. *Defense Analysis*, **8**, 3–27.

Samurcay, R. and Rogalski, J. (1988) Analysis of operators' cognitive activities in learning and using a method for decision making in public safety. In J. Patrick and K. Duncan (eds) *Training, Human Decision Making and Control*. Amsterdam: North Holland.

Samurcay, R. and Rogalski, J. (1991) A method for tactical reasoning (MTR) in emergency management. In J. Rasmussen, B. Brehmer and J. Leplat (eds) *Distributed Decision Making: Cognitive Models of Cooperative Work*. Chichester: John Wiley.

Samurcay, R. and Rogalski, J. (1993) Cooperative work and decision making in emergency management. *Le Travail Humain*, **56**, 53–77.

Santy, P. (1994) *Choosing the Right Stuff. The Psychological Selection of Astronauts and Cosmonauts*. New York: Praeger.

Sarna, P. (1984) Training police commanders and supervisors in the management of critical incidents. *Washington Crime News Services, Training Aids Digest*, **9**(12), 1–6.

Saunders, T., Driskell, J., Johnston, J. and Salas, E. (1996) The effect of stress inoculation training on anxiety and performance. *Journal of Occupational Health Psychology*, 1, 170–186.

Saville, P. and Holdsworth, R. (1992) *Occupational Personality Questionnaire Manual*. Surrey: Saville Holdsworth Ltd.

Scanlon, J. (1994) The role of EOCs in emergency management: a comparison of American and Canadian experience. *International Journal of Mass Emergencies and Disasters*, **12**(1), 51–75.

Scanlon, J. and Prawzick, A. (1991) Not just a big fire: emergency response to an environmental disaster. *Canadian Police College Journal*, **15**(3), 166–202.

Schmitt, J. (1994) *Mastering Tactics. Tactical Decision Game Workbook*. Quantico, VA: Marine Corps Association.

Schraagen, J. (1989) Requirements for a damage control decision-support system: implications from expert–novice differences. Paper presented at the Second European Meeting on Cognitive Science Approaches to Process Control, Siena, Italy, October.

Schraagen, J. (in press) Obtaining requirements for a naval damage control decision-support system. In C. Zsambok and G. Klein (eds) *Naturalistic Decision Making*. Hillsdale, NJ: Lawrence Erlbaum.

Schwid, H. and O'Donnell, D. (1992) Anesthesiologists' management of critical incidents. *Anesthesiology*, **76**(4), 495–501.

Scott, M. and Stradling, S. (1992) *Counselling for Post-Traumatic Stress Disorder*. London: Sage.

Scottish Ambulance Service (1990) *Arrangements for Civil Emergencies*. Edinburgh: Common Services Agency.

Sefton, A. (1992) Introduction to the First Offshore Installation Mangement Conference: Emergency Command, Robert Gordon University, Aberdeen, April.

Serfaty, D. and Michel, R. (1990) Toward a theory of tactical decision making expertise. In *Proceedings of the Symposium on Command and Control Research*, Monterey, CA, pp. 257–269.

Serfaty, D., Entin, E. and Volpe, C. (1993) Adaptation to stress in team decision making and coordination. In Proceedings of the Human Factors and Ergonomics Society 37th Annual Meeting. Santa Monica, CA: The Human Factors and Ergonomics Society.

Serfaty, D., Macmillan, J., Entin, E.E. and Entin, E.B. (in press) The decision making expertise of battle commanders. In C. Zsambok and G. Klein (eds) *Naturalistic Decision Making*. Hillsdale, NJ: Lawrence Erlbaum.

Shackleton, V. (1995) *Business Leadership*. London: Routledge.

Shackleton, V. and Newell, S. (1991). Management selection: a comparative survey of methods used in top British and French companies. *Journal of Occupational Psychology*, **64**, 23–36.

Shalev, A. (1994) Debriefing following traumatic exposure. In R. Ursano, B. McCaughey and C. Fullerton (eds) *Individual and Community Responses to Trauma and Disaster*. Cambridge: Cambridge University Press.

Silver, M. (ed.) (1991) *Competent to Manage*. London: Routledge.

Simpson, J. (1992) Testing command skills with simulation. *Fire International*, November, 42–43.

Sinclair, J. and Cook, D. (1994) OIM emergency assessment and development. Paper presented at the Third European Seminar on Human Factors in Offshore Safety, Aberdeen, September.

Skriver, J. and Flin, R. (1996) Decision making in offshore emergencies: are standard operating procedures the solution? In Proceedings of the Society of Petroleum Engineers 3rd International Health, Safety and Environment Conference, New Orleans, June (SPE 35940).

Slaven, G. and Flin, R. (1993) Learning from offshore emergencies. *Disaster Management*, **6**, 19–22.

Slim, W. (1956) *Defeat into Victory*. London: Cassell.

Smith, A. and Jones, D. (1992) Noise and performance. In A. Smith and D. Jones (eds) *Handbook of Human Performance*, Vol 1: *The Physical Environment*. London: Academic Press.

Smith, M. (1989) Selection in high-risk and stressful occupations. In P. Herriot (ed.) *Handbook of Assessment in Organizations*. Chichester: John Wiley.

Smith, M. and Sutherland, V. (1996) *International Review of Professional Issues in Selection and Assessment*, Vol 2. Chichester: John Wiley.

Solomon, Z. (1993) *Combat Stress Reaction*. New York: Plenum Press.

Stead, G. (1995) Personality on the flight deck. In N. McDonald, N. Johnston and R. Fuller (eds) *Applications of Psychology to the Aviation System*. Aldershot: Avebury Aviation.

Stewart, E. (1995) Naturalistic decision making. *Scottish Police College Newsletter*, **24**, April, 1.

Stewart, K. (1996) Managing emergency response: naturalistic decision making. *Journal of the Fire Service College*, **1**(2), 89–99.

Stewart, K. and Skriver, J. (1996) Emergency response: command and control on offshore installations. In R. Flin and G. Slaven (eds) *Managing the Offshore Installation Workforce*. Tulsa, OK: Penn Well Books.

Stokes, A. and Kite, K. (1994) *Flight Stress: Stress, Fatigue and Performance in Aviation*. Aldershot: Avebury Aviation.

Sugiman, T. and Misumi, J. (1988) Development of a new evacuation method for emergencies: control of collective behavior by emergent small groups. *Journal of Applied Psychology*, **73**(1), 3–10.

Svenson, O. and Maule, J. (eds) (1993) *Time Pressure and Stress in Human Judgement and Decision Making*. New York: Plenum Press.

Swezey, R. and Salas, E. (eds) (1992) *Teams. Their Training and Performance*. New York: Ablex.

Syrett, M. and Hogg, C. (1992) *Frontiers of Leadership*. Oxford: Blackwell.

Tang, T. and Hammontree, M. (1992) The effects of hardiness, police stress and life stress on police officers' illness and absenteeism. *Public Personnel Management*, **21**, 493–510.

Taylor, H. (1994) Post traumatic stress disorder – a consideration of perceptual perspectives of fire service officers with implications for training. MA thesis, University of Warwick.

Taylor, H. and Shevels, T. (1995) Post traumatic stress disorder (PTSD) in the fire service. *Journal of the Fire Service College*, **1**, 17–22.

Taylor, P. (1989) *The Hillsborough Stadium Disaster. Interim Report*. Home Office. London: HMSO.

Taylor, P. (1990) *The Hillsborough Stadium Disaster. Final Report.* Home Office. London: HMSO.

Thomas, R. (1994) Human factors training for flight crew in British Airways. In Collected Papers of the Third Offshore Installation Management Conference, Robert Gordon University, Aberdeen, April.

Thornley, F. (1990) Major disasters: an ambulance service view. *Injury: The British Journal of Accident Surgery,* 21, 34–36.

Toft, B. and Reynolds, S. (1994) *Learning From Disasters.* Oxford: Butterworth.

Toplis, J., Dulewicz, V. and Fletcher, C. (1991) *Psychological Testing. A Manager's Guide,* 2nd edn. London: Institute of Personnel Management.

Turner, B. (1994) Flexibility and improvisation in emergency response. *Disaster Management,* 6(2), 84–90.

Tversky, A. and Kahneman, D. (1974) Judgement under uncertainty: heuristics and biases. *Science,* 185, 1124–1131.

Ullman, M. (1994) A funny thing happened to me on the way to the forum. In Collected Papers of the Third Offshore Installation Management conference, Robert Gordon University, Aberdeen, April.

Ursano, R. and McCarroll, J. (1994) Exposure to traumatic death: the nature of the stressor. In R. Ursano, B. McCaughey and C. Fullerton (eds) *Individual and Community Responses to Trauma and Disaster.* Cambridge: Cambridge University Press.

US Marine Corps (1994) Command and control. Concept Paper. C41 Division, Washington, DC.

Vaernes, R. (1982) The defence mechanism test predicts inadequate performance under stress. *Scandinavian Journal of Psychology,* 23, 37–43.

van Creveld, M. (1985) *Command in War.* Cambridge, MA: Harvard University Press.

van der Kolk, B., McFarlane, A. and Weisaeth, L. (1996) *Traumatic Stress.* New York: Guilford.

van Leeuwen, E. (1993) ANDES: a real-time damage control system. Paper presented at the Tenth Ship Control Systems Symposium, Canada, October.

Vaught, C. and Wiehagen, W. (1991) Escape from a mine fire: emergent perspective and work group behaviour. *Journal of Applied Behavioural Science,* 27, 452–474.

Von Clausewitz, C. (1968) *On War,* translated by J. Graham. London: Routledge and Kegan Paul (first published 1833).

Wallace, A., Rowles, J. and Colton, C. (eds) (1994) *Management of Disasters and their Aftermath.* London: BMJ.

Walton, K. (1988) Crisis management. A command post perspective. *FBI Law Enforcement Bulletin,* February, 20–24.

Weather, F., Litz, B. and Keane, T. (1995) Military trauma. In J. Freedy and S. Hobfoll (eds) *Traumatic Stress. From Theory to Practice.* New York: Plenum Press.

Weaver, J. (1995a) *Disasters: Mental Health Interventions.* Florida: Professional Resource Press.

Weaver, J. (1995b) Morgue operations: disaster mental health interventions. Paper presented at the American Psychological Association conference, New York, August.

Wegner, D. (1987) Transactive memory: a contemporary analysis of group mind. In B. Mullen and G. Goethals (eds) *Theories of Group Behavior.* New York: Springer-Verlag.

Weisaeth, L. (1987). Mestring av lederstress under ulykker og krisesituasjoner [Control of leader stress during accidents and crisis situations]. In S. Larsen, T.

Skjerveongen, and L. Ostigaard (eds) *Handbok i Sikkerhetsstyring [Handbook of Safety Management]*. Oslo: Norwegian Management Publications.

Weisaeth, L. (1989) A study of behavioural responses to an industrial disaster. *Acta Psychiatrica Scandinavica*, suppl. 355, **85**, 13–24.

Weisaeth, L. (1994) Psychological and psychiatric aspects of technological disasters. In R. Ursano, B. McCaughey and C. Fullerton (eds) *Individual and Community Responses to Trauma and Disaster*. Cambridge: Cambridge University Press.

Wellens, R. (1993) Group situation awareness and distributed decision making: from military to civilian applications. In J. Castellan (ed.) *Individual and Group Decision Making*. New Jersey: Lawrence Erlbaum.

Wembley Stadium Health and Safety Department (1995) Emergency planning the Wembley way. *Emergency*, May, 8–9.

Wenger, D., Quarantelli, E. and Dynes, R. (1990) Is the incident command system a plan for all seasons and emergency situations? *Hazard Monthly*, **10**(3), 8–12.

West, M. (1995) *Teams*. London: Routledge/British Psychological Society.

Wickens, C., Stokes, A., Barnett, B. and Hyman, F. (1993) The effects of stress on pilot judgement in a MIDIS simulator. In O. Svenson and J. Maule (eds) *Time Pressure and Stress in Human Judgement and Decision Making*. New York: Plenum Press.

Wiener, E., Kanki, B. and Helmreich, R. (eds) (1993) *Cockpit Resource Management*. New York: Academic Press.

Williams, H. and Rayner, J. (1956) Emergency medical services in disaster. *Medical Annals of the District of Columbia*, **25**(12), 655–662.

Williams, R. (1994) Occupational testing: contemporary British practice. *The Psychologist*, **7**(1), 11–13.

Wilson, J. and Raphael, B. (eds) (1993) *International Handbook of Traumatic Stress*. New York: Plenum Press.

Wolfe, T. (1991) *The Right Stuff*. London: Picador (first published in 1979).

Woodruffe, C. (1990) *Assessment Centres: Identifying and Developing Competence*. London: Institute of Personnel Management.

Woodward, S. (1992) *One Hundred Days. The Memoirs of the Falklands Battle Group Commander*. London: HarperCollins

Wright, G. (1984) *Behavioural Decision Theory*. London: Penguin.

Wright, P. (1974) The harassed decision maker: time pressures, distractions, and the use of evidence. *Journal of Applied Psychology*, **59**(5), 555–561.

Wynne, D. (1995) Expert teams performing in natural environments. How flight crew training programmes can help the fire service to improve team performance. International project report, Brigade Command Course, Fire Service College, Moreton-in-Marsh.

Young, P. (1993) *Disasters. Focusing on Management Responsibility*. London: Herald Families Association.

Yukl, G. (1994) *Leadership in Organizations*. Englewood Cliffs, NJ: Prentice Hall.

Zsambok, C. (in press) Naturalistic decision making research and improving team decision making. In C. Zsambok and G. Klein (eds) *Naturalistic Decision Making*. Hillsdale, NJ: Lawrence Erlbaum.

Zsambok, C. and Klein, G. (eds) (in press) *Naturalistic Decision Making*. Hillsdale, NJ: Lawrence Erlbaum.

Zsambok, C., Klein, G., Kyne, M. and Klinger, D. (1992) Advanced team decision making: a developmental model. Report for the US Army Research Institute for the Behavioural and Social Sciences, contract MDA903-90-C-0117. Fairborn, OH: Klein Associates.

Index